COMING TOGETHER / COMING APART

Routledge
New York and London

COMING TOGETHER / COMING APART
Religion, Community, and Modernity

Elizabeth M. Bounds

Published in 1997
by Routledge
29 West 35th Street
New York, NY 10001

Published in
Great Britain by
Routledge
11 New Fetter Lane
London EC4P 4EE

Copyright © 1997 by
Routledge
Printed in the
United States of America
on acid-free paper.

Library of Congress Cataloging-in-Publication-Data

Bounds, Elizabeth M.
  Coming together/coming apart: religion, community,
    and modernity / Elizabeth M. Bounds.
  p. cm.
  Includes bibliographical references and index.
  ISBN 0-415-91261-X. — ISBN 0-415-91262-8 (pbk.)
  1. United States—Religion—1960–
  2. United States—Social conditions—1980–
  3. United States—Politics and government—1993–
  4. Liberalism (Religion)—United States—History—20th century.
  5. Liberalism (Religion)—Protestant churches—History—20th century.
  6. United States—Church history—20th century.
  I. Title.
BL2525.B68 1996   95-26368
277.3'082—dc20   CIP

ACKNOWLEDGMENTS

IN THE JOURNEY these thoughts have made from blank paper to dissertation to book, I have been graced with much support and many homes. Thanks, first, to my parents Harrison and Betty Bounds. At Union Theological Seminary (New York), I enjoyed the mentorship and friendship of Beverly Harrison and Larry Rasmussen. Thanks to Auburn Theological Seminary, especially to Bob Reber, Barbara Wheeler, and Laura and Mark Wilhelm. The Religious Studies Program at Virginia Polytechnic Institute and State University has supported completion of both dissertation and book (special thanks to Guyton B. Hammond). And thanks to Glen Stassen for his support and to Marlie Wassermann and Mary Carol de Zutter at Routledge.

bell hooks has written that you must "tak[e] … nourishment in that space where you find it." I have found it with Joan Bolker, Pam Brubaker, Judy Burns, Anne Gilson, Jerri Hurlbutt, Sally Johnston, Marilyn Legge, Sally MacNichol, Margie Mayman Park, Susan Quass, Roger Powers, Laraine Sommella, and the late Ju Ling Tan.

This book is dedicated to Michael T. Bradley, Jr. who has had to live through its creation and evolution.

CONTENTS

CHAOS OR COMMUNITY?
Setting the Scene

Here is a map of our country:
here is the Sea of Indifference glazed with salt
This is the haunted river flowing
we dare not taste its water...
These are the suburbs of acquiescence silence rising fumelike
       from the streets
This is the capital of money and dolor whose spires
flare up through air inversions whose bridges are crumbling
whose children are drifting blind alleys pent
between coiled rolls of razor wire
I promised to show you a map you say but this is a mural
then yes let it be these are small distinctions
where do we see it from is the question
                    —Adrienne Rich[1]

This is the great new problem of mankind. We have inherited a large house, a great "world house" in which we have to live together—black and white, Easterner and Westerner, Gentile and Jew, Catholic and Protestant, Moslem and Hindu—a family unduly separated in ideas, cultures and interests, who, because we can never again live apart, must learn somehow to live with each other in peace.
                    —Martin Luther King, Jr.[2]

chapter 1

WHY COMMUNITY? WHY NOW? AN INTRODUCTION

Community is, at the moment, a powerful word in the United States. It is invoked in seemingly contradictory places: among conservative leaders championing "traditional values"; among blacks trying to reclaim a ghetto neighborhood from poverty and despair; among Christians or Jews describing their congregations; among middle-class persons seeking a spiritual experience or connections along the "Information Superhighway"; among lower- and middle-class whites trying to keep a homeless shelter from being built in their neighborhood.

When invoked in these economically and politically varied locations, *community* is a powerfully suggestive, yet vague, term. Are all of these people who use this word talking about the same thing? I believe that while all are reacting to common features of our current situation, their responses differ significantly.

Sifting through the variety of uses for the concept of community, I find a few related, yet distinct meanings:

1) a desire for "immediate relations," an arena of meaningful love and solidarity and/or spirituality, in contrast to reified social roles;

2) a desire for collective connection (often rooted in ethnic and racial heritage) in reaction to what is perceived as a dangerous, conflicted and/or confusing pluralized society;

3) a desire for the experience of a unified transcendence, a meaningful whole, so that life is lived in relation to something *greater* than the self (often expressed in religious or nationalist language);

4) a desire to reaffirm a lost or eroded set of traditions and practices;

5) a desire to create a new set of practices in the face of a society that denies or negates the existence of one's self and one's group;

6) a desire for effective political participation, seeing oneself as citizen among fellow citizens with relations and responsibilities.

I have described all of these possible meanings as "desires," since all point to a yearning for change from current social conditions, or from what is perceived as the dominant characteristics of contemporary society. They are reactions to a sense of "uprootedness" which is countered by seeking roots/connections, "through forms of association which preserve particular memories of the past, a measure of stability in the present, and particular expectations for the future."[3] Yet the means for creating these connections differ. Meanings 1–4 imply a notion of community as a safe place of harmony and homogeneity. Meanings 3 and 4 suggest, in addition, a nostalgic yearning for a simpler time in the past. Meanings 2, 3 and 4 point to an assumption that a coherent social order depends on a common social (or in the case of Meaning 3, religious) morality. However, Meanings 2 and 4 might imply not nostalgia and homogeneity but challenge and difference, if the speaker were trying to reclaim a marginalized tradition over against the dominant tradition(s) (and, in the eyes of the dominant culture, it would be virtually indistinguishable from Meaning 5). Meanings 5 and 6 suggest a more complex and pluralist form of common life which explicitly recognizes the existence of marginalized or subaltern publics.

The variety of current meanings of community show that it must be understood as a complex term, simultaneously personal and social, symbolic and institutional. These apparently contradictory qualities and contradictory readings attached to the notion of community are, in fact, a clue to its importance. Although a term with a long heritage,[4] "community" has taken on a new life as bellwether of changing social conditions. We live in a time and place when community seems vital to our individual and social well-being. Yet, simultaneously, we live in a time when what have been ordinary communal relations are scarce in the face of social and geographical mobility, lost tradi-

2

tions, and the experienced pluralism of U.S. society. My claim here is that "community" is a trope for civil society. The renewed desire for community is based in the current problems of civil society under the conditions of modern advanced capitalism—problems variously described as "the crisis of capitalism," "the end of liberalism," "the crisis of modernity," or a "legitimation crisis."[5] Community, in this context, serves as "a metaphor for those bonds among individuals that the market is eroding" and is a reaction to globalization.[6] Specifically, it is a discourse responding to the cracks and conflicts of liberal capitalist modernity.[7] At its worst, the discourse of community is a flight from the challenges of the problems of capitalism and pluralism; at its best, it is an effort to assert the value of solidarity in the midst of forces eroding connection.

The crisis of the institutions of civil society lies behind all the different meanings of community depicted above and provides the postmodern context for my work which seeks to evaluate certain competing claims about community current in Christian ethics and social theory. The multiple meanings of community point to its current function as a "terrain of struggle" among different conceptions of society, where "historically necessary [ideologies]... 'organize' human masses and create the terrain where [persons] acquire consciousness of their positions, struggle, etc."[8] The discussion of community is an ideological discourse, that is, an area shaped by material institutions where "meaning is produced, challenged, reproduced, transformed."[9] As an ideological discourse, it arises out of the current problems of civil society in the liberal capitalist state, problems that affect understandings of morality, identity, and membership.

This context, I argue, forms the preconditions of any discussion of public ethics, including public religious ethics. Without regeneration of civil society, there can be no regeneration of public ethics. Citizenship is no longer understood as "a great extension of common culture and common experience" and thus the ethics of citizenship, public forms of morality, appear at best confused, at worst nonexistent.[10] While there is agreement that the previously dominant norms (including religious ones) have lost their legitimating and unifying meanings, some mourn this loss while others celebrate it. And in the midst of our disagreement, we struggle over which normative sources will be considered personally and collectively authoritative and legitimate within the public spheres of civil society. To understand the call for community as part of this struggle, it is essential to trace the simultaneously reactionary and emancipatory potential of the "political, cultural, and social practices that [seek] to reinforce local community solidarity and tradition in the face of the universalism and globalism of money power, commodification and capital circulation."[11] A glance at the "communitarian" debate will help clarify my point.[12]

Drawing on a long history of responses to modernity which have sought to protect/(re)create forms of communal life believed to be endangered or erased,[13] communitarian writers attack liberalism for creating a society where there is "a lack of concern for character and moral education, the displacement of parental authority, and the erosion of any vestige of shared values."[14] Liberalism, they claim, has assumed an "unencumbered self," a self which is hollow, goes against our intuitions, and avoids our unavoidable "situatedness." Rather than a self aimed at pursuing her/his own self-interest within a neutral state, communitarianism describes a self shaped by its pursuit of goods, goods only found within particular historical communal practices. Under the liberal model of selfhood, communitarians say, not only can we not develop ourselves as good persons, we cannot develop good (or stable) societies, because there is no possibility of common moral discourse or idea of the common good.[15]

What is perhaps most striking in much communitarian discourse is the intense tone of nostalgia, loss, and despair. Communitarianism is a discourse of lamentation which rewrites liberal optimism and faith in progress as alienation and dissatisfaction. The magic of community—membership, tradition, "embeddedness"—is the proffered antidote to these liberal modern diseases. Discourses and institutions of moral formation are to be established on normative experiences of relation which "champion the particularist claims of groups, families or 'traditions of shared meaning'."[16]

The limitations of most communitarian discussions, such as the valorization of a homogeneous model of community and society, the fear of "politicization," the refusal to connect a critique of liberal politics and culture to an analysis of capitalism, and the failure to take into account the historically privatized or ignored alternative public discourses of women's and other's marginalized experiences, are examples, I assert, of efforts to renegotiate dominance in a fragile situation. There are, however, other discussions of community, outside of mainstream communitarianism, that suggest different possibilities.[17] My task is to evaluate aspects of both the dominant and alternative discussions through a materialist approach which allows an understanding of the social context of communitarian discourse and helps us evaluate the different solutions proposed.

Religion is a critical component, although often ignored, of these postliberal shifts in community/civil society. As José Casanova points out, the privatization of religion is "constitutive of Western modernity" as it is the precondition of all liberal individual freedoms and central to the institutional differentiation of modern societies.[18] The liberal model of society which conflates state/public/political defined religion as private, nonpolitical, and marginal. Yet certain assumptions about the character of this privatization have proved incorrect. While religion no longer structures the taken for granted world view (ideology) of any Western society, it does not necessarily take a private role and it certainly has *not*, as has been realized in the past two decades, "withered away."[19] Americans' recent search for community has included increased participation in religions, such as a renewed interest in orthodoxy and alternative spiritualities, particularly among the more educated and affluent, and in charismatic religious experiences, generally among the less affluent. As Michael Dyson remarks, "Given the erosion of moral community across our nation, religion continues to provide moral strength and insight for millions of people through narratives of personal transcendence, ethical responsibility, and spiritual nurture."[20]

In the context of both these new perceptions and the sense of crisis in moral formation, many nonreligious intellectuals look to religion as offering the necessary transcendence which they believe will solve broadly experienced dislocation and alienation.[21] They argue that religion acts as a "sacred canopy" which provides the foundation of both personal and corporate life, binding and legitimizing the social order;[22] consequently, it is essential for the cohesion, and indeed for the survival, of any society.[23] Thus religion can encompass both the transcendental (Meaning 3) sense of community *and* seem to offer, as church, sect or cult,[24] the lived experience of community that many crave (Meanings 1 and 2).[25] It thus appears as a "solution" to the experienced loss of community. Yet this solution must be examined to see what kind of religious connections and traditions are being valorized. Religious institutions and their teachings, like any other institution of civil society, can reinforce exclusionary hierarchies *or* generate communities open to difference and connection.

In some ways, liberal Protestantism, the religious discourse highlighted here, would seem to be the least likely candidate for a communitarian discussion. In contrast to evangelical and fundamentalist Protestantisms, it seems to be a weakening player, unable to generate communities of much passion or conviction. Further, it lacks a strong heritage of teachings concerning public community such as the one enabling the U.S. Catholic Bishops to produce public moral statements on nuclear and economic issues.[26] However, discussing liberal Protestant thought in conjunction with a range of liberal arguments (from neoliberal and neoconservative to radical democratic and feminist) illuminates the problems of modernity and civil society with, I believe, a special clarity. The current dilemmas of liberal Protestantism are at the core of the problems of modernity since it was the religious body that most fully engaged with modernity and enjoyed a hegemonic status on the basis of that relationship. Now, no longer able to assume this cultural dominance, its struggle for identity and direction, its problem in constructing forms of public ethics, is paradigmatic of contemporary moral difficulties of the mostly white liberal middle and upper-middle classes who are the bulk of liberal Protestant membership.[27]

My suspicion is that the current discourse of community and public has been conducted primarily by and for males from the white middle or professional-

5

managerial class (PMC).[28] This contention emerges from a conviction that much of the discussion of the crisis of modernity and the wider communitarian debate which form the context of this work are rooted in a profound loss of community and identity among the white middle-class intellectuals who coin these theoretical accounts of community.[29] The PMC are products and producers of a liberal modernity which leaves us[30] with the "tradition of no tradition," that is, as participants in the traditions which have been most compromised by (if not eliminated by) the corrosions of modernity. Capitalism has erased the communal norms and traditions of most white Anglo-Saxon groups (or any group that has been "upwardly mobile"). Thus it is difficult to determine what communal forms can serve as sources for change.

At the same time, the white PMC faces challenges of submerged communities and traditions which have become more visible at the moment they are being incorporated more fully into the modern capitalist state. The newly-visible marginalized voices often bear different notions of community than the ones held in the dominant mainstream. For the marginalized, community may not be connected with power-as-dominance, but with the empowerment arising from resistance to that power (Meanings 5 and 6). For the privileged, community *is* connected with power as dominance. In both cases, the invocation of community is a claim of power, but to different forms of power. Thus the communitarian/communal discussion is inescapably about power and the effort to ensure social cohesion.

This initial discussion suggests the direction of my work that aims to highlight implicit assumptions about community present in current intellectual discourse. A concern for public ethics and its forms of solidarity is the thread that ties together the variety of authors, Christian and secular, evaluated in the rest of this book. Each of them asks whether some form of public morality is possible (or desirable) in our fragmented and plural society. And if it is possible, what kind of morality (or moralities) might it be? Each of them may be classified as seeking some sort of "communitarian" solution to problems understood to have been created by liberal modernity. They are all social critics, whose texts renegotiate and contest the nature of community, social morality, and common good. Although the dominant group within the PMC are white males, white women and men and women of color are also significant participants. While all share certain educational and economic resources, there are differences in their relation to the dominant discourse. The perspective on the problems of liberal modernity differs if the PMC member participates in a religious tradition or does not, is female or male, is Euro-American or African-American. Thus, while some attack liberal politics and philosophy as the culprits responsible for destroying morally necessary experiences of personal connection and common obligations, others highlight experiences of racial and gender oppression which "trouble the waters" of any simple claim to a common good. While some seek a homogeneous social morality, others call for a solidarity based upon the recognition of difference.

I begin with three important assumptions: (1) The discourse of community is a reaction against the nature of civil society in a social formation which includes a capitalist economy, a liberal polity, and a modernist culture in crisis. Common to "communitarians," critical theorists, postmodern theorists, and feminists is a deep criticism of liberal modernity and a search for some form of postliberal framework. To explore the context of this formation requires understanding capitalism, liberalism, and modernity as interrelated and to understand the shifting forces of postmodernity as they affect the formation of civil society. Persons in different social locations are positioned differently amidst these forces, and so the distinctive perspectives of white men, white women, and women and men of color need to be considered. (2) The texts / authors discussed here represent "contesting interests at stake in discursive constructions of the social."[31] Their arguments have to be analyzed in relation to the overall social formation. (3) Dialogue between religious and nonreligious discussions of community is essential. Religious ethics, most particularly liberal Protestant ethics, cannot engage with the current "moral crisis" without a grasp of social context and secular debates. Simultaneously, without an awareness of religious notions of community, nonreligious communal discourse is simply irrelevant to many members of U.S. society. I will use the rest of this chapter to discuss further these assumptions and to describe more fully a materialist methodology.

COMMUNITY AND CIVIL SOCIETY

Civil society is the social arena emerging within early capitalism distinct from both the market and the state.[32] Although its exact configuration is historically shaped, it includes cultural production, household life, some economic activities, voluntary associations and public discourse.[33] The dimension of civil society connected to the discourse of community discussed here is the public sphere, the arena where "individuals construct together with others the social meaning through which they interpret reality." These interpretations form our personal and social identities, connecting us to one another and to the state, thus forming the basis of our social order.[34]

My use of the term "community" corresponds both to this notion of civil society and to Jürgen Habermas's conception of lifeworld, a connection demonstrated by Jean Cohen's and Andrew Arato's extensive critical discussion of civil society as a contested terrain.[35] As Habermas has argued, the current legitimation crisis of advanced capitalism is rooted in the ways in which the differentiation and rationalization of social spheres has occurred as part of modernization. Society can be viewed as divided between system, that is, spheres directed by media of nonnormative instrumental rationality (such as money), and lifeworld, the stock of knowledge which "supplies members with unproblematic, common, background convictions."[36] The lifeworld is the realm, connected to but distinct from state and economy, where socially integrated values, norms, and beliefs are generated and transmitted.[37] It includes three functional components—culture, society, and personality—which involve "mutual understanding" [culture], "coordinating action" [society] and "socialization" [personalities].[38] Habermas argues that these functions make up the symbolic/communicative world in which we find our identities and on which the legitimation and cohesion of society rests. These processes occur both in the private sphere of family life and the public sphere of citizen deliberation, "of societal communication and voluntary association."[39]

With modernization, system and lifeworld become uncoupled from each other and increasingly differentiated. This in itself is not an inherently negative process as it has, for example, subjected norms to greater critical scrutiny and produced a greater capacity for reflective common consensus. However, as part of this development of modern capitalism, "spheres of communicative action [the differentiated lifeworld], centered on the reproduction of values and norms, are penetrated by a form of modernization guided by standards of economic and administrative rationality."[40] The instrumentalization of the lifeworld is dangerous because it destroys the social consensus foundational to the legitimation of the state, a consensus based upon our common store of moral, cultural, and social knowledge which shapes our view both of our social world and our place/identity within that world. As Habermas puts it, the systems of economy and state have "colonized" the lifeworld.

Habermas's notion of lifeworld, especially of the public sphere of the lifeworld, is a valuable conceptual tool which allows an entrypoint into connecting changes at the level of institutions with the types and possibilities of moral discourse. The diagnosis of legitimation crisis allows us to see the very specific material location of our concern for community, and the ways in which destabilized personal identity is linked with destabilized social legitimation.

Its usefulness increases if we alter Habermas's own focus on a single, liberal, bourgeois, public sphere.[41] Liberal thought has required some sort of unified public sphere constructed in opposition to a varied and particular set of experiences contained within the private sphere. What is important to realize is that in liberal theory, public has had a variety of meanings. It may mean only the state, or the state and the political sphere, or some sort of conflation of the state, the political and the economic spheres.[42] In virtually all of its configurations the public sphere has been the sphere of a particular group—bourgeois Euro-American men—and existed in relation to a variety of alternative or "subaltern counterpublics"[43] (working class, African-American, etc.) and semipublic private realms (women's groups, neighborhood connections, etc.).

The liberal discourse of politics has operated through exclusion, since the public/private distinction defined certain social relations and institutions as "beyond the realm of politics." As Nancy Fraser puts it, "[L]iberalism assumes the autonomy of the political in a very strong form....For liberals, then, the problem of democracy becomes the problem of how to insulate political processes from what are considered to be nonpolitical or prepolitical process-es."[44] Since issues in these realms—religion, family, marginalized cultures, sexuality, etc.—were excluded from public debate, the power and interests involved were, in spite of their importance to the public realm, invisible.[45]

The current concern for community is based in the exhaustion of the liberal capitalist consensus, the foundation of the nation state. The liberal presumption that the political community is coextensive with the cultural community can no longer be tacitly assumed, as newly recognized cultures and actors enter into the public political arena. As Seyla Benhabib puts it:

> All struggles against oppression in the modern world begin by redefining what had previously been considered private, nonpublic, and nonpolitical issues as matters of public concern, as issues of justice, as sites of power that need discursive legitimation.[46]

In our postmodern context, with a more fluid sense of "public" and "private," there is the possibility of multiple public spheres, both dominant and subaltern. The public sphere can then be understood as "the structured setting where cultural and ideological contest or negotiation among a variety of publics takes place," where both opinion and social identity are enacted and formed.[47]

Tracing the fortunes of the public sphere/community/civil society inevitably leads to a problem at the heart of this work (and the discourse of community). How do we evaluate the heritage of liberal capitalist modernity? Frequently, my account may sound like standard communitarian lamentation. And indeed there is much to lament. But it is important to understand the mixed heritage of modernity which is wonderfully captured by Marshall Berman: "To be modern is to find ourselves in an environment that promises adventure, power, joy, growth, transformation of ourselves and the world—and, at the same time, that threatens to destroy everything we know, everything we are."[48] This question of evaluation and categorization is key to postmod-ern/communal theories, most of which define themselves as antimodern.[49] Most evaluative discussions of modernity are dichotomized, presenting it as an unqualified good or an unqualified evil.

What is essential to my work—and what has been one of the most difficult issues to assess—is the morally *ambivalent* heritage of modernity/liberalism/capitalism. This ambivalence is noted by Jean Cohen and Andrew Arato when they speak of the "two-sidedness" of modernity and its two histories. One history is the development of "a more universalistic, inclusive, and pluralistic public life" (the liberal claim), while the other is "the penetration of culture through money and power" (the context for communitarian and postmodernist claims).[50] I acknowledge both of these dimensions, and argue that they both must be read in light of an ongoing history of exclusion.

Most of those who reject modernity are full participants in and beneficiaries of its heritage. As Charles Taylor remarks, "how inescapable this modern identity is for us, how much of it is involved even in what is seen as the most radical opposition to it."[51] Few of us would want to give up the political, social and material gains of modernization. Even as conservative and antimodern a theorist as Edward Shils remarks about Enlightenment modernity,

> The exercise of the capacity to reason and observe, disciplined into scientific activity, is one of the greatest we have cultivated in our civilization....The tradition of emancipation from traditions...has made citizens out of slaves and serfs....Sympathies have been broadened, the worth of human beings has been acknowledged and improved. Societies have become more human and more just....[52]

Although acknowledging the massive problems of inequitable access to goods and services, few would want to give up the material possibilities of better health care, more comfortable living, and broader access to education,[53] and increased acknowledgment of human rights and liberties. Further, it is by no means the case that *any* community or *any* tradition is, in and of itself, a good to be cherished. Modern discourses of equality and freedom helped to undermine traditions which treated people as inferior according to race, sex, class, sexuality, mental/physical ability. Indeed many movements of emancipation (Civil Rights, women's liberation, Solidarity, Third World decolonization, South African anti–apartheid) have used these discourses to bring their oppositional identities into national and international public arenas.

Nevertheless, any assessment of modernity must contend with the ways in which a liberal society was constructed by exclusions and oppressions that were not incidental but fundamental to its structure. Any reconstruction of civil society as community has to acknowledge the historical reality that under modernity this public sphere was constructed through the deliberate exclusion of selected groups of people and on the massive exploitation of what became the "Third World."[54] The liberal construction of civil society as a contract among equals not only concealed dependence upon ongoing institutions, but also concealed the reproduction and maintenance of domination by these institutions. John Keane writes that,

> This might be called the paradoxical achievement of the new contractarian theory of legitimacy. Its remarkable influence and its ability to induce

voluntary servitude flowed from its capacity to sustain widespread belief in its emancipatory claims through the systematic concealment of those internal and external impediments—such as psychic neuroses, or class, gender, and political inequalities—whose exposure would have revealed those claims to be self-contradictory.[55]

The ramifications of these exclusions live on in the liberal division between public and private spheres, which leaves politics as an activity generated only in the public life of individual citizens. Since the lives of women and minorities were considered as private matters, they were not considered participants in discourses of equality until they began to claim public space, or, in the case of feminist movements, began to redefine the nature of the private and public spheres.

Two dimensions of the exclusionary politics of liberalism are particularly relevant here: (1) the exclusions were not identical, i.e., the ways in which working-class white men were excluded from equality differed from the exclusions of middle-class white women and of African-American women and men. Since the exclusions are not identical, the corresponding issues of inclusion are similarly not identical. (2) As deconstructive theories have helped us understand, the exclusions do not mean simply that these groups were absent, but that the structures and categories comprising civil society were partially formed by this absence. As a result, inclusion can never be the liberal model of "add X and stir," but requires profound rethinking and reformation of the institutions involved. Since the "subaltern counterpublics" to be discussed in later chapters are those of white women and African-American women and men, these will be the groups highlighted here. Then I will return to the specific problems of liberal Protestantism.

Women: Outside the Social Contract

"Women," as Ruth Smith says, "are not just left out of the social contract; by design the contracts are arrangements of subordination."[56] The concept of the individual citizen participating in the social contract "was constructed via a series of oppositions to 'femininity,' which both mobilized older conceptions of domesticity and women's place and rationalized them into a formal claim concerning women's 'nature.'"[57] Viewing the changes from this historical perspective, it appears that the public developed not merely in ways which happened to exclude women and family, but that the emergent nature of modern constructions of the public, citizenship, and individuality *depended upon* the exclusion of women.

This argument has been most forcefully made by Carole Pateman, who argues that citizenship in the public sphere only gained its meaning, and thus was legitimated, through the presence of women in the private sphere. "The

11

fraternal social contract," she writes, "creates a new, modern patriarchal order that is present as divided into two spheres: civil society, or the universal sphere of freedom, equality, individualism, reason, contract, and impartial law—the realm of men or 'individuals'; and the private world of particularity, natural subjection, ties of blood, emotion, love, and sexual passion—the world of women, in which men also rule."[58] Liberal theory has theorized the public and political as a realm of equals which by excluding any form of particularity, and thus any participation by women, relies upon a world of structured inequalities. Correspondingly, even though domestic reproduction within the household was thoroughly shaped by capitalism, the bourgeois home and family were represented as "havens in a heartless world," where white women presided over a nest of natural harmony, separated from the necessary but morally questionable male world of power. Discussions of community among white feminists that highlight bonds of intimacy and care bear the positive and negative marks of this heritage. The incorporation of women into civil society requires thorough restructuring and rethinking of the institution of the family, the nature of politics, and the division of public and private spheres.

African Americans: Outsiders Inside

The term "black community" is commonly used to refer not to a geographical but a racial location. Historically, it was, of course, also a geographical location, as explicit segregation enforced separate black communities in the South, and implicit segregation has maintained black ghettoes in the North. For blacks and whites, "black community" has referred to an identity, a heritage of struggle and of invisibility. From the dominant perspective, just as the bourgeois family represented what must be cherished, the African-American community often represented what must be ignored or rejected. Ralph Ellison wrote,

> Since the beginning of the nation, white Americans have suffered from a deep inner uncertainty as to who they really are. One of the ways that has been used to simplify the answer has been to seize upon the presence of black Americans and use them as a marker, a symbol of limits, a metaphor for the 'outsider'.... But this is tricky magic. Despite his racial differences and social status, something indisputably American about Negroes not only raised doubts about the white man's value system but aroused the troubling suspicion that whatever else the true American is, he is also somehow black.[59]

The absence or acknowledgement of African Americans as part of the U.S. community or civil society reveals important presuppositions underlying calls for new community or moral order.

However, African-American communities have not and do not exist merely as the "shadow sides" of white dominance. Under slavery and segregation, African Americans forged their own relational bonds, creating a rich heritage of alternative publics. That heritage, like so many other communal bonds, is under siege and its condition is a vital part of any communitarian discourse.

Liberal Protestantism: No Longer Custodians

The disruption of civil society has very particular effects on current Christian ethics, most specifically "oldline" liberal Protestant ethics.[60] The dominant model of liberal Protestant religion has been based in the moral consensus Bellah has called civil religion, "the religious symbol system which relates the citizen's role and American society's place in space, time, and history to the conditions of ultimate existence and meaning."[61] This tradition, dominated by liberal Protestantism, was classically summed up by Will Herberg as commitment to the American Way of Life.[62] Yet its synthetic capacity depended upon an underlying coherence of Christian churches and modern U.S. culture, evident, for example, in the works of the Niebuhr brothers. For much of this century, liberal Protestant churches have served as bridging institutions "by mediating religious meanings and values broadly in the culture, and by expressing concern for society as well as the cure of souls…providing a meaningful transcendent vision embracing personal as well as social existence."[63]

However, liberal Protestant Christianity has lost its position as the "custodian" for the dominant culture. With the Enlightenment and the rise of capitalism, Christianity had long ago lost its direct, established political power in the West. And now with the growth of techno-consumer culture, liberal Protestantism has increasingly lost its moral authority. The rapid proportional decline of membership in these churches from the 60s until the present suggests that the bridge no longer holds and that civil religion no longer serves as civic cement or as vital community.[64] Michaelsen and Roof remark, "No longer the custodians of the culture in quite the way they once were, [liberal Protestants] must now truly accept the fact of pluralism and face religious and secular realities unlike any before."[65]

The loss of cultural and social dominance has posed peculiar problems for liberal Protestants and for liberal Protestant ethics. Since liberal theory locates religion within the private sphere of civil society, liberal Protestant intellectuals have generally viewed it as separate from material (economic and political) realities.[66] Further, given its location at the center of a social consensus, liberal Protestantism had little need to ask itself questions about public role, politics, or relations to those different than itself. In other words, as Beverly Harrison has argued, liberal Protestant religion, has "operate[d] with ideological blinders."[67] Through its dominance, liberal Protestant culture and morality have been neutral and invisible.

13

With the loss of hegemonic status of liberal Protestantism, these blinders no longer function. The public arena, already opened through modernity to scientific claims against religion, has now opened to claims of other cultures and religions. The social relations which formed the (unacknowledged) foundation for mainstream ethics no longer exist, which reopens Protestant Christianity as an arena of political, social, and religious contestation. On the one hand, the voices of conservative and fundamentalist Christians, and, on the other, voices of submerged critical traditions such as African-American Christianity have become more visible. So what types of social relations should now be assumed (if not acknowledged), as liberal Protestant Christian ethics struggles to determine its identity from a new location?

This new and uneasy awareness expresses itself as the question of what kind of public voice is possible for the liberal Protestant Christian church in the United States. Under Protestant hegemony, the question of Christian public ethics was a nonquestion, as the public culture itself was primarily an Anglo-Saxon Christian culture. The answer to this newly-posed question includes, necessarily, a description of Christian community and the relation of that community to the national community and its pluralized social order. It also requires liberal Protestant Christian ethics to face the question of its own marginality. As Jeffrey Stout poses the question, "can theology retain its distinctiveness as a mode of utterance without ceasing to speak persuasively to the culture it would like to influence?"[68]

14

In this troubled situation, Protestant ethicists are understandably attracted to the claim found in many "communitarian" writings that a religious framework is vital for society, providing the essential resource for restoration of a shared communal moral order or common good. Such a model of religion usually rests upon Durkheim's idea of religion as a force uniting disparate elements of society into an "organic" community. It also assumes a nation–state–community identity that, if it ever existed at all, is no longer valid now. Most of the communitarian models of religion are nostalgic recreations, I contend, of the old model of liberal Protestantism as civil religion which "create[s], maintain[s] and express[es] the national community."[69] The obsolescence of this model is shown in the way that the messy institutional realities of religious life are avoided in favor of a view of religion as an unproblematic homogeneous moral tradition. The type of religion and the theology presumed in such accounts continues to represent the Christian heritage as a smooth and undifferentiated line of development.

Yet depending on its social and ideological location, religion can equally well be a force disruptive of the status quo. The communitarian model runs the risk of ignoring social differences, banishing politics from morality, affirming a continuous and unified historical tradition, and privileging a harmonious model of community. Critical analysis of the ideological dimensions of these claims will enable Christian ethicists to avoid what Harrison describes as "a naively uncritical use of philosophical assumptions" that does "not correlate with our sociohistorical theological assumptions and accountabilities."[70]

MATERIALIST METHOD

The conceptual tools of civil society and lifeworld are, as I have indicated, multifaceted. I wish here to develop the materialist dimension of these concepts by connecting them to notions of ideology and hegemony which describe processes occurring in the lifeworld. These connections will help focus my later discussion of the contesting interests present within the discursive constructions of community in the texts analyzed.

Morality emerges from our common life. It is, as Birch and Rasmussen put it, "a kind of social glue...It keeps society sufficiently intact to let people get on with the living of life...."[71] Or, in the words of Alan Wolfe, it "is a socially constructed practice negotiated though learning agents."[72] In current discussions of morality, neither of these are necessarily controversial claims. In the past decades there has been a turn against the definition of ethics as a set of abstract and universalizable principles which exist outside of any given historical framework. And there has been a corresponding turn, an essential part of the communitarian tendencies discussed here, towards notions of morality as social, embedded, particular—as Alasdair MacIntyre puts it, "I can only answer the question 'What am I to do?' if I can answer the prior questions 'Of what story or stories do I find myself a part?'"[73] This shift is broad enough to encompass neo-Aristotelians such as MacIntyre, semisectarian Protestants such as Stanley Hauerwas, revisionist Hegelians such as Michael Walzer, liberation theologians such as Sharon Welch and Cornel West, and socialist feminists such as Iris Young.

Although the statement that morality is an embedded social practice is no longer daring, what is more controversial is the way the matrix of social reality is described and understood. "Moral theory," Seyla Benhabib writes, "is limited, on the one hand, by the macroinstitutions of a polity, politics, administration and the market....On the other hand, moral theory is limited by culture, its repertoire of interpretations."[74] To understand the possibilities of moral theory requires understanding the current state of both "macroinstitutions" and culture.

This materialist approach to moral questions contrasts with other current approaches. One approach, held by several of the figures discussed in this work, evaluates morality in relation to a goal of a harmonious social reality. What is lacking in these accounts of morality stressing harmony is an acknowledgement of the role of politics, power and material economic forces. Society is a realm shot through with different forms of power, a realm of conflicting and contradictory social and cultural forces rooted in forms of economic production. What is at stake is the construction of postliberal ethics that model a civil society/community where difference, conflict, and negotiation are accepted as processes essential to personal and social formation, rather than a mark of "politicization" of morality.

The invisibility of power, politics, and material reality is a particular problem for Christian ethics which has used the privatization of religion as a shield against the possibility of publicly contested morality. "All basic theological and moral questions," says Beverly Harrison, "are about power-in-relationship."[75] However, mainstream theology and ethics have generally refused to examine this material reality and rejected any notion of the ideological nature of their stances. An excellent example arises in Dennis McCann's response to the political stances of liberation theologies. McCann says we must distinguish religious transcendence (the foundation of theology and religious ethics) from partisan politics or praxis.[76] He assumes the capacity of Christian ethics to separate neatly (a privatized) faith from social life, politics, and, consequently, from issues of power. Any faith stance that explicitly names its political accountabilities is compromising the "purity" of religious belief.

In contrast, I argue that we need not, in fact, we *cannot*, simply divorce religion from considerations of power. Religion is about our human relations and our relations to God which are relations occurring in specific times and places. As Harrison puts it, "Christian ethical discourse is not, in the first instance, language about faith. It is language about ourselves in relation to our world, our agency or action in a social context, as that action is understood from 'the moral point of view'."[77] In using this language we are shaped by the particularities of our location. As Juan Luis Segundo has demonstrated, faith is inextricably mixed with ideologies, so the challenge is not to find a "Christian" position above the conflict, but to clarify the location and accountabilities of particular Christian commitments.[78]

Ideological critique is also to be distinguished from a deconstructionist/post-structuralist approach generally derived from the work of Michel Foucault. Foucault's work has, of course, had an enormous impact upon all forms of social theory and ethics, including revised marxist approaches. It has clarified ways in which our reality, especially our subjective reality, is socially constructed and shot through with power. Power is not unidimensional but "something which circulates...It is...never in anybody's hands.... Power is employed and exercised through a net-like organization... [individuals] are always in the position of simultaneously undergoing and exercising this power."[79] Foucault's concept of discursive power, as Rosemary Hennessy puts it,

> makes available a way to examine how power is exercised concretely and in detailed ways.... It also advances the critique of humanism and intervenes in discussion of language and subjectivity among poststructuralists

and marxists by considering power as a positive and discursive force rather than the property of an individual or group.[80]

By demonstrating the complexity of discourse, "the very form of action inhabited by thought," made up of language, itself a social structure, Foucault's work allows a greater understanding of the ways morality can embody power.[81]

On the basis of the greater subtlety of a discourse model of language and texts, much current academic work dismisses or ignores revised marxist notions of ideology as "totalizing" and "deterministic." In spite of the value of discourse theory, I argue for a continued use of an ideological critique model. Although marxist notions must be criticized, such as the obsolete notion of the proletariat as the sole revolutionary subject [82] and the deterministic model of economic base and ideological superstructure, these concepts have, over the course of the twentieth century, been profoundly revised. Revised marxist theory considers a variety of transformative agents operating within a social formation where there is interactive relationship among the different spheres of economics, politics, civil society, etc.[83]

At first glance, these marxist revisions seem to be leading me to the very poststructuralist position I am criticizing, stressing the "microphysics" of power played out in sites of discursive difference. Yet approaches relying solely on discourse often avoid confronting the structured nature of power and its relation to economic forces which a marxist or materialist theory insists upon.[84] As Hennessy argues, in a poststructuralist discursive model, power is so fully dispersed that it becomes difficult to analyze any organized forces of oppression, particularly their economic components.[85] If everything is power, it is difficult to make moral and practical distinctions about different kinds of power.[86] As several critics of Foucault have pointed out, the loss of any kind of normative agency, social or individual, in favor of a multiple play of forces may reproduce the oppressive relations it intends to critique. Speaking of the deconstructive turn of postmodern theory, David Harvey remarks that it "has us accepting the reifications and partitionings, actually celebrating the activity of masking and covering…while denying that kind of metatheory which can grasp the political-economic processes…that are becoming ever more universalizing in their depth, intensity, reach, and power over daily life."[87]

Many critics, generally either white women or women of color, have remarked that it is, in fact, those who still gain the most from (capitalist) modernity who are most interested in attacking it. Kumkum Sangari comments on the irony of a postmodern radical deconstruction that has not halted the radical material deconstruction/destruction capitalism continues to carry out in the third world. And Nancy Hartsock expresses suspicion of the loss of the modern category of the self, just as those who have been excluded from

17

that category (white women, women and men of color) begin to visibly claim that selfhood.[88] Both of these observations can help us see the ways in which communitarian antimodernity may be part of a reconstruction of privilege and power.

To consider community as an ideological discourse is to study it as part of the "array of sense-making practices which constitute what counts as 'the way things are' in any historical moment."[89] Within this array, it is also necessary to identify dominating ideologies:

> which function—though never fully successfully—to render the power relations of civil society invisible and, thus, to insulate them from public questioning and social and political action...[Ideology] functions as a condition of false compromise and unity among conflicting social groups....[90]

As a dominant ideology, therefore, morality can serve to legitimate the power of particular groups by presenting their interests as general. Yet these forms of morality and power are never simple reflections of these interests, but often contradictory discourses emerging from a variety of attempts at domination and resistance to that domination. As Gerald Fourez puts it, "ethical codes seem to be the result of a multitude of localized strategies that, little by little, give rise to ethical structures linked to a given society" and thus cannot be understood simply as a coherent imposition of a given set of interests.[91] Ideology is never merely the ideas, beliefs and practices of dominant groups, but a contested arena of differing forms of power.

To evaluate the complex relation of contesting ideological forces, Gramsci's notion of hegemony is helpful. Revising Marx's notion of civil society as merely a forum for bourgeois interests, he defines civil society as the arena for a struggle for hegemony, or domination. To him, hegemony explained the subtle noncoercive ways in which the capitalist state maintains and legitimates its authority.[92] The goal of those with power, he wrote, was "the attainment of a 'cultural-social' unity through which a multiplicity of dispersed wills, with heterogeneous aims, are welded together with a single aim, on the basis of an equal and common conception of the world...," a notion remarkably close to some current notions of community and common good.[93] Gramsci's insight was that this welding often did not happen through force but through an apparent "spontaneity" which was brought about through the activity of intellectuals and "the power of attraction" of their ideas.[94]

Hegemony, operating through cultural formations such as religious institutions, schools, family, and media, allows the domination of the interests of a few over the interests of many, not through the kind of repression that can foment rebellion, but through the multitude of social processes that make up our ongoing sense of ordinary reality: "It is a whole body of practices and expectations, over the whole of living: our senses and assignments of energy, our shaping perceptions of ourselves and the world. It is a lived system of meanings and values—constitutive and constituting—which as they are experienced as practices appear reciprocally confirming. It thus constitutes a sense of reality for most people in the society."[95] Hegemonic ideologies allow us to envision our fractured world as a smooth and seamless whole.

In spite of appearances, the ongoing maintenance of hegemony is not a smooth manipulation, but an uneven process involving conflict and compromise, selection and rejection.[96] Through cultural activity, ruling interests can mediate potentially disruptive conflicts in ways that can reaffirm the overall social consensus. Jim Merod writes that this consensus

> embodies the negotiated compromises that allow competing interests to transform potentially violent eruptions into agreements about larger 'national' or general social interests that must be preserved for the 'benefit' of all. Inescapably, within or underneath that putative coherence, disruptive forces remain with considerable volatility.[97]

Thus the exploration of hegemony and ideology asks us to consider the key areas of conflict, the "slips and cracks."[98] My contention is that the discourse of community is currently one of these areas, where "cracks" in the institutions of civil society are being addressed. If this is the case, then it is important to ask, where is there an effort to reassert the power of ruling ideas? Where is there resistance? What is at stake are which ideas, experiences and traditions are to be authorities, shaping our social life together.

Raymond Williams's specification of the workings of hegemony is a helpful tool for distinguishing among different forces within a hegemonic formation. Cultural processes, he argues, can be categorized in three ways: dominant, residual and emergent. Dominant is the hegemonic, legitimated world view at a given time. Residual views are elements of the past which continue to shape culture and may, in fact, offer an important criticism of current society. Emergent practices are new meanings, values, and relationships. Williams specifies certain difficulties in discerning different elements within residual and emergent practices. Within residual practices, it is "crucial" to distinguish between the potential oppositional nature of "certain experiences, meanings and values which cannot be expressed or substantially verified in terms of the dominant culture, [that] are nevertheless lived and practiced on the basis of the residue...of some previous social and cultural institution...." and "that active manifestation of the residual...which has been wholly or largely incorporated into the dominant culture." Similarly, within emergent practices, it is, he admits, "difficult to distinguish between those which are really elements of some new phase of the dominant culture… and those which are substantially alternative."[99] Cornel West has reappropriated these distinctions as hegemonic (dominant), prehegemonic (residual), neohegemonic (incorporated residual and emergent) and counterhegemonic (oppositional residual and emergent), which are the terms I will use here.[100]

What is relevant here, in relation to the discourse of community, is what Williams terms the "difficult" distinction between oppositional and incorporating practices. In its origin, the current discussion of community tends to be backwards-looking / residual, trying to retrieve elements from a nonmodern past. Some notions of community are residual / neohegemonic practices which appear to oppose the dominant world view but actually reaffirm and renew ongoing structures of power. Others participate in counterhegemonic culture, both residual and emergent, which develops as actual opposition to the existing order, consisting of practices and understandings that cannot be contained or realized within the established order. The communal proposals considered here generally purport to radically critique the liberal status quo—which would probably signal neo- or counterhegemonic discourses.[101]

The challenge neohegemonic work offers to the status quo can conceal the underlying effort to reassert older forms of domination. For example, many of the communitarian efforts, undertaken primarily by white male PMC intellectuals, purport to reformulate a liberal homogeneous model of society. Yet the communitarian emphasis on historically-rooted, pluralized identities must be put under critical scrutiny. In communitarian discourse, pluralism can operate as a term that implies a harmony of different interest groups, a use which conceals loss of hegemony and struggles for new forms of power. As Craig Owens puts it, "Pluralism reduces us to being an other among others; it is not a recognition, but a reduction of difference to absolute indifference, interchangeability."[102] In other words, pluralism is a way to recognize the inescapable existence of different others, but to avoid the challenges their communities, traditions, and ways of life may offer. The communitarian pluralist community and its people are "constituted retrospectively as something homogeneous."[103] Society and its moral formations are constructed as sites of harmony, a process of ideological closure seeking to repress conflict, contestation, and struggle. Thus, what appears as a critique of the dominant liberal capitalist social formation may turn out to be an attempt to maintain the power of those benefitting from this status quo. The call to community can be a call to resistance or a call to preserve dominating power.

Williams's categories are heuristic aids to help us sift through the complex, multiple and contradictory world of community and civil society. Attention to ideologies and forms of hegemony allows critical analysis of positions, discerning both their overall location and possible contrasting or conflicting strands within the position itself. It also leads to suspicion of accounts of community (or of tradition, history, or society) that suggest smooth and homogeneous social relations. This suspicion can be further refined with the help of the work of Seyla Benhabib. In her discussion of communitarianism, Benhabib describes two different communitarian forms which she labels "integrationist" and "participatory." According to the integrationist view, disruptions of community life have led to destructive individualism, egotism, anomie and alienation which "can only be solved by a recovery or a revitalization of some coherent value scheme" (such as religion or a form of civic republicanism) which stresses reconciliation, harmony, and value homogeneity. From the participationist perspective (which Benhabib prefers), what is at stake is not "the loss of a sense of belonging" but "a loss of *political agency and efficacy*" resulting from the contradictions between the various spheres of a divided modern society.[104] Meaningfulness, the remedy for alienation, is not a matter of putting together a coherent framework of pregiven values, but reducing contradiction through political and institutional changes which occurs through our participation with others in a process producing collective norms.

The integrationist stress on meaning reproduces a liberal notion of culture in opposition to a realm of politics defined as either a jockeying for power or the official business of government and state. The related model of community and membership is one where commonality of shared beliefs and heritage is prized over and against conflict, difference, and negotiation. The participationist view, on the other hand, depends upon a notion of politics as involving contestation and power. This model of community and membership would see commonality as an ongoing process of conflict and negotiation of differences, where there can be no simple fixed or pregiven traditions and identities.

An ideological approach suggests that any theory of community that proposes a normative model of smooth, harmonious and homogeneous social relations must be treated with critical suspicion. Yet such proposals are evident in many of the communal frameworks analyzed here which are often explicitly aiming to counterpose a model of normative harmony in contrast to what is perceived as the fragmented and alienated individualism of liberal modernity. Evident in a wide range of theorists is the presumption that the closeness of community, the desired harmony of "spontaneous" and "immediate" social relations, the transparent relationship to 'tradition' are all only possible in a homogenized context.[105] The nostalgia evident in the idea of *Gemeinschaft*, "the longing for that simpler, ordered, homogenized world that once satisfied the 'wholeness-hunger' of individual, subculture and larger culture"[106] continues in many of the writers discussed here.[107] Underlying the vision of homogeneous community is a romantic, often nostalgic, model of community, which looks to a world, in either a past or a future golden age, where there was no conflict, no challenge, no difference to mar intimate and immediate relations.

One of the most powerful symbols of homogeneous community is often the family. Both feminist and communitarian views of community are often rooted, implicitly or explicitly, in the model of the family, where blood ties are presumed to offer the most immediate, fulfilling, and satisfying relationships. "Community is a fusion of feeling and thought, of tradition and commitment, of membership and volition....Its archetype, both historically and symbolically, is the family."[108] For many, the family is the "haven in a heartless world," the source of intimate and supportive relationships in a frightening, draining and alienating society. As used in communal discourse, family also denotes a major source of collective moral education. It has stood for "a profound collective yearning for enduring emotional bonds and a fear that the social fabric ha[s] become dangerously frayed."[109] Thus it has served as a potent symbol of all the fears about society's condition and a barometer for society's health.

Often the effort to reassert "family" includes an agenda of retreat from all of the positive changes in women's status achieved in modernity. While more conservative communal theorists acknowledge this agenda, more liberal ones often are silent about possible implications of their proposals. As Susan Moller Okin puts it, "The communitarian critics of liberalism have by and large compounded liberal theory's blindness to the facts of gender and neglect of the family as a politically relevant institution."[110]

This discussion of method suggests two criteria essential for assessing the hegemonic implications of any communal proposal. The first is the issue of inclusion/exclusion or the problem of difference. As Iris Young puts it, the harmonious model of community "exemplifies the logic of identity...desire for fusion of subjects."[111] The second criterion emerges from the way in which this model excludes issues of power and politics. John Keane describes communitarianism as a "deep ideology of homeostasis" in which the issue of political power is rendered invisible. What is at stake here, I believe, are two different conceptions of politics. The first presumes a liberal notion of politics and power as the balancing between competing interest groups, each advocating its own self-interest (as can be found, for example, in Reinhold Niebuhr's sense of justice as the necessary balance of corrupt interests in a sinful world).[112] Culture and history are reduced to interests which are subsumed under politics. As I have suggested, the entrance of marginalized cultures into the public political sphere has forced both liberal and communitarian intellectuals to recognize the problems with this reduction of culture. However, I have argued that many communal thinkers make the same separation of politics and morality, citizenship and communal membership. Instead of privileging politics, they privilege culture and history, but end up, as do liberals, with truncated definitions of both which serve to exclude those marginal to the dominant forms of politics and culture.

For a contrasting conception, I point again to Benhabib's notion of participationist community which suggests that community as a meaningful form is constructed through the conflict, struggle and compromise of groups with different needs and different abilities to realize those needs. It resonates with many of the concerns of liberation ethics, one of the important background sources of this work. In a liberation-oriented theology and ethics, the concern for meaning, as a category separated from politics, is a concern peculiar to the privileged, and serves as an ideological cover for their own maintenance of power. In contrast, a perspective that tries to include marginalized voices will stress the need for agency. Speaking from a feminist liberationist viewpoint, Ruth Smith gives a participatory definition of agency:

> Agency involves responding to the needs, responsibilities, and choices within the constraints of our experiences and situations. Agency also involves the changing historical conditions of our particular nexus of relations and the critical self-consciousness and activity through which we become aware of our relations and seek to change them....To become a moral subject is itself a moral task, if not the central moral task.[113]

The desire for community is not simply a desire for acquiring a set of pregiven cultural traditions and forms of meaning, but also a desire for shared, purposeful participation that positively shapes one's own life and that of others. Participation in relation to others is the basis for solidarity, where the ties of community do not demand sameness, but foster care and responsibility across difference.

QUESTIONS AND CRITERIA

As is doubtless evident by now, my purposes in this text are complex and multifaceted. To return to where I began, community is currently a powerful term because of the perception (often partial and unconscious) of the crisis of our institutions of civil society. I have suggested that tracing the components of different models of community will reveal underlying forms of power. For example, to return to the list of different communal definitions at the beginning of this chapter in light of the previous discussion of method, Meanings 1–4 are likely to be part of integrative, neohegemonic models of community that suppress material realities such as economic structures and political conflict. Meanings 5 and 6, on the other hand, are much more likely to be part of participatory, counter-hegemonic models that seek to realize the equal worth of all involved. And, given a marginalized social location, Meaning 4 could also have counter-hegemonic possibilities. Further, the same position could contain a mix of models requiring the sorting out of different strands.

23

The task for the remainder of this work is to sort out some of the strands through examination of the communal / communitarian debate among intellectuals who are social / cultural critics, seeking to diagnose and cure the problems of society. I have deliberately not restricted the selection only to those writers identified as "communitarian," because of my sense of the limitations of that discussion. The "communitarian debate" is a discussion particular to the discipline of philosophy—and the problem of civil society goes beyond any discipline. Further, in even the most "popular" forms of communitarianism, there is little dialogue with those who are not white and male. Women of all colors and African Americans appear more often as problems (of family and urban communal life), and their thoughts on civil society are not solicited.[114]

American tradition has suffered and, to a large extent, still suffers from selective memory which constructs a model of civil society whose harmony is achieved through "strategies of depoliticization and amnesia" which "obscure or distort the collective memory of minority traditions."[115] Sadly enough, the form of religion in which I participate, liberal Protestantism has been part of this amnesia. A small hope of restoration and renewal lies in dialogue about all parts of civil society among all citizens of this country, a dialogue that seeks not only to acknowledge the impact of racism, sexism, and heterosexism, but also names the ways in which liberal capitalist modernity, the bringer of many riches, has had serious consequences for our collective moral lives.

My work here is a modest contribution to this dialogue, by someone who seeks to understand her contradictory and confusing role as an intellectual who is, in alphabetical order, Christian, female, PMC and white. In the following chapter, I will discuss more fully the context of liberal capitalist modernity that I claim is the precondition to any discussion of community. Although this chapter draws on a variety of sources, I turn most to Jürgen Habermas's critical theory of modernity and David Harvey's marxist analysis of postmodern culture. The next three chapters will bring three contrasting groups of "dialogue partners" into play. In chapter 3, I discuss the most visible communitarian positions, those of white males. To reveal the limitations and possibilities of this area of discussion, I have chosen a spectrum of thinkers, ranging from neoconservative (Daniel Bell and Richard Neuhaus) to radical democrat (Michael Walzer and Larry Rasmussen) with an "in-between" position (Christopher Lasch and Stanley Hauerwas). The secular thinkers (Bell, Walzer, and Lasch) respond to the problems of liberal modern individualism, pluralization, and alienation with proposals for renewed communal moral order. The liberal Protestant intellectuals (Neuhaus,[116] Rasmussen, and Hauerwas) seek to recast Christian public ethics in light of a revised sense of Christian community.

White feminist thought is the focus of chapter 4 where I explore the ways in which feminist approaches to community straddle the morally ambivalent heritage of modern liberal capitalism, affirming gains made by many women within modernity, while pointing to new forms of oppression women experience.[117] I will examine these ambivalences in a combination of secular and Christian white feminists: Jean Bethke Elshtain, Lisa Cahill, Iris Young, and Sharon Welch. From their marginalized location as women, they offer critiques and alternative visions of community that have not yet been taken into consideration by the male theorists of public order. Yet these writers still must be evaluated in relation to the white privilege of a homogeneous understanding of community. Within this group of women I have tried to match a Christian and secular writer, according to political position. Thus I study neoliberal political theorist Jean Bethke Elshtain, along with liberal Catholic Lisa Sowle Cahill.[118] Both women, I demonstrate, tend to emphasize the value of the distinctiveness of "women's" nature. And I examine social democrat Iris Young who seeks to emphasize difference over commonalities, along with liberation theologian Sharon Welch who tries to resolve the issues of white middle-class women by a turn to the narratives of black women. Their works, as I will show, carry on some of the problems found in the other figures considered here, but also begin, I believe, to suggest some new possibilities for community.

My final group of "dialogue partners" is drawn from the voices of the African-American community. I first discuss the distinctive historical experience of oppression and separation which has resulted in two dominant models of community: integration and nationalism, represented here by the thought of Martin Luther King, Jr. and Malcolm X. Then I consider how contemporary black intellectuals struggle to revise community in light of the post-Civil Rights black experience. Again I consider a range of views from neoconservative Glenn Loury to radical democrats Cornel West and bell hooks, with special attention to the womanist expression of community in the work of Emilie Townes and Delores Williams.

Of all these dialogue partners, I will be asking a similar set of questions, derived from the considerations of context and method discussed in this chapter:

— How is the problem of community diagnosed? Why does an author believe community has been 'lost'? Does this account acknowledge the role of capitalism, or focus only on the cultural and philosophical aspects of modernity?

— Does the author locate community in the public or private sphere? What relation does is there between community and nation?

— What is the role, if any, of religion in community/civil society? In the case of the Christian theorists, how do they define the relation between church community and social or political community?

— How does the author define and discuss politics? Is politics viewed as antithetical to a hoped for integrated morality? Or are participatory politics seen as central to the formation of community?

25

— Does the suggested vision of community recognize issues of power, domination, and difference? Or does it assume that immediacy of relationship requires homogeneity? What are the criteria for inclusion and exclusion within the community? Are these viewed as "natural" or historical? What tradition(s) or other forms of authority does the theory acknowledge (or include)? Does it recognize different traditions?

Finally, in the concluding chapter of this work, I will assess what has been learned and suggest some beginning criteria for models of community/civil society that seek to embody the solidarity necessary for an emancipatory Christian community ethics.

ALL THAT IS SOLID MELTS INTO AIR
A Brief Account of Modernity and Postmodernity

All fixed, fast-frozen relations, with their train of ancient and
venerable prejudices and opinions, are swept away, all new-
formed ones become antiquated before they can ossify. All
that is solid melts into air, all that is holy is profaned, and man
is at last compelled to face with sober sense, his real conditions of life, and his relations with his kind.
—Karl Marx and Friedrich Engels[1]

chapter 2

THE DISCOURSE of community as a postmodern discourse counters, either
implicitly or explicitly, some of the effects—if not the entire project—of
modernity. Most specifically, the language of community highlights through
reaction what have come to be considered problematic dimensions of modernity, such as ceaseless innovation, autonomous individuality, privileging the
universal over the particular. Yet, what is often left unsaid in these communitarian accounts is that Western modernity is *capitalist* modernity, inescapably
bound to changing conditions of production, circulation, and consumption.
The radicalized consciousness of modernity is the product of the "creative
destruction embedded in the circulation of capital itself."[2] The pervasive
spread of modern capitalism has uprooted social formations based on interdependent subsistence production and stable (albeit often oppressive) traditions.
The ambivalent heritage of this development, the context for the language of
community, is the focus of this chapter.

Over the past few centuries, capitalism has uncoupled economic production and exchange from the constraints of tradition, kinship, and government, slowly "rationalizing" the many facets of everyday life. As the organizing force of our social order, capitalism has, over time, restructured community-based societies into economic markets, social contractual relations, and state relations.[3] Although aspects of modernity, such as the development of individualism and the challenge to feudal forms of authority, can be discerned in Europe as early as 1500,[4] the rapid and radical transformation of social orders must be seen in conjunction with the development of industrial economy and technologies in the seventeenth and eighteenth centuries. At that time the Great Western Transmutation "set off westerners decisively from the rest of mankind. "[5]

The prerequisite for the social changes affecting community was an increasingly rapid rate of economic transformation and technological innovation. Capitalism slowly transformed family-based agricultural and artisanal production to factory-based industrial production. Capitalist development meant the gradual disappearance of old forms of village communal life. Instead of sharing a village green where everyone's animals could graze, individuals went off to factories nearby or in the expanding cities to make their living. Livelihood was measured by individual salaries, rather than by the amount of crops and livestock a family or community could produce. "Market-regulated activities, managed and controlled by a handful of Europeans [and, eventually, also Americans] began to eat into and break down older social structures in nearly all parts of the earth easily accessible." [6]

Rooted in these economic developments, the Great Western Transmutation or modern western capitalism encompassed changes and trends at all levels: technological, economic, social, political, intellectual, emotional, and relational. Summing up the complex process, Jürgen Habermas writes,

> The concept of modernization refers to a bundle of processes that are cumulative and mutually reinforcing: to the formation of capital and the mobilization of resources; to the development of forces of production and the increase in productivity of labor; to the establishment of centralized political power and the formation of national identity; to the proliferation of rights of political participation, of urban forms of life and of formal schooling; to the secularization of values and norms....[7]

This process has, as I will discuss, powerfully shaped the nature and possibilities of legitimizing foundational social and communal forms within civil society.

Capitalist development has meant an overall process of rationalization that is at the heart of many aspects of modernity. Habermas's distinction between system and lifeworld, discussed in the previous chapter, helps clarify the immense societal impact of this rationalization. To use his terms, capitalism both reoriented the *nature* of what he describes as system and lifeworld, and reoriented the *relation between* system and lifeworld. With modernity, these realms, previously embedded in one another, began to uncouple as each underwent a process of rationalized differentiation and growth in structural complexity. As Habermas has described it, the realm of system or material reproduction becomes organized according to purposive-rational action, that is, instrumental action governed by technical rules and empirical knowledge, which is the basis of both economic institutions and state bureaucracy.[8] For my purposes, however, what is significant is not so much the change in the system, but the accompanying transformation in the lifeworld, the realm of symbolic reproduction that constructs our world views, the order that shapes our own development and our interaction with others. Under capitalism, as Habermas explains it, the lifeworld (or civil society) becomes differentiated into different spheres:

> *On the cultural level*, the core, identity-securing traditions separate off from the concrete contents with which they are still tightly interwoven in mythical [i.e., premodern] worldviews. They shrink to formal elements....
> *At the level of society*, general principles and procedures crystallize out of the particular contexts to which they are tied in primitive societies.... *On the level of the personality system*, the cognitive structures acquired in the socialization process are increasingly detached from the content of cultural knowledge....[9]

This differentiation and rationalization, "the inner logic of cultural modernity,"[10] has had decisive implications for the themes of community and religion explored here. Religion lost its power as the source of legitimating symbolic tradition as "the authority of the holy [was] gradually replaced by the authority of an achieved consensus."[11] Rational forms of thought emerged which questioned all traditional assumptions on the basis of the authority of reason and the senses. In the name of scientific truth, bourgeois thought challenged many of the old hierarchies and assumptions: "Typically criticizing the past in the name of their own scientific and universally valid claims, bourgeois ideology radically weakened the objective, authoritative power of systems of myth, metaphysics, and customary ritual,"[12] that is, the forms that had previously constituted the foundations of society. Religion and its institutions became more marginalized as they appropriated or rejected these new forms of rationality. Instead of societies formed on the basis of sacred authority, societies began to rest upon ideas of achieved consensus, or some form of participatory social contract.[13]

Since constitutional governments gradually replaced monarchies, the key legitimating identity formation came to be based upon nationality. With the dissolution of the tight structures of local feudal life, the nation began to be viewed as the primary community. Benedict Anderson, who has brilliantly described this process, writes that "the idea of the nation ... is conceived as a solid community moving steadily down (or up) history. An American will never meet, or even know the names of more than a handful of his 240,000,000-odd fellow-Americans.... But he has complete confidence in their steady, anonymous, simultaneous activity."[14] This "confidence" is the basis for one's identity as citizen and for the ongoing legitimation of the social order.

However, as Habermas has pointed out, "One does not 'have' [nationality] in the way one has family background; it can be acquired and lost."[15] There is, necessarily, a built-in tension between citizenship and membership, which I would describe as a tension between what is understood as an "artificial" or chosen affiliation and a "natural" or given affiliation.[16] To maintain legitimacy, the modern nation must create conditions under which the chosen affiliation of citizenship appears as the natural connection of membership. Through this ideological transformation, citizenship becomes "a direct sense of membership based on loyalty to a civilization which is a common possession."[17] Thus, the question of legitimacy is based on the lived experiences of "recognition, identity and membership,"[18] the experiences constituting what we live as community.

Liberal nation states claimed allegiance not on the basis of the story of the divine right of kings, but on the basis of the story of the primordial consent of the "people," those who are born free and born equal. Seventeenth and eighteenth century contractarian concepts of legitimacy recast older corporate sense of the polity. Liberal theory "replace[d] allegedly natural social and political hierarchies with recognition of natural freedom and universal human rights."[19] The political community or public sphere of civil society was portrayed as consisting of sovereign individuals, the ultimate repositories of reason and of legitimacy, who voluntarily entered into contractual relations. Instead of legitimacy understood in relation to an objective order (the city of God or the *polis*), there was a turn to subjectively produced legitimacy where the newly-constructed individual was seen as the ultimate source of authority.

The new individuated person was "supposed to be free of constraints ... unbound in its inner life by any restrictions of group or of hierarchy."[20] In a perceptive account of the emerging sense of selfhood, Charles Taylor remarks that the liberal self is constructed as a rational individual who is "not to identify with any of the tendencies he finds in himself, which can only be the deposits of tradition and authority, but [must] be ready to break and re-make these habitual responses according to his own goals."[21] Now since this unrooted individual is "presumed to be sovereign ... the ultimate repository of reason from which sprang the state's legitimate authority,"[22] he is inherently a problem for any form of legitimate community as he by definition stands apart from community,[23] exemplifying Habermas's characterization of modernity as "rebelling against all that is normative."[24]

Developing in this context as a response to the need for a new nonreligious basis for legitimation for the emerging capitalist nation-states, liberalism has from the beginning had to face the question of how and on what basis individuals were to come together as society and state.[25] Although at the level of political theory, the answer stressed certain universal qualities of human beings (rationality, etc.), the actual historical answer lay in ongoing social relations. As Alan Wolfe puts it,

> A liberal theory of politics was linked to a conservative theory of society. By simply assuming that liberal citizens were tied together morally by tradition, culture, religion, family and locality, liberal theory was able to emphasize the benefits to be gained by the free exercise of political rights, since society could always be counted on to cement the moral obligations that politics neglected.[26]

In other words, liberalism's definition of politics as a procedural matter carried out in the public realm was only viable because society contained a mix of social institutions, ignored in liberal theory, that, until recently, continued to socialize groups into common moral norms. Liberal capitalism portrayed a world of non-relational, freely-consenting individuals, while it actually drew upon an ongoing collection of institutions and relations, that is, civil society.

Civil religion provides an excellent example of the ways in which liberal ideology and civil institutions worked together to ensure legitimation. Operating as the symbol system which related individual and society to each other and to ultimate existence, its vision managed to combine a celebration both of individualism and covenantal connection, all justified by America's divine mission.[27] For example, in his first inaugural address, George Washington said, "No people can be bound to acknowledge and adore the Invisible Hand which conducts the affairs of man more than those of the United States. Every step by which we have advanced to the character of an independent nation seems to have been distinguished by some token of providential agency...,"[28] a statement which neatly connects pursuit of individual interest to a framework simultaneously divine and national. This ideology was simultaneously open to incorporate persons of a variety of (Christian) beliefs and class experiences, *and* rooted in the social institutions of what evolved as mainstream bourgeois white Protestant churches. It was, says Peter Berger, *Kulturprotestantismus*,[29] an alliance between Protestant theology and liberal bourgeois culture, which

31

stressed religion as individual morality and envisioned Christianity as contributing to the progressive improvement of American society, "the working faith of our civilization" and nation.[30]

As I suggested in the previous chapter, the relationship between liberal ideology and the ongoing institutions was often contradictory. Liberal capitalist modernity, on the one hand, proclaims the equal worth and capacity of every individual, and on this basis challenges hierarchical tradition. On the other hand, the ongoing legitimation of this same order has always been rooted in traditions, communities, and relations (usually understood as the realm of women and family) that simultaneously nourish persons, shape them as members/citizens *and* render certain of them subordinate. Thus, the ideology of liberalism always contradicted the actual social and cultural practices of liberal society, practices essential for its maintenance.

This deception is particularly visible in the status of white bourgeois women in civil society. Carole Pateman has pointed out that not only was civil society distinguished from state, but also within civil society, there was a division between the world of men and the world of women, or a public world and a private, family world: "the realm of men or 'individuals'; and the private world of particularity, natural subjection, ties of blood, emotion, love, and sexual passion—the world of women, in which men also rule."[31] Thus, Pateman suggests, the legitimacy of the modern state requires the construction of an individual public citizen who is male / rational / social, opposed to and at the expense of private / female / irrational / natural. This legitimacy rests, ultimately, on the reproductive labor of the family which is "simultaneously the foundation of the state and antagonistic to it."[32]

The family "was reconstituted as an intimate sphere that grounded both the evaluative affirmation of ordinary life and of economic activity... and the participation of its patriarchal head in the public sphere."[33] Within the household, Elizabeth Fox-Genovese says, these economic and ideological transformations "tended to ... restrict women's access to political power by subjecting them to a more rigidly defined male authority within smaller families...."[34] However, such relations of power were hidden by an ideology of the family which presented it as independent of the market, tied by natural bonds of patriarchal authority and human intimacy.[35] The white bourgeois family form nourished and reproduced the citizens necessary for the liberal polity and capitalist economy through the ongoing nurturing work of women.

The subaltern counterpublic of African-American peoples had a different character. From their entry as slaves into the American continent, African-American life in U.S. society has been framed by exploitation of their labor and exclusion from the mainstream institutions of American life. This exclusion is perhaps best expressed symbolically in the Constitutional definition of African-American men as 3/5 of a white male citizen (which, of course, excluded women altogether). Although postbellum emancipation meant new possibilities of self-determination, these were almost immediately severely restricted through the imposition of Jim Crow segregation. Yet segregated black communities cannot be understood merely as locations of exploitation, but also as marginalized communities on the periphery of American society where black persons formed their own "counterpublic" of churches, schools, and politics. While their labor underpinned U.S. industrial and agricultural development, their lives were invisible from the perspective of the dominant public. In these marginalized communities, traditional ideas were nourished in resistance to the ongoing exploitation of the market-driven racist economy: "Notions such as … treating community as family … endured."[36] Although these practices had little direct effect on the broader U.S. society, they nourished patterns of African-American life.

Thus, as I have argued in the previous chapter, the effects of this modernizing process were ambivalent. On the one hand, it allowed critique of traditional hierarchical views of self, as Edward Shils puts it, "the tradition of emancipation from traditions," while perpetuating old and creating new forms of hierarchies. On the other hand, the changing world views were based on participation in new forms of labor which "presuppose … a capacity to separate (alienate) oneself from one's own product." The result was "an estrangement from the product of one's own experience, a fragmentation of social tasks and a separation of the subjective meaning of a process of production from the objective market valuation of the product."[37] While liberal ideology disregarded social relations, the institutions of liberal capitalism slowly eroded, displaced and destroyed these relations. Jon Gunnemann comments on the irony that since "liberals want to achieve membership by fiat," they became "parasitical upon other institutions for the moral formation a liberal society presupposes while at the same time undermining, unconsciously, or through conscious manipulation, those very social practices."[38] In our own time, we are beginning to become conscious of the consequences of this undermining.

33

MODERNITY IN CRISIS

Although capitalism's capacity to displace persons and destroy ways of life was evident from its origins, its impact varied according to class, race, gender and geography.[39] In spite of the ongoing thread of "communitarian complaint" from intellectuals who experienced or perceived the effects of changes such as urbanization or the development of a bourgeois class,[40] many persons living in the same time and place continued to live lives relatively untouched by capitalist bureaucracies.[41] There was, it was true, a shifting and steadily diminishing sense of community, as people became more mobile, more aware of the broader nation and world. But this was a slow process as pieces of local communal life slowly disappeared into more impersonal transcommunal networks (school systems, political parties, governmental bureaucracies, etc.). Throughout these changes, a vast number of people still retained something that they recognized as community.

The Second World War inaugurated, however, massive social and industrial change for the United States, forcing great numbers of people to leave the stable life of the countryside or town and enter mobile urban mass society. In the postwar boom, most remnants of agrarian ways of life were eliminated as bourgeois democracy and its accompanying commodity production, mass culture and mass consumption became completely dominant.[42] With these changes, "certain critical links with a precapitalist past were snapped."[43]

As capitalism became further developed, the institutions of material production, organized according to money and administrative power (capital and bureaucracy), became increasingly complex, as manifested in the development of a global financial system, multinational enterprises, and global markets which comprised a new international capitalist culture.[44] Capitalism penetrated more countries around the globe and more areas within already existing capitalist systems. It encroached further and further into the spheres of cultural/social reproduction: family, church, neighborhood organization, leisure, and education. Such penetration was necessary for the ongoing process of capital accumulation which required further rationalization of society. As David Harvey puts it, "mass production meant standardization of production as well as mass consumption, and that meant a whole new aesthetic and commodification of culture."[45]

As part of the "colonization of the lifeworld," structural or techno-rational forms reorganized areas of society which had been previously organized either on the remnants of premodern tradition or on newly emerging consensual foundations.[46] Thus, within civil society there has occurred a "monetarization" of the private sphere (constructing persons as consumers instead of workers) and a "bureaucratization" of the public sphere (constructing persons as clients instead of citizens).[47] In their new, reified form, accelerated by the post World War II economic reconstruction, these institutions could no longer provide the normative legitimation essential for the stability of the state and the integration of individuals within that state. Consequently, the postwar welfare states had to compensate for these legitimation-threatening disturbances by enhancing the roles of consumer and client through a variety of legal entitlements and benefits, which alleviated the burdens of alienated work and alienated domestic life.

Yet, ironically, these efforts by advanced capitalist states only intensified their problems, since they further bureaucratized whatever lifeworld activities they entered. As Habermas puts it, "The situation to be regulated is embedded in the context of a life history and of a concrete form of life; it has to be subjected to violent abstraction … so that it can be dealt with administratively."[48]

Thus, traditional family roles of health care, emotional nurture, and cultural training became bureaucratized activities of professional medical workers, psychologists, social workers, and educators. And, political identity as a citizen was swallowed up by consumption and administrative regulation, a process which seriously weakened the link between "given" personal and "chosen" national identity, membership, and citizenship.

Initially, the impact of these postwar changes was not fully evident here in the United States, in the midst of a postwar economic boom, social recovery and global hegemony. There was a concerted liberal effort throughout the 1950s and 1960s to present social and political life in terms of "a vision of unilinear and inevitable progress toward a rationalized and homogenized world" in which particularity would be considered outmoded or irrelevant in relation to the marvelous advances in technology.[49] Such an effort gained legitimacy from the enormous increase of prosperity for almost all sectors of society, apart from certain racial-ethnic groups and marginalized groups of whites.

By the 1960s, however, the dominant forms of capitalist accumulation were experiencing declining productivity and profitability, which meant a shrinking economic "pie" and the possibility of labor unrest. U.S. postwar economic dominance was also beginning to be challenged by new forms of multinational enterprises and more powerful foreign economies.[50] By the 1970s the devaluation of the dollar and the OPEC oil crisis signalled disruptions in the capitalist system. The rationalization and restructuring of the capitalist economy began to give rise to flexible capital accumulation which could move money globally at overwhelming speeds, and which moved production away from traditional industries to the new "intangible" industries of services and knowledge.[51]

These changes inaugurated the postmodern period, a still inchoate time which is both a continuation of and a transformation from modernity. Like community, "postmodernity" is a slippery concept. It may be used to describe the deconstruction of the subject, historical pastiche in architecture, hypermodern communications or the emergence of marginalized groups. Further, there is no agreement about when we became postmodern or indeed if we are postmodern at all. Following David Harvey and Fredric Jameson, I offer a minimal definition of postmodernism as a new phase of modern development where capitalism is able to penetrate new sectors of Western society and new areas of the globe.[52]

At the heart of the "postmodern condition" is the "new and historically original" penetration of capital so that its expanding horizontal global reach becomes matched by its vertical reach, moving into "Nature and the Unconscious … [through] the destruction of precapitalist third world agriculture … and the rise of the media and the advertising industry."[53] In a context of extraordinarily rapid economic changes, "the more flexible motion of

35

capital emphasizes the new, the fleeting, the ephemeral, the fugitive, and the contingent in modern life," overcoming all barriers—human, mechanical, geographical, etc.—that stand in its way.[54] Experiences of change, fluctuation, innovation, depthlessness have become central in a world where financial capital can move from one part of the globe to another through a few computer key strokes and where identity-shaping fashion can change from one week to the next.[55] Capitalism is able to organize the most intimate areas of lives and shape profoundly our consciousness. Generally, "cultural life in more and more areas gets brought within the grasp of the cash nexus and the logic of capital circulation."[56] Knowledge is now a commodity; indeed, the most expansive economic areas now involve the production, control, and distribution of knowledge.

With postmodernity, the geographical, historical, social connections which enable persons to integrate their personal identity within a social order have been eliminated, or else reappear in a commoditized form.[57] Without living traditions and experiences allowing some degree of integration of existence in all these different spheres, fragmentation and dislocation become predominant. We become "schizophrenic," with no spatial or temporal links among our varied experiences, "wander[ing] through these [plural] worlds without a clear sense of location, wondering 'which world am I in and which of my personalities do I deploy?'"[58]

36

CONTESTING FOR PLACE

Under such postmodern conditions advanced capitalist states face enormous difficulties in securing the stability of legitimation. To turn to Habermas's model, since legitimacy is rooted primarily in social relations, disruption in the other two realms of culture and personality, that is, in tradition and personal identity, occurs in order to protect and preserve the realm of the social order. The location of these disruptions, he says, helps to explain the particular manifestations of crisis currently occurring. Previously, legitimation crises were manifested in political struggles over work issues or citizenship rights. Now, the disruption of identity-producing institutions results in protest movements concerned with personal and collective identities, questions of culture and personality, "along the seam between system and lifeworld."[59] For many movements, what is at stake is not acquisition of more welfare state compensation or achievement of greater rights for workers, but "defending and restoring endangered ways of life" including home, territory, community, and nation, against the experienced dislocations of capitalist bureaucratic organization.[60] Thus, the longing for community is one effort to defend, restore, or create identity; it is a longing which is a reaction to "the systemically induced reification and cultural impoverishment" of advanced capitalism.[61] The turn to community as a symbol for new forms of collective, meaningful life can be seen as part of a general response to the overwhelming complexity of a world where agency seems impossible and collective resources seem scarce or nonexistent.

These changes of advanced capitalism are at the heart of the current crisis of Western modernity and liberalism. The infrastructure of civil society that liberal political ideology presupposed has been largely eradicated or disabled. The size and complexity of the bureaucracies that affect virtually every facet of lived experience threaten capacities for political participation in a "culture that promotes public deference and private orientation toward career, leisure, and consumption"[62]—whether or not one is able to achieve any of these goals. In such a context, liberal notions of politics and society are unable to be maintained. The participatory assumptions of liberalism, based on "ideas of individualism, free will and personal autonomy" come to seem implausible, that is, illegitimate.[63] Liberalism, as I have stated, seeks to insulate political processes from supposed "nonpolitical" or private concerns, so that the "political glue" is a neutral glue of procedure, not a stew of beliefs and identities. But the groups contesting for space within the many-sided public enter the arena on the basis of their identities, identities which are under pressure from the powerful reshaping forces of postmodern capitalism. In this disrupted culture, the political dimension of cultural movements becomes highlighted as groups seek to establish conditions for the participation of some, if not all persons, in a society that provides shared meanings and personal identity, as well as some degree of material well-being.

37

The breakdown of old structures has allowed submerged and marginalized forms of life, lives lived by minority men and women of all races, to gain new status and "public" visibility. As David Harvey puts it, "The idea that all groups have a right to speak for themselves, in their own voice, and have that voice accepted as authentic and legitimate is essential to the pluralist stance of postmodernity."[64] The mere recognition of the existence of a plurality of races and classes within the nation-community is in itself a challenge to what has been, in the history of the U.S., primarily a white Anglo-Saxon world view. Further, the entrance into the public arena of all these privatized groups with their claims for identity recognition redefines the liberal division between private and public, opening up both spheres for contestation.

To maintain its legitimacy, the state tries to incorporate these new forms, making them one interest group in the pluralized marketplace of interest groups, so that their difference does not challenge the dominant cultural consensus. The widening of the public means the incorporation of the experiences and communities of marginalized peoples into the capitalist market, a process which puts pressure on racial and ethnic identities. Earlier waves of incorporation in the late nineteenth and early twentieth centuries had altered white ethnic identities through cultural homogenization so that whiteness had lost its ethnicity. "By the mid-twentieth century," Manning Marable writes, "millions of white Americans had no clear ethnic or cultural identity beyond vague generalizations."[65] Yet "whiteness" was, nevertheless, dominant, the invisible "normal," rooted in the production and consumption of commodities.[66] While the incorporation of other ethnic groups generally occurred under conditions of capital expansion, current incorporation (mostly of persons whose skin color will never look "white") occurs under worsening economic conditions, where new technologies have increased the wealth and power of a small group in relation to declining economic conditions for the lower-middle to lower classes of U.S. society.[67]

To evaluate the different claims about community requires consideration of the ways in which the persons / groups making these claims are located within this overall framework of the state. Although the conditions of advanced capitalism are generally pervasive, different groups within society experience and react to them in differing ways dependent upon their location within civil society. Thus, of the broad range of communal movements and claims, some are counter-hegemonic movements of resistance and transformation, while others are neo-hegemonic movements of resistance and withdrawal, aiming "to build up and separate off communities, to establish subculturally protected communities supportive of the search for personal and collective identity"[68] in the face of capitalist bureaucracy.

At the farthest ends of the spectrum are those movements that completely withdraw or completely resist, such as the Branch Davidians or certain groups within radical / cultural feminism.[69] By contrast, the persons considered here all contest for places within the mainstream of society. To begin to understand their positions, it is necessary to look more closely at their differing social locations. All of them are members of a vulnerable segment of the middle class, the Professional-Managerial Class (PMC), who are dislocated from their families and communities, participate in the newest form of capitalist reorganization (knowledge production) and are constantly in danger of slipping out of the middle class.[70] Yet within the PMC, some are liberal Protestants (here white males), some white females, and some African-American.

The Professional-Managerial Class

The PMC are, to a large extent, a product of advanced capitalism, since the prerequisite for their appearance was the development of the new capital of knowledge, which they produce and organize. The member of the PMC is "the possessor of cultural capital, moves forward self-representation and becomes a contending force on the basis of knowledge which in our times is taken as truth."[71] She / he is there to provide the insider trading knowledge, the scientific and technological discoveries, the computerized systems, the media output. For the segment of the PMC who could be classified as intellectuals, their intellectual life is now lived almost exclusively in relationship to large state and/or capitalist organizations (communications conglomerates, government). Lost are conscious connections to ethnicity, neighborhood, and community.

One new area of capitalist penetration, relevant here, has been the reorganization of the universities which were always key institutions for transmission of culture / knowledge, but are now required to produce different forms of knowledge. The disruption of these formative social processes and shifts in the role of the university impacts the PMC university and seminary professors / intellectuals surveyed here.[72] David Harvey writes of "the uncomfortable transition in many university systems in the advanced capitalist world from guardianship of knowledge and wisdom to the ancillary production of knowledge for corporate capitalism."[73] They are part of the postmodern changes which demand a different subject as citizen and worker, so that universities no longer must produce the "humanist individual and agent of choice" but "a decentered, fragmented, porous subject."[74]

These changes render deeply problematic the role of the university intellectual whose function and allegiances are often unclear. An overwhelming emphasis on specialization has separated most intellectuals from any sense of accountability to society. As William Dean writes, intellectuals currently avoid public responsibility "because most of them now work in those societies called universities" where they are "blinded by their own academic method."[75]

In many ways the discussions of community analyzed here are not only discussions about society, but also implicit reflections on the difficult context of the university/seminary by intellectuals who are able to take a view beyond a particular discipline. The concern for the community and accountability necessary for social morality is, at one level, their own concern about their personal vocations and commitments.

Liberal Protestantism

To participate in the reforming public sphere, liberal Protestantism must also enter on the basis of a renewed identity. But this is, as I have suggested, a critical problem as an assumed hegemonic identity is no longer possible. The periodization of this shift is not a simple one-to-one correspondence with the historical changes outlined in this chapter. Among scholars of modern Protestantism, there is disagreement about exactly when liberal Protestantism lost its hegemonic status and, indeed, what kind of hegemony it actually enjoyed.[76] However, all agree that changes that began in the 1930s became more apparent and rapid in the 1960s.[77] The Supreme Court decisions concerning school prayer, civil rights, and censorship marked what Sydney Ahlstrom has called the "post-Puritan" era. In this era, says José Casanova, the one surviving hegemonic element of Protestantism, the Protestant ethic, was destroyed, leading to "the secularization of public morality and the emergence of pluralistic system of norms and forms of life."[78] The end of the dominant Protestant ethic was the end of the cultural hegemony of liberal Protestantism.

The loss of dominance is marked by the increasing experience of religion as a matter of personal taste. Participation in Protestant church life is, for many people, a form of shopping—choosing a church that suits one's tastes and interests. With their "willingness to pick and choose as individuals from a varied religious menu," most church participants have little sense of the traditions and teachings of their church's denomination.[79] Increased working hours and the growth in families with two adults participating full time in the workforce have also reduced active (or even marginal) church participation. The church community becomes a privatized haven rather than a place nurturing common moral and political agency. The deprivatization of evangelical Protestantism and Catholicism towards a new public identity (in defense of a threatened lifeworld or in criticism of state/market structures) means new competition for a shifting liberal Protestantism which no longer is the implicit "public" private voice. Thus, as the nature of the public has altered, so have the components of liberal Protestant identity. At all levels—congregational, liturgical, ethical—liberal Protestanism is forced to reconsider its identity.

White Women

Women's status is at the heart of the contradictions of these social changes. On the one hand, late modern to postmodern institutional changes have gradually freed the family of virtually all of its economic and many of its social functions. The destruction of family-based hierarchies has allowed women, particularly middle-/upper-class white women, new opportunities for participation in the economic, state, and public spheres. Middle-class white women have left their roles in a changing family, assisted by feminist ideologies and movements, and more women of all races and classes have entered the workforce from choice or necessity.

The renegotiation of private and public spheres has held both emancipatory and oppressive possibilities for women. On the one hand, these changes have allowed the potential for more egalitarian family relations. Yet, on the other hand, as the capitalist state has taken over many of the traditional functions of the family, the family has lost its socializing and legitimizing capacities and has become a contested area.[80] There is a new concern for "family values," which is, at bottom, a response to the erosion of "the political and legal foundations for much that membership could offer: roots, continuity, loyalty."[81] Rather than probing the sources of experienced instability, a quick solution is offered of a return to a "traditional" family, held together by a "traditional" privatized mother—a being who can no longer exist (even if we wanted her to) in light of economic change.

White women have been granted "an unprecedented, if still incomplete, freedom from involuntary community membership."[82] Yet this renegotiated identity holds some special difficulties. First, the entrance of women into the more public spheres of society has often meant an exchange of the power of an individual man for the power of a patriarchal corporation (at work) and a patriarchal state (through interaction with welfare workers, public schools, etc.). Second, the class and ethnic dimension of this new status is ambivalent. In most of first wave feminism and in the early days of second wave feminism, it was assumed that "sisterhood is global." Virginia Woolf put it: "As a woman, I have no country. As a woman, my country is the world." Yet it is mainly white women who strain for this universal—women of color feel themselves women of their country and community *and* women of the world. Unlike Jewish, black, Asian, and working class women, we white Christian middle-class women often cannot recognize ourselves as a people, as a community that includes men, women and children. Out of the resulting alienation, we may seek, along with middle-class white men, a community which we call univer-sal (whether brotherhood or sisterhood) and yet which is profoundly particu-lar. As Chandra Mohanty says, universal sisterhood "ends up being a middle-class, psychologized notion which effectively erases material and ideological power differences within and among groups of women … and, paradoxically, removes us all as actors from history and politics…."[83] Consequently, I argue that white women's models of community, while confronting the issue of women's oppression, may, like those of their male counterparts, continue to erase difference.[84]

41

African Americans

With the Civil Rights movement (whose heart was in the peripheral com-munities of the South) and integration, the alternative publics of African-American life were partially incorporated into the center of U.S. society. The process of incorporation has resulted in new forms of economic and political participation by African Americans, and by their new visibility as cultural par-ticipants. However, it has also meant the greater penetration of capital in the life of the black community with the result of the destruction of communal resources and traditions. The soul-searching over what William Julius Wilson termed the "underclass" is a sign of the ambiguity of new middle-class status for some blacks and greater impoverishment for many others.

Marginalized black communities, for example, had their own public of church and community organizations, which was never part of the dominant public of U.S. society. The price for greater recognition of this community in the dominant public has been its incorporation into capitalism which has meant the creation of a subproletarian underclass and the loss of "the social institutions created by working class Blacks to preserve a sense of collective humanity, culture and decency."[85] "The segregated ghetto is the product," writes William Julius Wilson, of such racist practices as redlining, zoning, and "the creation of public housing projects in low-income areas.... Many viable low-income communities were destroyed."[86]

Seeking to sum up the situation of poor black communities, Manning Marable writes that their consciousness is "the sum total of destructive experiences that are conditioned by structural unemployment, the lack of meaningful participation within political or civil society, the dependency fostered by welfare agencies over two or three generations, functional illiteracy, and lack of marketable skills."[87] Cornel West speaks of the nihilism present in the black community due to "the saturation of market forces and market moralities in black life." Through this saturation, there has been erosion, if not eradication, of "the black religious and civic institutions" that sustained those "familial and communal networks of support" which generated and sustained the traditional values of African-American communities.[88]

Thus, although black intellectual work is marked by paradoxes as is the work of white feminists, the nature of these tensions differs. Black traditional norms do not suffer from their ambiguous participation in oppressive racial history the way that concepts of white sisterhood do. Yet it is hard to reconstruct notions of black community in a world reshaped by capitalism, where the answers of the two traditional models of black community, integration and nationalism, seem to fall short. The inclusion dreamed of by integration has been partial and damaging, while the separation modeled by black nationalism must grapple with a complex, interstructured global society. African-American experiences offer both a resource for renewed civil society and a warning about the current level of social dissolution.

In this chapter and the preceding one, I have tried to demonstrate that the discourse of community is rooted in the problems of civil society under advanced capitalism. With this background in mind, I now turn to discussing different groups of intellectuals participating in discourse on community. I would characterize all of them as seeking some sort of "revitalized synthesis of political [and / or] religious themes as basis for crystallizing personal [and social] identities."[89] For them, community points to civil society, re-ordered on a different basis from the old liberal framework.[90]

Yet the question is on what basis is this reordering sought? Although the positions considered here all respond to liberalism, there are significant differences in the ways that liberalism is renewed, revised, reaffirmed and/or challenged. Such ideological differences are central to the critical framework proposed here. It is important to emphasize that my task is not to categorize a variety of positions simplistically as hegemonic, neohegomonic, or counterhegomonic. All of the positions considered here fall within what could broadly be defined as the intellectual mainstream. What is at stake are the specific aspects or tendencies within the complex mix of traits characterizing most movements or positions. Using the organizing questions posed in the preceding chapter, how do we begin to sort out emancipatory and defensive tendencies in discussions of community? I will begin to do this as I engage with different groups of "dialogue partners" in the next three chapters.

43

LIBERAL ILLNESS, COMMUNAL REMEDIES
White Men and Community

Liberalism is dissatisfying because it fails to provide what we yearn for most: fraternity, solidarity, harmony, and most magically, community.

—Stephen Holmes[1]

If we admit that the state and society, together with innumerable other forces, are still the main formative powers of civilization, then the ultimate problem may be stated thus: How can the church harmonize with these main forces in such a way that together they will form a unity of civilization?

—Ernst Troeltsch[2]

chapter 3

ALL OF the men discussed in this chapter understand themselves as responding to a crisis in public ethics. Each could be called a social critic, writing not just for his own discipline (although all are academics), but for a broader audience of intellectual readers, or, in the case of the Christian critics, the church. They all share "disenchantment with the liberal prospect"[3] and hold some form of modernity responsible for the decline of essential formative moral and political communities in the United States.

Although their agenda is common, each communitarian theorist discussed in this chapter represents a different position along an ideological spectrum concerning culture, politics, and economics. Their responses can be grouped under three headings, each represented by a secular and a religious intellectual: a neoconservative effort to reform civil society as a unified culture (Bell and Neuhaus), a radical effort to revive traditional communities (populism in

Lasch's case and semisectarian Christianity in Hauerwas's case), and a democratic effort to reconstruct civil society under acknowledged conditions of pluralism (Walzer and Rasmussen). Moving through this political spectrum means moving from models of community seeking to preserve integrative forms of morality and culture toward more inclusive, materialistic, and participatory possibilities.

FEAR AND HOPE IN A DARK AGE:
DANIEL BELL, CHRISTOPHER LASCH, AND MICHAEL WALZER

The Public Household with a Closed Door: Daniel Bell

To Daniel Bell, our society lacks "*civitas* ... the spontaneous willingness to make sacrifices for some public good,"[4] which shows our lack of cohesion as community. This disunity flows from the absence of a common philosophy and is a result, not of capitalism, or even political liberalism, but of modernist culture. In Bell's view, moral values, the core of any public philosophy, arise from a separate cultural realm to provide the "anchorage" of society. The ultimate anchorage, the source of all values, is what Bell terms the "transcendent." For him, religion—which he defines as a transcendent authority including rituals, boundaries, and obligations (the "mutual redemption of fathers and sons")—is essential for social or communal cohesion. Through religion, culture can simultaneously maintain the particular (which Bell characterizes as the "primordial ties of father and son") and the universal;[5] that is, the roots of concrete historical (evidently patriarchal) tradition and the transcendent bond that breaks open the limits of that tradition.

In Bell's eyes, modernity has shattered that bond. Since the nineteenth century, he says, culture has become distinct from religion and within culture, the experience of the autonomous self, "the radical I," has become the supreme value.[6] Modernity is an "adversary," anti-institutional culture opposing reason, knowledge, and order. Thus:

> the primary elements that provide men with common identity and affective reciprocity—family, synagogue and church, community—have become attenuated, and people have lost the capacity to maintain sustained relations with each other in both time and place[7]

For Bell, the corrosive character of modernity is exclusively cultural. He sees a capitalist economy as a positive good, the work of experts and industrialists, in contrast to dissolute artists and intellectuals.[8]

As a result of these cultural developments, our public sphere has, in Bell's eyes, no coherence, but is filled with contending groups, including blacks, "women's libbers," and "sexual nonconformists." Such groups negate community or common good because they see persons not as individuals, but as defined by their "attributes" (sex, skin color). Individuality and humanness do not, it seems, include race, class, and gender. Further, these groups do not seek "universal goods" (which Bell never clearly defines), but "politicized" group representation.

Race and gender contention are further proof of "the death of society" which is "the unacknowledged political fact of our century."[9] For Bell, community is a unified cultural and moral public sphere, bound by authoritative transcendent traditions.[10] Contestation is necessarily bad, a form of "politicization" in contrast to the good politics of problem solving. Such politics are the province of "experts" of the "Knowledge" class who direct the state according to "communal goals"[11] which are expressed in "neutral," not particular, terms.[12] Our only hope is, Bell believes, a renewal of liberalism as a social compact which will model a public household, "a rational standard as foundation for consensual principles" for a polity which rejects hedonism, emphasizes needs and acknowledges limits.[13]

Bell never overcomes the contradiction of his affirmation of modern liberal political and economic society combined with his condemnation of the modernist culture rooted in that society. His construction of the enemy modernity exemplifies Habermas's observation that neoconservative movements "shift onto cultural modernism the uncomfortable burdens of a more or less successful capitalist modernization of the economy and society."[14] Bell's image of a household appears, at first, to offer the potential integration of public and private. But in this household, all members of the family look and act in the same way. His integrative vision of order renders all different voices as invisible in the private sphere or disruptively "political." As Peter Steinfels comments,

> the refusal [by Bell] to acknowledge the unequal power already congealed in the political sphere makes it appear that [his] public philosophy is more likely a system of deference on the part of the have-nots than of restraint on the part of the haves ... his caveats appear aimed at those clamoring for a greater share of national wealth—obviously the established powers do not have to clamor.[15]

The transcendental authority shaping Bell's vision of a revived public community is, ultimately, a defense of the tradition of the "haves" which preserves their power over any form of democratic participation.

A Populist Haven: Christopher Lasch

Throughout his work, Lasch has been concerned with one problem: the loss of "all agencies of social cohesion" through the ravages of capitalist modern liberalism."[16] For Lasch, these agencies—which include work (with its accompanying class solidarity), political movements, church, and family—are the social, "legitimate" authorities which are foundational for personal identity, a sense of a common world and a capacity for moral agency. Through work and politics, through practice, we used to create a "durable, common public world" that bound us together as human beings and bound human beings to nature.[17]

Capitalism drove a wedge between handwork and brainwork, production and planning, which eliminated the possibility of labor as a source of meaning and education.[18] Workers have lost the particularity of skills and knowledges and control over the conditions and products of their work.[19] Lasch argues that since capitalism has destroyed the work and communal relations of proprietorship, the world we now create is only a world of "flickering images," a world of technique rather than morally creative practice.[20] Unless we find a way of developing a material institutional world that creates particular loyalties, "the flesh-and-blood love(s)," Lasch sees little hope for society.[21] These particularities provide the external standards and tradition, the discipline, which allows us to develop as fully moral persons who can continuously create civil society.[22]

Lasch's efforts to renew our common world have led him from marxist economics to Freudian psychology to, in his last work before his death, populism, civic republicanism, and transcendental religion. For him, Freud's work is a tool to reveal how the family, the site of moral formation foundational to civil society, has been eroded. The strength of a culture rests on the strength of its socialization process where the child learns "that the parents he wishes to punish and destroy are the same parents on whom he relies for love and nourishment," that he is both separate and dependent.[23] Successful socialization includes the recognition and overcoming of conflict, culminating in the Oedipal conflict, where the distinction between self and not-self, "the basis of all other distinctions" in our culture, is formed.[24]

However, capitalism and its accompanying consumerism have destroyed all collective institutions, especially the family, which have the capacity to raise children who can negotiate successful psychic development. The modern family is the "product of egalitarian ideology, consumer capitalism, and therapeutic intervention."[25] Its liberal world view assumes the unlimited potential of a rational capacity which, if nurtured, could lead to the perfection of self and society.[26] In a liberal society we are not raised to understand a sense of limitation, the ontological "tension between our unlimited aspirations and our limited understanding."[27] The liberal, rational approach to childrearing denies the power of authority and raises the child "permissively." The result, says Lasch, is a society filled with dysfunctional narcissistic selves. Not only our society but our very persons prevent us from engaging in the practices necessary to build durable morality. Worse yet, since we have no psychic experience of paternal authority and maternal love to nurture our superegos (internal

48

critical authority), we are vulnerable to fascist forms of authority which supply what we lack.

In *The True and Only Heaven*, the last book published before his death, Lasch moves on to sketch some solutions to the devastations of liberal modernity. He looks to populist politics and what he sees as a civic republican tradition of moral argument which "condemns the boundless appetite for more and better goods" and, instead, celebrates responsibility, proprietorship, the virtues of good work, and the "dependence of happiness on the recognition that humans are not made for happiness."[28] Lasch argued that "we need to recover a more vigorous form of hope, which trusts life without denying its tragic character."[29] It is a religious argument, using Reinhold Niebuhr and Ralph Waldo Emerson to point to the inescapable tragic sinfulness and limitation of human existence and seeing salvation in dependence on higher, transcendent powers. And it is grounded in a particular social location, the "sensibility of the petty bourgeoisie," the "lower-middle-class culture … organized around the family, church, and neighborhood," a culture preserving institutions and meanings capable of "demanding unselfish devotion to the common good"[30] and "subordination to communal standards," authorities given to us by history.[31]

Few have equalled Lasch's capacity for grasping the devastation of society at the hands of liberal capitalism. At the beginning of his work, redemption from this devastation seemed to be possible through participatory practices (good politics) and fulfilling labor (good work). However, Lasch's continued exploration of the effects of capitalism led him away from a materialist view of history into a drama of the inner world, where, unfortunately, Freud was his main guide. Unable to see any benefit in modernity, he dismissed all achievements of rights, as, basically, reinforcements of narcissistic selves over traditional authorities. Although he insists that "the justice of women's demand for equality remains too obvious to be ignored," he manages to ignore them as he stresses the negative impact these demands have had on the authority of the family. His judgment is clouded by an uncritical reliance on a patriarchal Freudian model and an uncritical assumption of an individualist liberal version of feminism.[32] He barely acknowledged the racial and sexual exclusion characteristic of populist tradition, nor did it seem to occur to him that neither Emerson nor Niebuhr were likely to be congenial "transcendent sources" in populist eyes.

Ultimately, instead of struggling to bring together meaning, economic life and political participation, Lasch imports an integrative transcendent solution. Affirmation of difference and new forms of identity are seen *only* as threats to authority, rather than possibilities of creating new, more reciprocal, forms of authority. In spite of his concern for social solidarity and participation,[33] restored community for Lasch, finally depended upon "subordination to communal standards"[34] given to us by a dominant version of history.

49

Communities of Shared Understanding: Michael Walzer

The body of Michael Walzer's work is an attempt to show that in the midst of mobility, pluralism, and conflict, some sort of moral and political community can be found and made. All of the themes of his writings—political involvement, community, the rights and obligations of citizenship, welfare and distribution—revolve around the political complexities of life in advanced welfare capitalist states.[35] Reading his most recent work, I find that his implicit purpose is to sketch a model of a justice and morality that honors dense, particular, communal cultures and provides an overall participatory democratic framework.[36]

Common moral understandings, "the culture we have collectively produced," constitute the community in which we all participate. Community is bound by culture, "the story its members tell so as to make sense of all the different pieces of their social life."[37] Walzer grounds his communal claims not in an ontological need for constraints on human egoism, but in an essential sociality, "our shared sense of what we are about."[38] Culture is what we have used, what we have chosen, and what we have transformed according to our changing needs and purposes. The connections are always there—even in liberalism which Walzer describes as "a theory of relationship, which has voluntary association at its center."[39]

Walzer does, however, admit that this sociality is under great strain. Our society is characterized by "four mobilities": geographical, social, political, and marital. Liberalism, Walzer remarks, is the "theoretical endorsement and justification of this movement," yet it contains an "underside of sadness" since we are often alone.[40] "[U]nder a democratic regime," he says, "no one has a fixed place ... a society of misters is a world of hope, effort, and endless anxiety."[41] Living in this kind of world, we "*want*," he claims, "a home, a dense moral culture" in which we "can find some sense of belonging."[42]

Unlike most communitarians, Walzer believes we do still have this dense culture and still speak a language thicker than the language of individualism. No one is out there, he says, except "our liberal selves ... yet it is good to teach these selves to know themselves as social beings."[43] Community, he remarks, is "conceivably the most important ... good that gets distributed."[44] Walzer does not accept an organic notion of community/nation/state (distinguishing himself from integrationist communitarians such as Alasdair MacIntyre or Michael Sandel), but sees community as simultaneously "chosen" and "given," voluntary and inherited.[45] This definition of community does not highlight ethnicity, but speaks more generally of "historically stable, ongoing associations of men and women with some special commitment to one another and some special sense of their common life."[46]

But what, exactly, is this community? The answer to this question points to the doubled idea of community in Walzer's work. One notion of community is equivalent to the nation state, the generally liberal framework of Western political communities, which is based upon "chosen" covenantal participation.[47] On the other hand, he also uses community to refer to particular local groups, bound by ethnicity, race, neighborhood, the differing communities of civil society which are "given" to us.

From the perspective of "chosenness" or public life as voluntary covenant, Walzer treats the authority of state/community as stemming from its participants who must all have "ultimately" an equal say in determining the structures that govern their lives.[48] The place to begin, he says, is with the "liberal idea of voluntary association" which, he admits, is not perfectly voluntary, but still includes the "freedom to leave the groups and sometimes even the identities behind." He suggests that the only community all of us (Westerners) know is, in fact, this kind of liberal community.[49]

The liberal state "provides a frame, a protective structure," within which "individuals and groups [can] cultivate diverse forms of life."[50] The common good of a democratic state is a pluralist good which overrides "local ethnic enclaves" and the power of a dominant ethnicity. "The crucial problem," he says, "of the politics of difference is to encompass the actually existing differences within some overarching structure."[51] Yet Walzer's general attitude to the state is cautious. The citizenship offered by the state "provides a frame," "liberal in the strict sense." He notes that we need the state to foster associative activities but that these social unions must, simultaneously, be strong enough to limit the state's power.[52] Within this structure "individuals and groups [can] cultivate diverse forms of life" so that there is cultural manyness and political oneness.[53] Walzer is keenly aware of the dangers of the claims of a state that declares itself culturally homogeneous. For him, the tension lies between the "closure" any culture or group must have to maintain its identity and the democratic principle that "if [men and women] are subject [to the state's authority], they must be given a say and, ultimately, an equal say in what that authority does."[54] "National character," he writes, "is obviously a myth; but the sharing of sensibilities and intuitions among the members of a historical community is a fact of life."[55]

Walzer seems to envision a tolerant state that fosters a civil society comprised of local communities of ethnic or other groups, combining the chosenness of the liberal vision of the state with the givenness of communitarianism. Thus the democratic freedom of the nation state guarantees the rich particularity of neighborhood and local community. Simultaneously, the diversity and difference of "families, nations, and communities of faith" provide the political competence necessary for democratic politics.

When we accept "the norm of basic respect," we respect the "particular creations" of men and women, that is, their given traditions, norms and other cultural creations, and thus we "do justice" to them.[56] For Walzer, this respect

51

entails both a plurality of traditions and an equally necessary mutual correction. He stresses that from the interplay within and among traditions, there arises what he terms "internal" criticism.[57] A communal moral discourse emerges from critical interaction among the religious, cultural and political traditions of a variety of historically-shaped communities and spheres within a complex egalitarian / liberal framework. Domination is prevented through "complex equality" since "every social good or set of goods constitutes ... a distributive sphere within which only certain criteria and arrangements are appropriate."[58] Thus not only are goods particular to communities, they are also particular to spheres within the communities. Instead of ruling and being ruled in turn, citizens will rule in one sphere and be ruled in another.[59] Power, which for Walzer means getting the largest share of the goods, is legitimate when it both rests on the consent of the governed and is kept within a specific sphere.

The model Walzer provides is, I find, enormously appealing, as it fosters communal bonds within frameworks of equal respect for difference in multicultural, multireligious modern states. Walzer's insistence on the importance of ongoing immigration as foundational to the diverse nature of U.S. society is, at this historical moment, especially commendable.[60] However, there are still some questions to be raised. Since Walzer suggests that moral authority rests in our "shared understandings," his use of "we" in many of his works to include himself and his audience is extremely suggestive. However, I continue to be puzzled about just who *are* the "we" involved in "shared understandings." "We" are certainly Western, probably U.S. citizens, presumably well-educated. Yet it is not clear whether Walzer's community/audience, his "we," is identical with *all* of those who make up the United States or with a particular subgroup. More recently, Walzer has tried to engage more directly with the question of difference, the "others" who might be excluded by reliance on "shared understandings." He has stressed that we can draw on many different traditions, including the "tradition of discontent,"[61] since the conversation, as he repeatedly states, is open-ended and ever changing, "vulnerable to shifts in social meaning."[62] Considering the place of gender and ethnicity in Walzer's work helps clarify the ways in which his notion of "shared understandings" can accommodate the necessary politics of difference.

Far more clear-eyed than many male political theorists on power relationships in the family, Walzer sees it not only as a private world of affection, but as the place where "favoritism begins." He also recognizes that there must be intervention "in the case of neglected children ... or of battered wives."[63] Yet he neglects the power of patriarchy when he writes, "The real domination of women has less to do with their familial place than with their exclusion from all other places."[64] Feminist scholarship has shown that the two spheres of inequality are intimately connected, arising from the division between the public and the private that is foundational to patriarchal capitalism. Walzer's division of society into multiple spheres seems to obscure the significance of the public/private split and again makes it difficult to name "trans-sphere" forms of power.[65]

While Walzer is deeply aware of the need for respect for different races and cultures, it sometimes seems that difference tends to be reduced in favor of commonality. For example, he suggests that the symbols of the U.S. state are culturally neutral. While it is possible that they may become neutral (think of the image of the Statue of Liberty being raised in Tiananmen Square), they are mostly Western and Christian in origin (for example, the U.S. Congress still retains a Christian chaplain). Discussing "Third World citizens" in the United States, Walzer remarks that there is nothing inherently unjust in their studying the dominant (presumably Western) culture.[66] It is hard to understand just what he means by Third World citizens—aliens who are actually citizens of other nations? recent or first generation immigrants? Non-European people with long histories in the U.S. such as African-Americans, Hispanic-Americans, Asian-Americans? Although I do agree that learning Western culture is necessary for participating in the heritage and history of the United States, it is not sufficient for preparing us as citizens of a multicultural state. I am troubled by Walzer's unilateral concern for preserving Western thought, as he offers us only images of Third World U.S. citizens studying Euro-American texts, black Algerians studying French history, Israelis of European and Middle-Eastern backgrounds studying Plato.[67] Surely the history and heritage of any substantial group who are permanent residents in the nation must be part of public education and culture. In his recent work, Walzer has pushed harder on these issues, stating that community rests upon "the American values of a singular citizenship and a radically pluralist civil society."[68] Although it seems at first that this recreates the liberal division between a universal public and a particular private, Walzer checks this split when he writes, "it is not the case that Irish-Americans, say, are culturally Irish and politically American.... Rather, they are culturally Irish-American and politically Irish-American."[69] Yet this is the point where much of the tension over civil society and the public sphere rests, as we seek to renegotiate the liberal division of spheres.

Walzer does not always acknowledge that the way disagreement occurs in this society is not through measured discussion, but through often painful conflict that challenges "shared understandings." This tension shapes his discussion of religion. For Walzer, religion needs to be considered as a cultural not a theological tradition. "Bracket[ing]" god, splitting theology and culture, allows Walzer to take the most liberal interpretations of religious traditions and avoid difficult questions of exclusion and domination. In *Exodus*, he deals with God's command to annihilate the current inhabitants of the future Israel by suggesting that contemporary Israelites and later rabbis had "anxiety" about the text.[70] Although this approach allows Walzer the opportunity to oppose some

53

of the extreme right-wing interpretations current in Israel, it avoids the theological problems. Even if the text did not really mean annihilation, there have been quite an assortment of people (such as colonizing Afrikaaners and frontier white Americans) who *did* understand the command in just this way and whose views cannot simply be dismissed as "misinterpretation."[71]

What is frequently at stake in our polity are radically *disjunct* understandings, whether they be between women and men, lower- and upper-classes, racial-ethnic and white peoples. In Susan Moller Okin's recent book, *Justice, Gender, and the Family*, she asks what criteria Walzer could bring forth to adjudicate such conflicts—"deeper" understandings? Are not these criteria usually only the understandings of the powerful? Perhaps, as Okin suggests, there are indeed virtually *no* shared understandings at this point in our social history on a topic such as gender.[72] Any model of community that does justice to the experience of all members of U.S. society must be sufficiently complex to account for past and present domination, conflict, and resistance.

Walzer understands that liberalism is a tradition with certain important values to which most Americans assent and want to continue to assent. And he is committed to a conversational process that minimizes "authority, conflict and coercion."[73] One of his most helpful comments is his insight that "we do justice to actual men and women by respecting their particular creations."[74] Yet, as Stephen White puts it, "The question … is how one does this."[75] It is hard to see how Walzer can offer this respect when his cultural assumptions lie within a certain limited range which may block him from recognizing the authority of identities shaped by communities at odds with dominant traditions and understandings.

Walzer's work is marked, as Seyla Benhabib has pointed out, by a tension between the participatory and integrative dimensions of communitarianism. She remarks that while Walzer wishes to "further an egalitarian, participatory conception of justice," he often "slides into the integrationist language."[76] Pointing to the integrative dimension, Sheila Briggs writes, "like other proponents of a narrative ethics of community, Walzer assumes the existence of a shared world of social and moral meanings. This world is, I believe, the process of cultural hegemony."[77] While I myself see counterhegemonic forms of democracy present in Walzer's model (especially his most recent work), I would agree that his work is marked by forms of power that he does not fully acknowledge, possibly because his "conversation partners" tend to be representatives of majority not marginalized traditions. Walzer evidently believes that pluralism protects against domination, but a pluralist account rarely describes structural relationships of power. To see the public sphere as the site of contending and contradictory powers allows us to begin to map the location of conflicting voices within the state and to consider what kind of community is envisioned by these different perspectives.

QUEST FOR THE BELOVED COMMUNITY:
RICHARD J. NEUHAUS, STANLEY HAUERWAS, AND LARRY RASMUSSEN

In the early part of the twentieth century, liberal Protestantism could take its authority for granted in relation to its cultural context. Such authority allowed early modern liberal Protestant thought to maintain the ideal of harmony both *within* church and culture and, ultimately, *between* church and culture. In a culture that ordered and organized (white, middle-class) persons in relation to a relatively stable set of moral norms and goals, liberal theology could assume "a fundamental fit between individuals, their society and their history."[78] Even though the model of liberal Protestant community was a voluntary one, such choice did not pose a problem in an essentially homogeneous setting. As Stanley Hauerwas says, "the very characterization of Christianity as a system of beliefs ... was a correlative of our cultural establishment in liberal societies."[79]

The realization of the illusion of the "fundamental fit" became more and more evident as the twentieth century continued and Christian intellectuals came to assert, like Reinhold Niebuhr, that "society is in a perpetual state of war ... the dream of perpetual peace and brotherhood for the human race is one which will never be fully realized."[80] The ideal of a harmonious Christian community seemed increasingly invalid and useless in a complex capitalist secularizing world. Different levels of recognition of the problems at hand can be seen in the work of Ernst Troeltsch, and in the work of H. Richard and Reinhold Niebuhr which can serve to set the scene for contemporary proposals.

At the very beginning of the century, Ernst Troeltsch perceived more clearly than many contemporary Christian ethicists the danger to Protestantism inherent in the modern reality of "such a variety of interpretations, formulations, and syntheses that no single idea or impulse can dominate the whole."[81] He saw that "harmoniz[ing] with these main forces" of modern capitalism seemed to require the loss of any possibility for unified community, and thus the possibility of unified culture. His own age was, Troeltsch feared, increasingly dominated by what he called "mystical individualism" which "lives in and on communities ... it tries to transform these groups from confessional unities into mere organizations for administration.... It is opposed to the ecclesiastical spirit by its tolerance, its subjectivism and symbolism, its emphasis upon the ethical and religious inwardness of temper, its lack of stable norms and authorities."[82] Instead of community there was only fragmentation.

Troeltsch believed that the lack of stable Christian communities/institutions posed deep problems both for the future of the church and for Western social order. For him, religion was essential to the maintenance of society: "without a religious basis, without a metaphysic and an ethic, a strong self-consistent spirit of civilization cannot exist." And for his world, "the great

55

Anglo-Saxon portion of our modern world," Protestant Christianity was "the backbone."[83] Loss of traditional authority meant loss of an authoritative communal structure which, for Troeltsch, "eliminates the only center around which a Christian cult can be formed."[84] The authority of common culture, the *corpus Christianum* centered in the Christian church, was gone. Thus Troeltsch saw the contemporary dilution and confusions of Protestant communal life as threats to what he constantly referred to as the "power," "strength" and "vitality" of the civilized Western world. If the Christian church did not "harmonize with these main forces," there would not only be no church, but no "unity of civilization."[85] Without a strong Protestant Christian ethic, there would be no public ethic.

Troeltsch offers here one of the clearest statements of the dilemma that has faced liberal Protestantism throughout this century but has reached, at this point, a critical stage. The price of Protestant hegemony (without which, it is understood, "civilization" is not possible) is a capitulation to modernity that ultimately erodes the resources of Protestant tradition, threatening the cohesion of the Christian community and the moral order it undergirds.

As a remedy, Troeltsch sought the "strong sense of unity for common, positive ends and values"[86] that he believed to have been present in the earlier Catholic and Calvinist churches. The challenge was to develop a Christian community that would maintain both the spirit of the church-type "in its great conviction of an historical substance of life which is common to all" and the sect-type which embodies a diversity of "declarations."[87] One possible solution he considered was a new form of practical dogmatics which would be a confession of faith that presupposed scientific conclusions "establishing on the basis of a historical and philosophical comparison of religions the fundamental and universal supremacy of Christianity for our own culture and civilization."[88] Yet there is an uneasiness in Troeltsch's account of this possibility, since he recognizes that without institutional renewal, a reconstructed dogmatics was of little use.

From his doctoral work on Troeltsch, H. Richard Niebuhr had grasped the inescapable historicity of modern life, including human religious and moral life. For Niebuhr, the question of community was not so much a question of the coherence of culture as a question of the nature and role of the church. Recognizing the incoherence of society, he appeals to a single "Christian ideal" which is the kingdom, "the joy of the great community."[89] Community is determined, in Niebuhr's view, by the sharing of a common tradition, a "common memory" or "single epic."[90] There can be no coherent community or society without such unity: "Without a single faith, there is no real unity of self or of a community, therefore no unified inner history, but only a multiplicity of memories and destinies…. Where common memory is lacking, where men do not share in the same past there can be no real community, and where community is to be formed common memory must be created."[91]

By working through the historical past in light of revelation, Niebuhr believed we could find both personal and corporate unity. "To be a self is to have a god; to have a god is to have a history, that is, events connected in a meaningful pattern; to have one god is to have one history." "God and the history of selves in community belong together in inseparable union" which is "*sub specie aeternitatis.*"[92] Niebuhr does understand that "to be in the present is to be in *compresence* with what is not myself."[93] Yet in the "I–You" relationship he models as the foundation of community, the You's "not-I-ness" is never given any social historical specificity. The concrete other, the "individual being with specific needs, talents and capacities ... *different from the self*" disappears in favor of an abstract, generalized other.[94] As John Howard Yoder writes, for Niebuhr, "[c]ulture is first of all *monolithic.*"[95] Its unity depends upon the culture of white Protestantism.

In his modelling of a "responsible self" for marginalized African-American communities, Darryl Trimiew remarks upon the corrections necessary to appropriate Niebuhr in this context, since a marginalized self "has at least two societies [dominant and marginalized] that must be related to responsibly."[96] Such a recognition breaks open the power implicit in Niebuhr's presumptive unified community and suggests the rethinking that is required when "the members of a debased community" are taken seriously as "sources of moral insight."[97]

Throughout most of his life, Reinhold Niebuhr argued that liberal assumptions concerning progress and liberal optimism concerning the moral capacities of society were inadequate in a world constantly broken by the sinful struggle of the will to power where order is achieved by "adjustments of interest to interest" or "balance of vitalities and forces", and, if necessary, the application of coercive power.[98] Niebuhr's critique of liberalism, an important forerunner of the theories considered here, maintained many of the liberal assumptions it purported to dismiss. One key assumption, as Ruth Smith has pointed out, was Niebuhr's presentation of the individual as separable from society and history.[99] For Niebuhr, one of the triumphs of the bourgeois social order has been the full emancipation of the individual from the restraints of medieval community.[100] Running through Niebuhr's work is a tension between individual apolitical morality and collective immoral politics. For him, the person stands within history but is always also in an individual relation to faith, "an indirect relation to eternity."[101] The individual's transcendent relationship to an unchanging eternal moral ideal permits personal moral behavior, discipline and freedom.

The individual in society/group/community is, however, subject to the determinations of self-interested power present in nature and history. Inside society, in the world of politics, the reality is conflict or a forced subjection to "contingent, irrational and illogical forces."[102] "Power is a necessity of social cohesion," and thus, although the ideal is the harmony of love, "the complete identity of life with life," the proximate achievable ideal is not harmony but justice as an equilibrium among competing powers.[103] In spite of the fact that historical political conflict was Niebuhr's lifeblood, it always had a provisional moral status in his method, since the conflicts inherent in political life were never signs of human creativity and growth, but of human sinfulness and limitation. The basepoint of true moral community ultimately existed only outside of history.

All three Christian intellectuals, Troeltsch, H. Richard Niebuhr, and Reinhold Niebuhr, saw the Christian church playing a key role in the stability of society. From their perspective, that role was dependent upon the church and its theology being able to provide a normative center for social morality. For Christianity to accomplish this, all three believed the church itself must become a unified community. Yet as each intellectual understood modernity to reveal the profoundly historical and provisional nature of all social structures, including the church, they realized these forces challenged the possibility of any normative center.

Writing of the period 1920–60, the prime years in which H. Richard and Reinhold Niebuhr thought and wrote, Philip Hammond remarks that Protestantism's loss of cultural power was not immediately apparent because "the culture toward which Protestantism is powerless has only slowly lost its Protestant appearance."[104] But by the end of the 60s, it was evident that liberal Protestantism was no longer the bridge or mediator that united the dominant forces of society. For many, of course—conservative fundamentalist Christians, African-American Christians, non-Christians—it had never been a bridge but, rather, the dominant center to which they served as margins. Yet for those who thought, wrote, preached and taught in liberal Christian institutions, the loss of an assumed dominance left them unsettled and disoriented. There were no longer evident answers to the question of the particular role and activities of the liberal Protestant community in U.S. society. With the alteration of its public role in the private sphere, the liberal Protestant church has been forced to reconsider its place in both the private and public spheres.

In this context, Neuhaus, Hauerwas and Rasmussen face challenges of diversity, historical change, and modern alienation greater than those which confronted their predecessors. Rather than assuming that addressing the Protestant church is addressing society, they have to consciously consider whether their prescriptions are aimed at reform of the church or reform of society, determining the kinds of claims liberal Protestantism can make at a time when the hegemonic form of church and American society has been broken.

Resanctified Clothes for a Denuded Public: Richard John Neuhaus

In many ways, Richard John Neuhaus's life and work serve as a symbol for the travails of modern liberal Protestantism. Starting out as an ardent participant in the Civil Rights movement and a left-leaning liberal during the 1960s, he has over the decades become a political and religious conservative.[105] Neuhaus paints himself as a disillusioned liberal. He claims to have been consistently guided by his quadrilateral: "religiously orthodox, culturally conservative, politically liberal, and economically pragmatic."[106] In his eyes, change has occurred only in the "politically liberal" side of the quadrilateral.[107] Instead of seeking social transformation through religious involvement in social and political movements, such as the Civil Rights or anti-Vietnam movements, he seeks a religious and moral renewal which will overcome what he terms the "imperiousness of the political" in our culture. Indeed, instead of being polit-ically involved, churches must, he now says, function to "debunk the inflated importance of politics."[108]

American society, says Neuhaus, is now a *Kulturkampf*, a series of warring factions which have no basis on which to find agreement. What has been lost, he argues, is the central role of mainline Protestantism as "the culture—the shaping force that provides moral legitimacy for democracy in America."[109] Religion is "the morality-bearing part of culture, and, in that sense, the heart of culture."[110] He links religion and culture with citizenship and legitimacy, writing that without "the centering of religious dogma, there can be no *civitas*, the loyalty to the state that does not demonize the state, but keeps it in check under ultimate loyalty to God."[111] We have lost the overarching transcendent referent which was "the set ... for the political stage ... [the] continuing story or purposes that bestow meaning upon the action."[112] In other words, he rec-ognizes that the world of the Niebuhrs is truly gone. This loss has left America with no dominant public culture, and thus there is only what Neuhaus calls "the naked public square."

For Neuhaus, the moral disarray which threatens the ordered legitimacy of our society is not due to a tradition-destroying capitalist economy or an over-reaching state, but rather to a liberal culture in crisis. As in Bell's usage, culture is defined as absolutely separate from any economic dimensions and, also, any political dimensions. For example, it is clear that, for Neuhaus, *civitas*/citizen-ship is primarily a *cultural*, rather than a *political*, identity.[113] And, correspond-ingly, the church's role is stressed as a cultural role, providing the "sacred canopy."[114] The sin of liberal church bodies, such as the NCCCUSA, is that they engage in "political," not cultural, activities.

Neuhaus is anxious simultaneously to affirm America as a coherent moral community (bound by a sacred canopy), to affirm the distinctive (yet separate) role of the church guiding such a community, and to give some recognition to unavoidable plurality and difference. He endeavors to differentiate himself from fundamentalist *and* liberal Christians both of whom he sees as merging Christian community and public community, and thus endangering the plu-rality of American life—a plurality which appears to be religious, not ethnic.[115]

He argues that we cannot identify the sacred canopy with "one institutional united church" or even one religion: "The canopy is that to which Judeo-Christian religion points. Religion bears witness to it, but our religion is not to be equated with it."[116]

Indeed Neuhaus appears skeptical that any overarching American "community" exists as, he writes, "it can be argued that the idea of America as a community is problematic to the point of being meaningless. Church, family, friendships, professional associations, neighborhood, maybe even town or city—these are real communities.... America ... is altogether too various and amorphous."[117] The sacred canopy that covers the nation cannot be identified with any community, because, Neuhaus says, we need to see ourselves instead as members of "several communities" which "require discriminations in moral judgment." Such a recognition is an acknowledgement that one Protestant ethic can no longer serve for the United States. Indeed, he finds national community too "thin" to be a resource for moral values. Instead, he hopes for a renewal of the "thick communities of deeper allegiance" or institutions of civil society. These are the mediating cultural structures that simultaneously intervene between 'naked' state and 'naked' individual, and also provide moral education and connections.

In spite of Neuhaus's stress on particularity and diversity of the languages spoken, these communities do not seem to be very diverse places, and moral disagreement seems, finally, not possible. Disagreement is not possible because of the way in which Neuhaus constructs the moral apart from the political and the economic. Thus, he can label any disagreement with his own account as "political" and banish it from the moral realm in order to secure the unity of a dominant church.

A clue to Neuhaus's underlying model of the *corpus Christianum* can be found in his understanding of the church and its relation to society. Neuhaus completely dismisses the validity of any sectarian model of church community, claiming that "[r]eligion is incorrigibly interventionist. Judeo-Christian religion with its universalistic claims to truth relates to the totality of things."[118] However, he insists that the model of Christian church as the servant church, favored in liberal ecumenical Protestantism, is also not helpful because it requires the church to lose its power as a "culture-forming force." The church, says Neuhaus, is a "proleptic and anticipatory model ... for how the world is to be rightly ordered."[119]

In Neuhaus's own model the transcendent moral order of the church can unite the diversity and conflict of the world. Theology and morals are defined as transcendent of any political location or determination and thus capable of being absolute and unambiguous. Because of their transcendent status, they can shape political life, offering the "truth by which judgment can be rendered.... an agreed-upon authority that is higher than the community itself."[120] These "nonpolitical" "Christian" positions include support of "the family," presumed to be heterosexual and nuclear, and condemnation of "activist homosexual organizations" and feminists. Neuhaus offers, it may be noted, no real argument from Christian traditions and scripture for any of these positions. His separation of morality and culture from politics and economics allows him to label his own political position as moral (and universally true) and dismiss all opposing views as politicized (reflecting partial interests).

Neuhaus's model of politics, culture, and religion, in the end, allows him to bring in, under the guise of transcendent norms, a dominating form of politics and power. Like most neoconservatives, he is unable to see that American consumer capitalism has marginalized Protestantism and helped turn it into a marketplace of competing churches. For him, there is, ultimately, no conflict in the religious community which can then serve as the model for a common "American" morality.[121] At bottom, Neuhaus hopes for a unified *corpus Christianum*, that is, a homogeneous western Christian culture and civilization, a hope which explains why he has recently entered a church he understands still to be the *one* universal Catholic church.[122]

"Let the Church Be the Church": Stanley Hauerwas

Although Hauerwas is frequently described as "sectarian," he himself does not accept the label.[123] Unlike one of his mentors, the Mennonite John Howard Yoder, he never locates himself clearly within a radical reformation tradition, and, indeed, could be characterized as a high-church Methodist. However, he does use a sectarian approach to present himself as the underdog—as a nonconforming Christian and as a Texan. The best way, perhaps, to characterize Hauerwas is as an intellectual who uses a sectarian ecclesiastic perspective as a critical tool within the liberal tradition.

Liberalism, says Hauerwas, has assumed that "people do not need a shared history; all they need is a system of rules."[124] In his criticism of liberalism, Hauerwas is making two sets of arguments. First, he contends that liberalism is descriptively inadequate. We are by nature particular beings rooted in our time and place who find moral identity through a narrative understanding of our lives, an understanding that requires recognition of the history and community that one is born into or in which one finds oneself embedded. These descriptive inaccuracies are the basis for Hauerwas's second set of complaints against liberalism. Because liberalism cannot account for peoples' particularities, it cannot maintain sustaining moral community. It cannot offer the "truthful story" he believes we need to make sense of our confused and plural world.

Hauerwas sees community as depending on shared history and shared interpretation. He defines community as "a group of persons who share a history and whose common sense of interpretation about that history provide the basis for common actions."[125] Tradition is the ongoing set of judgments and interpretations of that community ("tested through generations") which form the internally-derived authority. Hauerwas contrasts "good" authority with "bad" power. "Like power," he writes, "authority is directive; unlike power, however, it takes its rationale not from the deficiencies of the community but from the intrinsic demands of a common life."[126] The authority of the community "of which we find ourselves a part" allows us not the liberal freedom of choosing our stories, but the freedom of "being formed by a truthful narrative,"that is, a narrative intrinsically related to our communal context.[127]

In contemporary America, there is in Hauerwas's view, no such truthful narrative. We live "in a world of moral fragments" which is a life always on the edge of violence, since there are no means to ensure that moral argument in itself can resolve our moral conflicts.[128] And when we try to refer to a universal standpoint, we are actually referring to the false departicularized universalism of the Enlightenment which, he says, is embodied in the nation state and its wars. Arguments justified by reference to such a universal standpoint are necessarily false and inherently violent. The only possible universal for Christians is the *telos* of Jesus Christ, "the one alone who is worthy of worship."[129]

What Hauerwas claims to be at stake in his attack on liberalism is the character of the Christian community which is his primary audience. He understands that liberal Protestantism's "identification with that [liberal American] civilization has been so complete that we have tended to forget that the church's future is not the future of 'western democracies'."[130] Thus we have allowed the overall program of the liberal church to serve as legitimization for the *telos* of the nationstate.[131] Hauerwas's particular gift is to challenge liberal assumptions about the meanings of religion, polity, culture, and family that have been an integral part of the Protestant worldview. The question remains, however, as to what he proposes as new possibilities for liberal Protestantism.

For Hauerwas, the most deadly result of the partnership between liberal Protestantism and liberal democracy has been the "domesticat[ion] of the gospel in the hopes of controlling, if not dominating, the ethos of this society."[132] To "liberate" the gospel is to separate it from *any* connection to liberalism and its concepts (rights, democracy, equality, politics). In his criticism of feminism, he casts it as championing a liberal notion of rights destructive of family ties.[133] He dismisses equality as egalitarianism which he calls the "opiate of the masses and the source of the politics of envy."[134] A society where all are considered equal is a society that devalues the "extraordinary."[135] It also makes impossible the "hierarchy of goods" essential to a good life. Past appreciation of democracy "has been only a justification for why we should rule. It now functions primarily to give Christian liberal societies the illusion that we continue to rule."[136]

One of the core questions considered here, the possibility of a Christian public ethics, Hauerwas dismisses as a nonquestion. There is not and should not be a Christian public ethics—any ethics that claims to be such is simply perpetuating the modernist captivity of liberal Protestantism. Christian politics is a different politics than the nationstate's politics of violence and coercion. The politics of the true Christian community, Hauerwas suggests, transcends private and public, since the community acts not to exalt itself and its power, but to serve as a mirror and servant to the world, demonstrating its authority by "showing to the world what it means to be a community of grace."[137]

In Hauerwas's Christian community, all moral questions must be determined in relation to the Christian *telos* which is found in the life of Jesus as represented in scripture. Yet this allegiance, he insists, is "not to an abstract story but to a body of people formed by the life of Jesus."[138] Given a moral basepoint supposedly rooted in the historical life and tradition of a community, an obvious question is what process the community might use to come to its judgments and interpretations. However, on this point Hauerwas is completely opaque. In his customary gnomic style he writes, "Christians do not believe that there is no truth; rather truth can only be known through struggle. That is exactly why authority in the church is vested in those we have learned to call saints...."[139] This firm-toned statement leaves the reader with more questions than answers. Who *are* the "saints"? On what basis has the community determined them to be authoritative? What kind of moral leadership do they model? Presumably Hauerwas finds a difference between a Jim Jones and a Martin Luther King, Jr., but he never tells us what it might be. This omission would be acceptable if he saw the determination of actual practices to be community-based, and thus plural, but his confident evocation of "Christian" moral positions suggests that he *does* have criteria which are not being put forward.

It all seems so simple—one story, the "super-story" of Jesus Christ,[140] one community, one politics. This homogeneity lies at the heart of both the attraction and danger of Hauerwas's work. The attraction lies in the offer of a model of grounded, relational community so desparately sought by white, middle-class (often male), liberal Protestants. Within that community, the basepoint is simple: we are Christians who follow Jesus Christ. Thus, "the Christian way of life forms people in a manner that makes abortion unthinkable."[141] Enduring marital relations are not founded on love but on Christian commitment.[142] We are not even responsible for the evils of history: racism is an evil of the *American* story, rather than the *Christian* story.[143]

Instead of the postmodern historicism he is seen to embrace, Hauerwas responds to the problem of social complexity, the many forces and roles present in our lives, by returning to a simple, homogeneous absolutism. This move

63

doubly distorts our material, embodied existence. First, Hauerwas puts "Christian" as a category separate from any other portion of our identity (gender, class, race or ethnicity, sexual identity). Yet people's understanding of themselves and their communities is always *simultaneously* Christian, Asian, working-class, female, etc. Hauerwas models a church set completely apart from history and society which commits sin *only* as it participates in a corrupt world (currently the modern liberal one).

Second, the Christian story that Hauerwas tells is *one*, not *the* story. For him, the Christian narrative is a simple, homogeneous moral marker—a position which nicely avoids encounter with the abundant and ambiguous messiness of Christian history.[144] A closer look at Christian history reveals strand of different stories which presumably must be honored if we are to live the thick moral lives Hauerwas loves to celebrate. Gloria Albrecht describes Hauerwas's understanding of "the Christian story," as an "essence ... [which] floats above the concrete embodiment of Christian life and history."[145] Michael Dyson has insightfully pointed out how Hauerwas's understanding of sharp church/state separation as essential for "the Christian story" excludes from that story any part of the black church experience which "presents a vital vision of the relationship between faith and politics that preserves Christian identity while expanding the possibilities of democracy."[146]

In spite of his criticisms of liberalism, Hauerwas seems condemned to repeat what he cannot acknowledge. First, he repeats the liberal move of abstraction away from historical particularity, specifically the particularities of those who are not white and male. Second, by rejecting any public participatory role for the church in civil society, he reproduces the very public / private split he is trying to overcome. The church, he says repeatedly, is beyond public and private. But what this seems to mean, if we follow Hauerwas's examples, is a withdrawal from any form of meaningful public participation.

Hauerwas's church is a hazardous possibility at a time when the church is one of the few institutions of civil society that still demonstrates responsibility towards the social order.[147] The church community Hauerwas constructs, separate from the challenges of difference and politics, offers, I believe, a dangerous haven for white liberal Protestants. They are given a communal identity without the challenge of ethnicity. And they are able to justify a retreat from politics when they are tired of the turmoil of social involvement.

At Home Among the Fragments: Larry Rasmussen

Like Neuhaus and Hauerwas, Larry Rasmussen diagnoses our society as suffering from a loss of moral coherence. In his main work on community, *Moral Fragments and Moral Community*, he says that since we no longer experience "the moral formation done in local communities," we "[live] from moral fragments and community fragments only, and both are being destroyed faster than they are being replenished."[148] Without this personal and local moral formation "there is," he writes, "hardly a vocabulary for public moral discussion, much less the skills needed for pursuing the common good together."[149]

Like Neuhaus, Rasmussen addresses in this diagnosis both church and society; however, like Hauerwas, he sees his primary purpose to be addressing the church, particularly the liberal Protestant, white, middle-strata church. Knowledge of society is essential to be able to answer the question driving his work: "Given the claims of Christian faith, and given the requirements of moral formation in a society like ours … what is the shape proper to the church?"[150] That shape, though proper to the church, is intimately bound to the situation of the broader society.

The source of fragmentation is, of course, modernity. But unlike Hauerwas and Neuhaus, Rasmussen sees modernity not just as a cultural institution, but as a phenomenon including culture, technology, and economy. Rasmussen gives modernity a mixed review, since he acknowledges the way it has "extended moral obligation to millions of people" through global interconnection and "rescued significant populations from the whims and crude injustices of entrenched local ways of life." It has produced "worthy moral capital—individual freedom, human rights, critical thought itself, tolerance, voluntary association." Nevertheless, it is "killing us."[151]

The main culprit is not individualism but the market and, secondarily, the state. During the "Second Bourgeois Revolution" (which Rasmussen never quite pinpoints historically), the market came to substitute for moral communities as "the moral order and culture [were] organized on the same principles as the economy and share[d] its ethos."[152] When "capitalism became a culture and a society and not simply the means for economic exchange," it destroyed communities of civil society and could not itself provide any compensatory formation. The result is a bureaucratized society, since "society could not handle in more informal ways the array of problems … when its human bonds are atomized and its moral base thinned."[153] The market numbs our sense of personal and social responsibility so we leave our social problems unsolved or to be handled by the state.

The challenge, as Rasmussen sees it, is to figure out "how modernity's strangers can muster the social practices and settings by which they come to know and live by the morality they have created."[154] Like Hauerwas and Lasch, he sees the revival of practices as central to a reformed morality. Practices are "focal actions … that belong to a way of life as means to appropriate ends (eating, resting); are worthy ends in their own right (breaking bread together, the communion of hospitality); and are the mediums whereby our lives are centered, ordered, and sustained."[155] They are sustained through the connections with others experienced in intimate communities.

However, unlike Hauerwas and Lasch, Rasmussen sees these communities as only one part of the complex societies we inhabit. He emphasizes that there are two kinds of relational bonds in our modern societies: "face-to-face" or intimate communal bonds and "associational connections." One set is local and particular, the other more global and abstract. In Rasmussen's eyes, although the intimate bonds are the ones most endangered, both are necessary for the health of social morality. In a globally connected world, "face-to-face relationships cannot serve society at large" and thus "segmental" relationships, more limited and open-ended, are also necessary.[156] However these associational ties are hollow without the underlying support of more intimate associations of civil society which provide moral formation, mediating relations between simple personal experience and complex social institutions. The global connections our postmodern world requires can only be sustained through ongoing particular local relationships.

Rasmussen's caution about the limits of communal ties is matched by a caution about the type of community and communal tradition endorsed. "The very last thing this nation needs," he writes,

> as multicultural, multiracial, and multireligious as it factually is (though is not in its dominant consciousness, habits, or story), is to return the moral life to the homogeneity of like-minded, little communities who value the social harmony which comes by shunning, even excluding, the neighbors we don't want as our neighbors.[157]

66

Implicitly, Rasmussen evaluates traditions and communities in light of their treatment of different others, emphasizing that middle-strata Americans must move outside their particular "cultural experience and sense of history."[158] He also views traditional notions in light of our socioeconomic context when he writes that the loss of family life cannot simply be solved by the revival of "family values," because "the forces maiming family life are the very economic and technical ones conservatives largely support."[159]

Attention to diversity and economy demonstrate Rasmussen's post-hegemonic assumptions concerning liberal Protestantism. Further evidence is the way he sees the church not as the only, or even the prime, moral institution. Although both Rasmussen and Hauerwas see the church as potentially providing a paradigm or model of revived community, Rasmussen sees this role as a partnership with other social institutions—while Hauerwas dismisses these institutions as irrelevant, if not harmful, to Christianity. Although both Hauerwas and Rasmussen criticize the "acculturation" of liberal Protestantism, Hauerwas speaks in generalities about liberal democracy, while Rasmussen specifies middle-class whiteness as the source of much of the church's captivity. Where Hauerwas sees the church as a "beacon on the hill", Rasmussen sees it as one institution among others in civil society which continues to have an "explicit moral vocation."[160] In contrast to Neuhaus's interest in a revived *corpus Christianum*, Rasmussen says that liberal Protestant church should absolutely *not* see itself as a Constantinian universal community. While Neuhaus criticizes any humility on the part of liberal Protestant Christianity, Rasmussen thinks that "a chastened Christianity ... now might be the Christian gift and treasure."[161]

For Rasmussen, the gifts the Protestant church can renew for itself and for society are its egalitarian membership, its "pioneering creativity," its function as a haven, and its role as moral critic.[162] To do this, he is clear, the church cannot preserve itself as a homogeneous community. Moral critique, he says, requires "hearing disparate voices" through "openness to difference, to revelation, to perspectives and stories other than our most familiar and comforting ones."[163] It also requires Christians to not only learn from their own traditions and identities but to "learn from those who dwell beyond church borders." Unlike Hauerwas, who sees important knowledge coming only from the Christian tradition, Rasmussen insists that "the word from the world (which, we are all reminded, is God's) is often a correcting and teaching word, a revelatory and sometimes saving one."[164] Tradition always requires renewal and correction as part of the ongoing life of the community.

Rasmussen's model of church as community, like Hauerwas's model, is a haven for persons contending with a harsh and confusing world. But it is a place of refreshment, not retreat, where the emphasis is not on boundaries and exclusion, but on connection and inclusivity.[165] Authority and commonality do not depend upon a unified moral order but on fragments of love shared amidst struggle.

67

Moving from Daniel Bell to Larry Rasmussen has meant traversing a spectrum of communitarian thought. Drawing on the questions raised at the end of the first chapter, we can mark the differences amidst their diagnoses of moral illness and communal cure. While all, as I said at the beginning of this chapter, point to liberal modernity as the source of our ills, Rasmussen and Walzer also see it as a source of many of our strengths. This recognition leads them to insist upon the continued importance of ideas of equality, justice, and rights, understood in a nonindividualistic framework, in contrast to the others who generally dismiss all appeals to these values (Lasch and Hauerwas) or define these values so abstractly they have little relevance (Bell and Neuhaus).

These views of justice are connected to underlying assumptions about the nature of moral order. Thus, for Neuhaus and Hauerwas, the Christian community is formed around a unitary tradition, which offers a clear set of guiding norms, and rejects alternative interpretations as nonChristian (or "political"). For Neuhaus, his version of Christianity represents the "agreed-upon authority that is higher than community itself." In Hauerwas's case, the appeal to historical narratives and embedded, communal selves conceals a neoconservative preservation of power, represented in his authoritarian Jesus. For them, the Christian community plays an exemplary role in the moral life of society, understood, of course, as completely separate from political life. Similarly, Bell and Lasch seek to resolve the diagnosed problem of cultural and moral disintegration through a renewed normative harmonious communal framework. For them, religion also operates as an ultimately transcendent guarantee of unity. However, their ideas of religion are highly abstract, since it serves as stand-in for the patriarchal forms of authority they see necessary for social order.

If there is a presumption of a unified moral order, there can be little room for claims on justice and the common good made by those defined as external to this order. For Bell and Neuhaus, difference is a dangerous group-based particularity breaking unity. Lasch and Hauerwas appear to enter the particular as they affirm membership in rooted, particular communities as a foundation for the moral renewal of citizenship and nation. Yet both are reluctant to engage communities based on nonwhite heritages, which suggests that the notion of citizenship or discipleship they hold is, ultimately, a liberal, standardized version, unshaped by marginalized political cultures. Lasch's reappropriation of populist tradition may be an important resource for citizenship, but it needs major transformation from a tradition that excluded others to one that can incorporate difference.

68

Walzer and Rasmussen, in contrast, are searching for ways to preserve difference in tension with connection and commonality. Walzer draws the most detailed picture of the relation of differing communities within a complex nation state, since he highlights the importance of doing justice towards cultural traditions different than our own. For him, the shared assumption of a liberal political order can accommodate, yet be corrected by, a civil society full of difference, although, as I have suggested, the potential richness of the difference is sometimes overiden by the move to "common understanding." Rasmussen emphasizes more clearly than anyone else in this chapter the need to engage with different experiences. Although he never specifies any source of commonality, a certain given sense of a shared society and shared church is suggested that can help us face the challenges of difference.

Those who search for a unified culture not only exclude those who are different, but, generally, also avoid economic questions. Bell's and Neuhaus's avoidance of capitalism allows them to attack culture and the "culture producers" as the source of our woes while generally ignoring exploitation and poverty. Indeed Neuhaus, like other neoconservatives, suggests that the problems of poverty are solely cultural and bear no relationship to economic conditions. Although Lasch began his work by emphasizing the impact of shifts in economic structures, in his later books, issues of meaning become more distant from issues of economy. Walzer's references to economic questions are indirect as he criticizes the movement of money out of its proper economic sphere to other spheres of society. Rasmussen is the most clear in stating the need to understand the ways in which the economy shapes our experience of fragmentation.

Cutting across these issues are efforts to renegotiate the relations of the public and private spheres. For Neuhaus, the Christian church is the transcendent public institution "by which all positions—right, left, or unlabeled—must be evaluated" providing the moral content for what would otherwise be a "naked" public square. Similarly, Bell creates a public household, where all particularities of gender and race stay outside in a private world. In contrast, Hauerwas sharply distinguishes between Christian identity and citizenship, claiming that in its location apart from the world, the church is neither public nor private, but "a mirror to which each culture can compare itself." A mirror, however, does not image a responsible relationship to society, especially as Hauerwas tacitly accepts the heritage of religious privatization. Walzer works with an ambiguous division of public/private in his distinction between the common political sphere and the diverse world of civil society. When he speaks of the common symbols of U.S. public life, the division seems sharp and universalizing. But when he insists that Irish and American are both political identities, the division becomes more blurred and becomes a potentially rich area in his reconstruction of a just political and social order. Although Rasmussen does not explicitly address the public/private division, his appeal to a church that spans both public and private lives, working with differences and commonalities in both spheres is also suggestive. Returning to the problem of a broken Protestant synthesis of public and private roles, while Neuhaus has maintained the public role and Hauerwas has maintained the private role, Rasmussen endeavors to construct a new nonhegemonic synthesis for liberal Protestantism where it is one institution among others trying to reconstruct a civil society providing moral resources to all persons.

Comparing the discussions of the family reinforces those observations as it appears to function either as a symptom of disorder or an invisible entity. For Neuhaus and Hauerwas, the family is an institution whose moral coherence and unity is closely tied to that of the church. Family and church are expected to be communities of harmonious relations ordering the private sphere of morality. For Bell and Walzer, family is not a significant consideration. Bell simply leaves family as a realm of assumed normative importance. Walzer finds family less key in his discussion of cultural and political membership, focusing more on women's possibilities for public participation than their private identities. As a result, he leaves the family invisible within the private sphere. For Lasch, the family is the central institution of moral formation where, if "natural"—patriarchal—authority is not instilled, we are left unable to function as part of a coherent moral order.

All of the men discussed here exemplify differing ways in which white males of the PMC seek to maintain or renegotiate power. Bell, Lasch, Neuhaus, and Hauerwas all believe a integrative morality (and, ultimately, a religious morality) is required to maintain social order. Participation and politics, ways in which power is shared, represent a threat to transcendental norms under-girding that moral order. Walzer and Rasmussen, by contrast, understand the moral and egalitarian dimensions of participatory politics, where interaction with fellow citizens (and, for Rasmussen, fellow Christians) provides a foun-dation for developing a strong moral, democratic society where differences are respected and protected.

SISTERHOOD, FAMILY, AND SOCIETY
White Women in Search of Community

Women's communities are seldom the original, nonvoluntary,
found communities of their members.
                                —Marilyn Friedman[1]

Perhaps women are the "fools" in Western political thought
and practice whose official powerlessness grants them a paradoxical freedom from full assimilation into the dominant public identity whose aims, in our day, are efficiency and control.
                                —Jean Bethke Elshtain[2]

chapter 4

WHITE MIDDLE-CLASS women, among whom I include myself, are in a contradictory position. On the one hand, the crisis of Western whiteness is,
unavoidably, our crisis, since it is our culture. On the other hand, the traditions in crisis have always excluded us and denied our participation as
women.[3] Sharon Welch expresses well the complexity of this status: "As a
woman I am oppressed by the structures of patriarchy. Yet as white, I benefit
from the oppression of people of other races. As a person whose economic
level is middle-class, I am both victim and victimizer of others." We live in a
"double identity—oppressor and oppressed," collaborators and critics.[4]

Community in many ways appears as a "natural" topic for white feminists.
Foundational to feminist practice and theory has been a stress on women's
relational or communal capacities. The assumption of women's concern for
nurturing relation can be seen from the nineteenth century bourgeois cult of

domesticity through "Second Wave" consciousness-raising groups, on to the most recent work on women as possessors of a distinctive "caring" moral perspective. The most vivid visions of community built on these qualities have emerged from the radical and cultural feminist movements. For example, Mary Daly calls "Crones" to join together in "The Fire of Sisterhood." Most recently Sarah Lucia Hoagland has continued the vision of a separate women's community in her *Lesbian Ethics* which suggests that a completely alternative moral and political structure emerges from lesbian community.[5]

Feminists find themselves in an ambiguous relationship to both liberal and communitarian discussions. The norms of equality, rationality, and freedom, the liberal division of public and private spheres, the model of a social contract have all been subjects of feminist criticism.[6] In response to liberalism, feminist and woman-oriented work often invokes community as a norm reflecting both women's relational nature and a vision for the future. While on the surface these proposals would seem to agree with communitarian perspectives, there is, however, a corresponding concern about community to be found in a variety of current feminist critiques of communitarian proposals. Much feminist work has joined with communitarians in a critique of the individualist liberal self. However, the particularity that is denied that self, from a feminist perspective, is not merely a "rootedness," but, more specifically, a location in the experience of *women*. As Marilyn Friedman puts it, the communitarian community "harbors social roles and structures that have been highly oppressive for women" and "manifest[s] a troubling complacency about the moral authority claimed or presupposed by these communities."[7] Reflecting on the problems of authority and community within a historical framework, Elizabeth Fox-Genovese remarks that the "close association between community and the unity of wills that results from inequality has left an inadequate model for community based on gender equality."[8]

In reviewing the equivocal relation of community and women, two key issues must be highlighted.

WOMEN, COMMUNITY, AND THE PRIVATE SECTOR

As I have discussed in chapters 1 and 2, the creation of modern civil society depended upon the relegation of bourgeois women to a newly-emerged private sector, the realm of "natural" relations outside of the world of abstract, interchangeable citizens bound by the social contract. Describing liberal theory's view of the domestic world, Carole Pateman writes, "In the family, individuals appear as unique and unequal personalities and as members of an undifferentiated unity grounded in sentiment."[9] From the perspective of dominant morality, the private family sphere, as a number of feminist commentators have pointed out, has been rendered either invisible or morally suspect. The presumption was that the "disorder" of women, whose bodies and emotions could not be fitted into the mold of rational autonomous citizenship, had to be kept in a sphere separate from the political world.[10]

Yet, simultaneously, the world of bourgeois women was seen as essential for social life, the place where there could be "a sense of belonging and bonding in contrast to the ruthless pursuit of self-interest."[11] These emotional family bonds were one of the key sources of ongoing socialization, always at odds with the dominant liberal ideology. Thus in spite of the fact that it ignored or dismissed women as citizens, liberal polity depended upon the existence of women's reproductive labor in the private, domestic sphere.[12] This dependence makes any change in women's status a question that challenges the legitimation of society. The challenge is implicitly understood by communitarians who frequently (as with Lasch, Hauerwas, and Neuhaus) are anxious to reaffirm the traditional role of women in the family.

The double existence created by the split between public and private spheres bequeaths an ambiguous heritage to white feminists. On the one hand, white feminists seek participation in the public sphere, the arena of politics and power. But since it is an arena constructed for the activities of white, bourgeois men, they are forced to question the terms of that participation. On the other hand, feminists who advocate the special values and virtues of women seem to still be trapped in the private sphere, assuming the possibility of relations of intimacy and immediacy and neglecting the ways the public world shaped and continues to mediate these relations.

This tension between autonomy and relation, between liberal individualism and communitarian merging, is at the center of much feminist theorizing. Elizabeth Fox-Genovese finds the roots of these capacities, gathered together in the communal vision of sisterhood, in the ambiguous heritage of women's family experiences. She argues that there is a problem about community and family inherent in (white middle-class) feminism. She points out that feminist organizing and theory grew originally from seeking to participate equally in liberal modern individualism. Yet, "for feminism to thrive, the male model of individualism must be replaced by a female model of sisterhood," a model, Fox-Genovese contends, is rooted in the female experience of unequal gender relations in the family which includes emphasis on immediate relations and nurturance.[13]

Further complications arise from the reality, central to this work, that these discussions are carried out within the context of modern advanced industrial capitalism. As I have demonstrated, the structures of the bureaucratized capitalist state have altered both the public and private spheres, so that participation seems impossible at the public level and intimacy impossible at the private level. Since the state has already taken over most of women's family roles, women now are subject to public, rather than private patriarchy.[14] In this context, do women's notions of community depend more upon a reconstructed public or a reaffirmation of the private sphere? Does women's entrance into the public threaten the communal values of their domestic tradition? Are these notions of community, rooted in the values and experiences of the bourgeois private sphere, really able to offer resources for the problems of liberal modernity? Are women's citizenship and community compatible?

THE PROBLEM OF DIFFERENCE

A key question, as with the male theorists discussed in the previous chapter, is whether these feminist theories and models are based primarily on the experience of white, bourgeois women, or acknowledge the traditions and experiences of women of other races and classes. The split between private and public which has determined the heritage of so many white women has operated in very different ways for white bourgeois women, as opposed to women of color and poor white women. While the bourgeois woman was trapped as a "doll-wife" in a doll's house,[15] for less privileged women, the restrictive home of the white middle-class woman was the site of paid labor and exploitation. Their own homes, while places of patriarchal oppression, were also sites of resistance, often linked to marginalized communities. Yet, they have also always been sites open to the intervention of white capitalism, whether through slavery, legal segregation and illegal lynching, or, most recently, state intervention through police and social workers.[16]

Given this different history, white feminist theories that assume a uniform women's experience necessarily invoke communities of exclusion. The issue is not simply invisibility, but the nature of the experience claimed as essential for communal life. Elizabeth Spelman remarks that "the claim of commonality may be very arrogant indeed: the caller may be trying to appropriate the other's identity."[17] The acknowledgement of difference within the category of woman will be an important criterion to differentiate among the views presented in this chapter and to determine which might hold out possibilities for our multicultural society.

My discussion here suggests several important points by which to compare and contrast the four women considered here. All four join in the criticism of liberal individualism and its capitalist roots. Yet each proposes different alternatives. Elshtain and Cahill seek to maintain and renew the traditional institutions of family and church, putting them at the more conservative end of my spectrum. For Elshtain, this renewal occurs by revaluing women's domestic nature, while Cahill balances individualism and Catholic community. Young and Welch, both socialist feminists, seek more radical change. Young constructs a radical nonhomogenous pluralistic public; and Welch looks first to Foucault and then to black women as sources of community resistance.

SOCIETY AS A CARING PLACE:
JEAN BETHKE ELSHTAIN

Jean Bethke Elshtain is a woman who calls herself both feminist and communitarian.[18] From her first book, *Public Man, Private Woman: Women in Social and Political Thought*, Elshtain has pursued what she sees as the ambivalent situation of women, defined by the private sphere, now entering the public sphere. Developing these concerns in terms of women's values has led her to extensively examine the family as the site of the positive contribution of women and war as the site of the negative contribution of men. She has seen women's values and capacities as the source of whatever renewed communal vision is still possible in our disintegrated society. Most recently, however, she has moved away from a focus on women to a discussion of the problems of civil society and democracy in the midst of what she sees as dangerously weakened political discourse.

For Elshtain, the source of our social woes is "ultraliberalism." It is, she writes, "what has helped to sicken us ... the final rationality and disenchantment of all aspects of social life; deeper dependence of the self on antidemocratic bureaucracies and social engineering elites; a more complete stripping away of the last vestiges of personal authority (construed as domination), and of traditional identities (construed as irrational and backward)."[19] However, in her most recent work, *Democracy on Trial*, the source of our moral problems is defined not as liberalism, but as a politics of difference and displacement.

Although the shift in names is significant, certain themes have remained constant in Elshtain's communitarian account:

1) A concern with an isolated self, which is stripped of all relational or embedded qualities through the loss of "social webs." This self focuses on its rights and freedom to choose its own mode of life, unbound by belonging, obligation, or tradition.[20] Elshtain calls our current society "a world of triumphalist I's."[21]

2) A model of community as voluntary, bound by "the conviction that all relations that are not totally voluntary, rational and contractual are irrational and suspect." This community has not, until recently, been dominant since "American life was stitched together historically by a dense web of communities whose glue was religion, ethnicity, shared associative purposes, and immersion in substantive civic moralities to which the broader framework was officially agnostic."[22] Now these intermediary institutions, or civil society, have been seriously eroded, leaving atomist selves facing a powerful state bureaucracy.

3) The loss of the consensus furnished by Protestant civic religion which, to Elshtain, means the loss of "certainties surrounding familial life and authority as a secure locus for the creation of democratic citizens."[23]

4) The loss of the social space and personal capacities of political participation.[24] This loss is tied, in Elshtain's view, to the loss of the distinction between

public and private spheres. While she recognizes the damage of a "rigid pub-lic-private dichotomy," perhaps the primary concern of *Democracy on Trial* is the impact of a blurring of public and private which, in her eyes, has meant the loss of both communal politics and moral selfhood. In our current "poli-tics of displacement," "everything private ... becomes grist for the public mill" while "everything public ... is privatized and played out in a psy-chodrama on a grand scale."[25] This displacement allows for the development of selves without responsibility to others since one's private concerns are pri-mary. It also destroys politics, since without any public/private distinction "there can be no differentiated activity or set of institutions that are genuine-ly political, the purview of citizens and the basis of order, legitimacy, and pur-pose in a democratic community."[26]

Although Elshtain is very clear about the dangers of state power, she is silent about the ways that power is rooted in capitalism. For example, it never seems to occur to her that the world of "triumphalist I's," where our desires are pri-mary, is a world which benefits capitalism since we consume (and are urged to consume by all the different media shaping our lives) to satisfy these desires. Elshtain's concern is meaning (and its loss) which to her does not involve questions of economic exploitation and commercialization. Yet she shares with Walzer a concern for democratic participation, which, as in his case, stands in some tension with the desire for ongoing, stable traditions of meaning. These tensions are perhaps most clear when we consider how Elshtain has treated feminism and issues concerning women.

For Elshtain, the family is the key site of liberal destruction and potential communal renewal, a renewal based upon the moral roles and capacities of women. Similar to other social institutions, the family has been "weakened by market forces that eroded communal ties and severed work from communal life." As part of this process many of the family functions have become the work of the state.[27] While other theorists, such as Jürgen Habermas, see this development as but one example of the results of liberal capitalism, for Elshtain the issue of family has been paramount. The family plays, in her view, the cen-tral role in producing and reproducing the moral relations, "the basic moral grounding" essential for the health and cohesion of a democratic society.[28]

Elshtain characterizes the importance of the family in several ways, which are all foundational to her notion of community. First, the family provides the necessary embedded particularity, the concrete sense of identity, which con-trasts with the abstract individuality presumed by liberalism.[29] That particular-ity is rooted in the givenness of the moral community of the family, which contrasts to the liberal voluntaristic model. For Elshtain, moral norms and commitments nurtured in this givenness have a strength and durability impossible with the "self-chosen obligations" of voluntarism."[30] Second, the strength of these given moral norms provides the foundation for an enduring moral authority. Like Lasch, Elshtain locates the authority necessary for social legitimation and cohesion in family relations: "Family relations could not exist without family authority, and these relations remain the best way we know anything about to create human beings with a developed capacity to give ethical allegiance to the background presumptions and principles of democratic authority."[31] Our childhood obedience to our parents and to the norms of social respect they taught us allows us to understand the meaning of limits to our self-oriented desires and capacities, experiencing the constraint of obligations and duties to all others. This training in the particularity of *Sittlichkeit*, Elshtain says, is our "launching pad" to the universality of *Moralität*.

Given this understanding of the importance of family, Elshtain concludes that we are powerless in the face of state bureaucracy, not only because of the lack of actual intervening institutions, but also because of the loss of the internal capacities that those institutions provided.[32] Her analysis differs from Lasch's in two respects. First, she does not rely on Freud; her arguments are based on social and political sources, rather than psychological ones. Second, she refuses to assign gender-specific roles to mother and father, and, instead, stresses that what is at stake is *parental* authority.[33]

However, although Elshtain tries to reformulate the traditional roles of mothers, she never reformulates the heterosexual family norm. Family, she says, must have "its basis in marriage and kinship.... To throw the honorable mantle 'family' over every *ad hoc* collection of persons ... is to diminish the genuine achievement of family men and women who have retained their commitments to and for one another."[34] What is at stake, in Elshtain's view, is the stability needed for the nurture of children. Although she accepts the existence of other forms, they should not, she says, be the focus of family debate and policy. Her underlying assumption is that only ties of blood and heterosexual marriage are "given," and thus have the necessary durability to sustain moral nurture. Equally absent in this harmonious model are any discussions of families of different cultures and races. Yet the maternal "powerless" virtues shaped in the private, household sphere have been primarily heterosexual white women's virtues. In spite of her strong sense of the historical development of the family, Elshtain preserves a "naturalized" view of the emotional world of the family which reproduces some of the public / private dichotomy of the very "ultraliberalism" she repudiates.

This tension about the status of women's "nature" runs throughout Elshtain's work. As a critic of liberal universalized individualism, Elshtain constantly emphasizes the *difference* of women: "women as a group experience their social worlds differently than men as a group."[35] The source of this difference lies in differing roles and responsibilities: "In the past when the household was the hub of human life, female power was more complementary to the institutions and juridical authority of men." Since liberal modernity

77

eroded this household, "the complementarity of powers has given way to an enhancement and expansion of institutionalized male authority accompanied by a simultaneous diminution of women's domestic, sacred, and informal authority."[36] Elshtain is suggesting that this authority was not only key to women's well-being, but also to the well-being of the social order. Although feminist research has certainly questioned the standard liberal account of modernity unilaterally improving the status of women, I still find it hard to celebrate a world where women had little or no legal entitlement or protection.

The irony, in Elshtain's eyes, is that feminism has contributed to the expansion of institutionalized male authority, doing the dirty work of capitalism. Since the public world of men is an ultraliberal world of "stripped-down individuals," the feminist desire for women's entrance into this world can only mean a loss of their particularity. "The demand," Elshtain writes, "for a shift in the social identity of women involves their full assimilation into a combined identification with the state and the terms of competitive civil society."[37] It would lead, ultimately, "to the final suppression of the female social world."[38] Consequently, feminist activity should not be aimed at women's public participation and at learning "hard-nosed, realistic talk about power,"[39] but at preserving and championing women's special maternal identity. Not only will public participation co-opt women's distinctive capacities, but it will "extend the annihilating public world into the private," increasing the power and penetration of the state.[40]

78

What women need to value, Elshtain believes, are not the liberal patriarchal values, but the moral qualities of the private world that have been the basis of their lack of participation in the public. This marginality is no longer a hindrance, but, under the conditions of "ultraliberalism," a valuable resource of resistance and renewal. Women, says Elshtain, are "fools" in Western political tradition "whose official powerlessness grants them a paradoxical freedom from full assimilation into the dominant public identity whose aims, in our day, are efficiency and control."[41] The virtues developed through the experience of nurturance, "the core concepts of maternal achievement," are "the animating ethos of women's familial and communal identity [which] may serve as a nucleus of an alternative to atomistic and technocratic politics."[42]

In her most recent work, Elshtain has broadened and revised her criticisms of feminist political agendas in order to assess more precisely the damage of the "politicized" claims of women and other minority groups. She links the loss of personal responsibility to the proliferation of groups which are organized according to a "politicized ontology—that is, persons are to be judged not by what they do or say but by what they *are*."[43] Although she remarks that these groups are found throughout the political spectrum, all of her examples are from the Left, most particularly radical feminist, gay liberation groups, and "multiculturalists."[44] Here the lack of an analytic framework encompassing the economy, civil society, and the state becomes evident, since Elshtain is unable to make several important distinctions. For example, not all feminists are radical (in fact, most aren't), yet by exclusively speaking of radical feminists, Elshtain gives support to those who like to reduce and dismiss all feminist claims. And she falls into contradiction she criticizes radical feminists for enlisting the police power of the state in support of battered women on one page, while praising inner city women for calling for police protection in gang areas on another.[45]

Although Elshtain has stressed women's difference from men, her current formulation of civil society emphasizes commonalities. If we do not perceive what we share, our common tradition, we will perish. That common tradition marks us as citizens, in contrast to the the differences marked as male or female, heterosexual or homosexual, black or white. Those differences, Elshtain says, are not "civically interesting."[46] But because the difference of race is not "interesting," she treats Martin Luther King, Jr. *only* as appealing to American notions of equality and biblical notions of human worth, while ignoring the specific black heritage of suffering and faith that also supplied King's moral vocabulary. While Walzer sees both "African" and "American" as crucially important, for Elshtain, the "African" simply does not exist. Elshtain is right to emphasize the importance of shared tradition, the fact that we share commonalities as U.S. citizens. But part of the heritage that connects us also divides us—thus the freedom and equality of "our" heritage was developed at the expense of the captivity of African-American slaves, the death of indigenous tribes, the labor of Asian and Hispanic immigrants. To acknowledge the complexity of this heritage is not to "flatter groups ... teaching exotic, mythic and 'foreign' pasts," but to truly make our tradition a common one, that includes the experience of all. It is not to make "a pitiless assault on the past," but to claim the past in all its hope and suffering.[47]

A key question for Elshtain, particularly in her most recent work, is the relation of the private and public spheres. Earlier, she has called for a "social compact," a model she believes lies in between liberal contract and conservative community. She hopes that the compact will avoid both the sharp liberal division of public and private spheres, and the undifferentiated hierarchy of conservative notions of community. It will envision society "as a caring place, one protective of specific ties, sustained by a sense of history and collective memory, valuing diverse ways of being, promoting a working reconciliation with nature."[48] Although this is a worthy image, participation and politics have vanished in favor of integration around a restricted definition of women and their moral identity. The private sphere, the repressed half of liberal polity, has been expanded to encompass society in a "compact" that negates, rather than integrates, the public sphere. Politics are described according to the liberal model as clashes of interest played out within the state and are evaluated in relation to a norm of harmony which assigns negative value to power and conflict.

79

In *Democracy on Trial*, Elshtain now argues that the spheres have melded together, so that "everything private ... becomes grist for the public mill" and "everything public ... is privatized and played out in a psychodrama on a grand scale."[49] While even the smallest sampling of daytime TV talkshows support Elshtain's analysis, the question is how she hopes to solve this problem. The solution seems to be a renewed sense of the citizenship and civil society we have in common. An important model for her is las Madres, the movement of Argentinian mothers, who broke through the political process, creating a group political identity in a voice that "fused the language of grief with the language of rights," rights that are immunities from harm and responsibilities, rather than entitlements.

Elshtain is right to ask us to reject the language of rights as individual entitlement and to turn to the common task of building a common civil society. Yet the gay and feminist groups she criticizes have also maintained the connection and solidarity that she so admires. Indeed it is on the basis of these common identities, that they have entered the public sphere, claiming a place for themselves and, necessarily, challenging the liberal boundaries of public and private spheres. Mary Dietz has argued that Elshtain "reinforces an abstract split between the public and private realms" which cannot link the practices she values with "the kind of 'ethical polity' she envisions, namely one informed by democratic thinking and the political practices of citizenship."[50] Elshtain seems stuck with the two alternatives of no public / private division (which she rejects) and a return to the old division. While her earlier work on the public importance of women's private language implicity challenged the split, in *Democracy on Trial* she is unable to push further.

Elshtain clearly names the current problems of civil society—lack of moral discourse, exposure to state administration, etc. But her resources for any positive proposal are limited by her omission of capitalism and her distorted notion of difference, so that, as with Bell, the culprits for our woes are these troubling, clamorous "groups" practicing "groupthink." She claims to seek a civil society that contains both the bonds of commonality and respect for differences but she never explains the grounds for either. While her model of harmony was earlier based on family ties, it now is a more general civic connection which, in spite of her criticisms of homogeneous "groupthink" seems unable to take into account any form of difference. The foundations for the primary virtue of solidarity Elshtain cherishes seem very fragile.

PERSON, PARTNERSHIP, AND COMMUNITY:
LISA SOWLE CAHILL

Lisa Sowle Cahill is a Catholic intellectual working within her religious tradition. Cahill would probably describe herself as primarily committed to the Catholic church, rather than to feminism, but her work in sexual ethics has sought to enhance the position of women in Catholicism through dialogue with both mainstream and feminist Catholic theologies. As she says, she hopes to recover "a positive message on sexuality" from Catholicism by joining the values of Catholic tradition with feminist critique.[51] While Cahill's own position is often hard to determine, since her preferred style is to sum up a variety of viewpoints with a small, suggestive conclusion, I will try to discern what kind of Christian community is at stake in her work.

Cahill's work on sexuality can be seen as part of her broader project which I would characterize as affirming a Catholic norm of community over against both the individualism of Western society and the inegalitarian traditions (particularly in relation to women) of Catholic natural law teachings. For Cahill, Catholic traditional notions of community and common good are important resources to counter the pervasive "Lockean individualism." The "liberal view," as she describes it, "stresses the rationality, freedom and autonomy of the individual ... the autonomous adult exists to fulfill independently his or her own interests and needs, and is limited in attempts to do so only by the parallel and sometimes competing rights of others."[52] Liberal theory provides a structure only of rights, while ignoring the ongoing responsibilities, "the traditional service-oriented and communal ideals" required by the Catholic understanding of our social / communal existence.[53] Even in American Catholic philosophy, the person comes to have priority over society and the common good.[54] This individualism is correlated by Cahill with a relativism, particularly in the realm of sexual ethics, which she believes to be damaging to human moral formation and the intrinsic communal nature of the person in general, and counter to Catholic moral tradition in particular.

Yet Cahill is aware that the Catholic traditional teachings on women demonstrate that any simple affirmation of tradition and community are not possible. She frequently expresses her difficulties with the continued papal emphasis on motherhood. Writing of the apostolic letter, *Mulieris dignatatem*, she notes that even though the pope affirmed the "essential equality" of women, he suggested that women's primary role is mother and that in other roles women seek "to fulfill their destiny of self-giving love ... by some analogous extension of motherhood."[55] Drawing implicitly on the norm of equality, Cahill criticizes the pope's stereotyped and romantic ideas about women.[56] These ideas are examples of what Cahill sees as "a continuing assault on Christian community ... [by] the patriarchy which distorts relationships not only in the culture, but 'even' (and more so) in the church."[57]

To develop her third, revisionist Catholic, way, Cahill starts from her primary moral basepoint: "The *community* itself, and the experience of its members in the Spirit, is the primary reference of moral evaluation."[58] Indeed, she says, "the absence of such community has been perhaps the glaring flaw of recent Roman Catholic ethics."[59] This communal experience, understood by

81

Cahill as historically conditioned, is her justification for revision in Catholic teachings.

Cahill, however, is cautious in her use of the category of experience. She insists that the appeal to women's experience must be justified within a natural law framework, following the traditional Catholic norm "that Christian ethics should continue to be informed by human values experientially discovered."[60] And she recasts Elisabeth Schüssler Fiorenza's claim that women's liberatory experience is the primary norm for evaluating scriptural canon in order to argue that there is a tension, which she defines as a complementarity, between the poles of "pluriform and changing" historical reality and scripture. The appeal to experience must finally be justified, Cahill suggests, by an authority internal to Christian canon and community.[61] The evidence of women's experience is not dismissed since Cahill draws on a variety of empirical biological and psychological studies of gender, on feminist theologies and psychological theories, and, to a far lesser extent, social theory. Yet the authority of that experience is understood as an immanent critique within Catholic tradition. Although Cahill does see the Catholic church as a community with historical variation, her emphasis tends to be on maintaining (with revision) the traditional contours of Catholic tradition. Her work is a feminist apologetic, implicitly widening the boundaries of Catholic community.

Like Elshtain, Cahill tries to steer a third way, between liberalism and a conservative communalism that negates the equality of women. Yet Cahill, far more than Elshtain, draws on feminist theories marked by an asocial liberal individualism, which, I suggest, creates some tension in her work. She rarely speaks of women as a differentiated group and stresses equality and partnership in roles, as opposed to justice. Although she emphasizes relationality continuously, drawing on both feminist and Catholic sources, her notion of relations makes no attempt to consider issues of power, conflict or difference.[62] Indeed, the non-Christian feminist sources she chooses, such as Gilligan and Chodorow, are theories which stress relationality, but within an ahistorical, asocial context, which, ironically, reprivileges aspects of the very liberal individualism Cahill wishes to criticize. Without, in fact, some sort of liberal notion of individual equality, Cahill's concept of partnership would not differ greatly from the papal notion of women's special role of motherhood within marriage and community. In Cahill's work, the tension between liberal and communal values that I have portrayed as fundamental to much white feminist theory is played out as a tension between an individualist feminism and a communal Catholicism.

Unlike her Protestant counterparts, Cahill can claim a tradition of community that has more historical weight than, for example, Hauerwas's invocation of communities of character. Cahill does not have to worry, as Hauerwas does, about what is the center of Christian community since Catholic tradition maintains a common and enduring set of essential norms, which may be appropriated in light of changing historical circumstances. As she puts it, "the Christian community should formulate criteria that define fidelity to the essence of [the] norm, while allowing variance in the ways that it is fulfilled."[63] She draws on certain values of liberal equality to revise Catholic tradition and on the communal heritage of Catholicism to reform liberalism.

In many ways, with its emphasis on common responsibilities and compassion, the Catholic church community invoked by Cahill is analogous to the social compact Elshtain seeks. Also similar is the emphasis on the role of common norms to bind and integrate the community. The question is whether Catholic tradition and community can be maintained in such a continuous and unbroken fashion when faced with the challenges of women's experiences.

THE HETEROGENEOUS PUBLIC:
IRIS MARION YOUNG

From her earliest writings, Iris Marion Young has identified herself as a socialist feminist activist. One of her first theoretical contributions, for example, was a discussion of the relations between feminism and marxism as grounding for a socialist feminist movement.[64] But, as Young says, in the context of the 1980s and the 1990s, "radical politics ... has become for me, and many others, more plural and contextualized than the simple label 'socialist-feminist' can convey."[65] Correspondingly, she has moved from an almost exclusive focus on feminism to justice issues based on a vision of coalition politics and normative solidarity.

Young's purpose in all of her writings is working to achieve a democracy based on participation and justice. "Justice," she writes, "is the primary subject of political philosophy." But the subject of liberal philosophy has been a justice focused only on the distribution of goods, never challenging the underlying structures that produce those goods.[66] Instead Young seeks to outline a justice that combats domination and oppression so that *all* are free to meet their needs and exercise their freedom. Young evaluates all notions of justice, community, and public by the criterion of difference, which she sees as a norm guaranteeing truly fair treatment, that is, treatment of people in their particularities. For her, the concept of justice coincides with the concept of the political, "since both seek to enable the fullest possible participation and negotiation about the variety of needs and interests of the members of a society."[67]

The focus of this discussion of Young, however, is not directly on her theory of justice but on the notions of community, society and public that are part of that theory. As I will show, Young shares with communitarians the critique of liberalism which she explicitly defines as capitalism and also the concern to restructure public life and public discourse. Yet she is also deeply critical of the notion of community, turning instead to the concept of a participatory

83

"heterogeneous public" which will recognize the structured differences of identity among the various groups within our society. She struggles explicitly with the prospects for meaningful and democratic social relations in a complex multicultural society.

In Young's view, welfare capitalism has resulted in a society of injustice, domination, and oppression. Following Habermas's analysis, she argues that state welfare capitalism has commodified all aspects of social and personal life. What is of particular concern to her is the way in which the colonization of the lifeworld has meant depoliticization of society, since there is "no forum within the public sphere of discussion and conflict where people can examine the overall patterns of justice or fairness."[68] Politics has dissolved into "interest group pluralism," which is based upon assertion of privatized self-centered interest and "lacks the element of public deliberation that is a hallmark of the political."[69]

The root of this disordered public is located by Young in the Enlightenment ideal of civic impartiality. She describes the emergence of this theory of the public in reaction to an actual vital, multiple public existing in Europe in the mid to late seventeenth century.[70] The republican vision constructed a public world centered around a homogenous norm of impartial reason whose ideal was "the universality of a general will that leaves difference, particularity, and the body behind in the private realms of family and civil society."[71] This norm, named "the logic of identity" by Young, presumes an objectivity based upon an abstraction from the particular. Thus the endpoint of public deliberation is a unity, a general will, transcending all particular experiences, needs and interests.[72]

This model of the civic public is not, says Young, about reason and deliberation, but about power and domination. Impartiality "supports the idea of the neutral state … legitimates bureaucratic authority and hierarchical decision making processes … [and] reinforces oppression by hypostatizing the point of view of privileged groups into a universal position."[73] Those who are excluded are, specifically, women and minorities "associated with nature and the body." Agreeing with Elshtain and a variety of feminist analyses, Young states that the realm of women, the realm of emotion and particularity, is both excluded and essential, a moral division of labor that simultaneously devalues women, excludes their participation, and enables the existence of the "rational" citizen.[74]

Young is especially concerned about the impact of these developments on citizenship, that is identity and participation within the nation-state. The important norm of universal citizenship, or citizenship for all, has been used, she says, to entail three different propositions. The first is the statement that all can be citizens, a presupposition that has empowered both the suffragette and civil rights movements. However, the norm has also been understood to entail that (1) citizenship is based on what all have in common and (2) citizenship requires equal treatment for all. Each of these propositions (which do not *necessarily* flow from the idea that all can be citizens) leads to the elimination of difference. If the norms and powers of citizenship are defined as what we all have in common, those norms and powers usually end up being the qualities of the most powerful. If citizenship involves absolutely equal treatment, then we have no way of remedying past unequal treatment of minority men and women of all races. If it requires and promotes independence as self-sufficiency, a model of a job-holding citizen is perpetuated that negates the role of caring and dependency, marginalizing those who need and who give care.[75] Citizenship ends up being correlated with one particular ethnic membership (white) and one particular gender (male) rather than including qualities of all different groups.[76]

Nevertheless, the problems with the liberal public do not lead Young to embrace community as a solution. She writes, "Liberal individualism denies difference … by levelling … separated individuals under a common measure of rights. Community, on the other hand, denies difference by positing fusion rather than separation as the social ideal."[77] Communitarian and civic republic notions of community assume, Young believes, the normative priority of a common good or general will that binds together community / republic. The existence of a general will implies that we can be fused together in transparent, unmediated relationships. This "illusion of face-to-face unmediated relationships," says Young, avoids the complex realities of social institutions, including racial, class, sexual and gender identities.[78]

85

As a result, communities are, Young believes, generally based on exclusion. Pointing to the tension between membership and citizenship, she argues that community cannot be used to describe the political relations of citizens because "for most people … a community is a group that shares a specific heritage, a common self-identification, a common culture and a set of norms … self-identity as a member of such a community also often occurs as an oppositional differentiation from other groups."[79] Thus, the social model must be more inclusive and more institutionally complex.

Young's alternative to community vs. civic public is the model of a heterogeneous public composed of a full diversity of different groups where difference is acknowledged and where she believes justice can be enacted. In contrast to the liberal model, the major participants in this public are not individuals, but groups which "are socially prior to the individual." Young is anxious to demonstrate that the groups involved are not the privatized groups of interest-group pluralism, but are shaped by special heritages. "Groups," she says, "are an expression of social relations…. Group identification arises, that is, in the encounter and interaction between social collectivities that experience some differences in their way of life and forms of association, even if they regard themselves as belonging to the same society." The bonds of a group are based, Young says, in "a specific affinity with one another because of their similar experience or way of life" and because of their difference from other groups.[80]

In her definition of groups, Young, I believe, struggles with the tension between identifying groups in relation to given traditions, as opposed to more fluid, possibly voluntary, certainly historically malleable identities. On the one hand, she says that group identity has "the character of what Heidegger calls 'thrownness,'"[81] so that the group fundamentally shapes the identity of its participants. On the other hand, Young sees this "thrownness" as open to change since she writes that a group arises out of "a social process of interaction and differentiation in which some people come to have a particular *affinity*." Young insists that this "thrownness" is not an essentialism: "There is no common nature that members of a group share. As aspects of a process, moreover, groups are fluid; they come into being and may fade away."[82] Not everyone constitutes a group: "Only those groups that describe major identities and major status relationships constituting the society or particular institution, and that are oppressed or disadvantaged, deserve specific representation in a heterogeneous public."[83]

There is some ambiguity in this notion of group that deserves further consideration. For example, *who* decides what "major identities and major status relationships are"? And how do we deal with the ways in which race, gender, and class cut through these groups? Also, Young's turn to deconstruction to delineate the fluid identities of the groups leaves me feeling that the groups no longer are participants in history and tradition. I have argued, it is true, against any unified notion of tradition, but Young's reaction against the power structure of unity is so strong that the groups begin to sound uncomfortably close to those participating in interest group pluralism.[84]

Young's model can, however, be corrected with the help of Nancy Fraser. At the end of her discussion of *Justice and the Politics of Difference*, Fraser argues for more refined notions of difference than found in Young's work. These are: the difference that is an "artifact of oppression" (and should be abolished), the difference that is seen as a mark of cultural superiority (and should be universalized), and the difference that is simply cultural variation (which should be enjoyed).[85] Fraser's analysis suggests that Young's category of group difference is too generalized to be useful in constructing a complex civil society. Nevertheless, a heterogeneous public of groups seems a starting point to counter many of the problems with the models of community and civil society observed so far in this study. Citizenship in the nation and membership within a group can be simultaneously affirmed, because the public realm is able to acknowledge the different needs and interests of group members. And groups exist as mediating institutions, but, because they are more fluid than community, and are not necessarily based on unified traditions and identities, they do not exclude and oppress. People are able to be members of more than one group, reflecting the complex social identities of most U.S. citizens. Society is not blurred into one homogenized community, but understood as complex and differentiated, including differentiation between public and private.[86] Through multiple memberships, greater solidarity among groups may be fostered. Young's communal vision is of a revitalized, differentiated civil society checking and correcting the power of the state.

HOPE AND COMMUNITIES OF RESISTANCE: SHARON WELCH

Sharon Welch is a white feminist Christian theologian and ethicist whose work has consistently sought to name and describe liberative communities within the U.S. Both of her books, *Communities of Resistance and Solidarity* and *A Feminist Ethic of Risk*, are written from an acknowledged doubled perspective of someone who participates in the privilege of being white, Christian, and middle-class, and who also experiences oppression as a woman. Speaking from this ambiguous location, she seems to express ambivalence about the location of her own communities of accountability, particularly her faith community. In her first book, she says that her matrix is her participation in "communities of faith" which include the church and "communities of faithful political resistance," particularly women's communities and peace communities.[87] As her work has developed, she has become less concerned with the specifically Christian (liberal Protestant) community, and more concerned about the resources for communal, political, and moral renewal of the U.S. white middle class. Of course, liberal Protestants are mostly a subgroup of the white middle class, but there has been a turn in Welch's thought from new forms of *ecclesia* to new forms of community in general. Throughout she has continued to name her own accountabilities to the white middle class.

In her first book, *Communities,* Welch focused specifically on exploring the *ecclesia* as part of a liberation theology to be realized here in the U.S. She was searching, she said, for "a particular form of *ecclesia*, liberation faith's reordering of the world of faith in light of oppression and resistance to oppression."[88] In sharp contrast to the Christian ethicists discussed in chapter 3, Welch's criteria for *ecclesia* have nothing to do with faithfulness to scripture, tradition, or the person of Jesus. The real *ecclesia*, Welch says, is a "community of resistance," that "appropriates the Christian tradition in the context of a political and social struggle." In other words, the norm determining Christian life is praxis, not theological dogma.

Welch's suspicion about the unifying tradition cherished by Neuhaus and Hauerwas is supported by her observations of Christian triumphalist claims filtered through lenses provided by Michel Foucault. Using him, she deconstructs

87

tradition as an identity-shaping force for Christian community and disciple-ship. In Welch's eyes, Christianity is another example of the "history of the will to truth" which Foucault finds in the Enlightenment. Thus, it is no expression of unified transcendent identity, but a multiple, contradictory construction of power. There are various trajectories of Christian tradition, and choices can be made as to which trajectory to follow. Through Foucault, Welch wants to name the "dangerous memories of human suffering," the massive denial of difference, the voices of the powerless whose pain can never be compensated.[89] In contrast with Neuhaus's and Hauerwas's homogeneous views of tradition, this is, potentially, an enormous contribution to the rethinking of a crisis-ridden lib-eral Protestantism.

Welch seeks a new basis for *ecclesia*, the transcendence of solidarity which "breaks the bonds of isolated individuality and forgetfulness ... and enables the creation of community and conversion to the other. The Christian mes-sage is interpreted as the hope of universal solidarity and the Christian faith is remembered and celebrated as a vehicle of that solidarity."[90] Such solidarity functions both as normative center, realized through practice, and as ongoing critique. The link among persons is not, however, Christian *tradition* but *praxis*, "communal struggles for a particular kind of humanity."[91] The communities of resistance are, it seems, marginal and resistant areas of society, bound by common political activity, possibly rooted in a Christian tradition.

After this first book, Welch apparently saw some of the problems inherent in relying so exclusively on the work of Foucault as the basis for a liberating communal praxis. While thoroughly deconstructing the unified power sus-taining most traditions and institutions, Foucault does not give us a place to stand to *build* community. Although he does force us to realize that there is no "innocent" or "pure" location of resistance, he also seems to foreclose any resistance at all. Even the partial, decentered group identities offered by Young as basis for communal grouping within civil society would be considered places for production and repression of power. Without some normative base-points, Foucault's theory cannot provide for constructive political transforma-tion, or even, ultimately, the deepest forms of critique. As Nancy Fraser says, "Without a nonhumanist ethical paradigm, Foucault cannot make good his normative case against humanism."[92]

Turning from Foucault, Welch sought a more concrete ground for com-munity. In her next work, *A Feminist Ethic of Risk*, she finds such grounding in the historical resources of African-American women's writings.[93] Still viewing community as a resource for white middle-class despair, she is able in this book to describe that despair more fully in terms of guilt and political paralysis. What is blocking white middle-class community, Welch says, is an ideology of uniformity that tries to control all aspects of life and repress all differences to ensure security. One example of this ideology, a powerful block

88

to empowerment, is, for Welch, the nuclear arms race, since the desire to use nuclear weapons is, at its heart, the desire for "the elimination of all evil and chaos and disorder" by utter annihilation.[94] In her post-Cold War writings, Welch has named this block more broadly as a general condition of privileged whiteness.

An ideology of security based in privilege negates the possibility of responsible action, especially action for others. Like Young, Welch suggests that at the heart of renewed communal life is full participation. What interests Welch is the possibility of responsibility on the part of the privileged which must, in her eyes, be grounded in some sort of community: "Responsible action as the creation of a matrix for further resistance is sustained and enabled by participation in an extensive community ... [which] provide[s] a haven offering support in struggle and constitute[s] the context for struggle that spans generations."[95]

For Welch, a model of such a community is found in the black communities portrayed in the works of African-American women writers. These works, she says, provide a moral framework that fundamentally "challenge[s] ... the presuppositions of Western moral theories." The ethics of African-American women's traditions involve different notions of rights, responsibilities, risks, and power.[96] Reviewing a selection of novels by African-American women, Welch traces themes of resistance, solidarity, struggle for dignity, communal joy, and tradition. These are all themes from her previous work which receive new embodiment when seen in the narratives of black women.

Welch uses the resources of black community to challenge the homogeneous tradition presented by dominant Christian theology and to criticize the communal ethics of MacIntyre and Hauerwas. Community is not, she says, a "cohesive" entity "with a shared set of principles, norms, and mores." This kind of community, in fact, "lacks the means to criticize constitutive forms of injustice, forms of exclusions and limitation...."[97] Lacking critical challenges, these theories can only reproduce domination. Truly critical norms emerge from interaction with those who are different than ourselves. Through this interaction we can understand solidarity which involves "granting each group sufficient respect to listen to their ideas and be challenged by them" and "recognizing that the lives of various groups are so intertwined that each is accountable to the other."[98]

There are, however, problems with the way in which Welch appropriates black communal traditions. First, she focuses only on literary accounts, leaving out the histories lying behind the narratives, particularly the histories of black church resistance and struggle. Second, I have difficulties with a one-way appropriation of black traditions by middle-class whites. In a cynical reading, one could say that because white people have lost their powerful traditions, they want to take over black people's traditions. I by no means believe that this is Welch's intention, but it never seems to occur to her that there might also be stories of white struggle and resistance that could be brought into consideration. In her most recent writing, Welch has acknowledged the problem of appropriation[99] and tries to draw on a variety of sources in her discussion of hope, failure, and risk as moral components of community. She has used antiracist training as a example of the struggles and perplexities that are part of a retraining of dominating selves and invokes "firm foundations" of "habits."[100]

Welch is moving toward some sort of notion of a public corresponding to Young's heterogeneous public, a public made up of a variety of different communities that could be described as members of civil society. Along with this pluralized public comes a renewal of white middle-class community since "as we become accountable for the limits of our vision and the damage caused by the violation of those limits, we become a different community."[101] Welch outlines the transformative praxis necessary for white middle-class people to develop the moral communities which would serve as a base for a revitalized civil society. Christian and other religious communities can come to recognize divinity as relation and compassion, developing a theology of immanence which simultaneously transcends suffering through transformation and celebration. All can participate in new / renewed habits, the "embodiments of ideals and visions, patterns of perception and response" which create practices of solidarity.[102]

90

Each woman considered here seeks to renew or transform some part of the liberal modern social order. However, unlike the men discussed in the previous chapter, they all understand that a revised role for women is essential to these changes. Elshtain and Cahill hope to maintain traditional forms (family and church), yet ensure an equality for women within those forms. Young and Welch radically question all traditional structures (state, family, church) and seek a new social order.

The ambiguous heritage of public and private spheres runs through all of their works in quite different ways. The approaches of Elshtain and Young mirror one another. Elshtain seeks to transcend the split between the spheres by reevaluating the entire social order on the basis of women's maternal capacities and values. Yet she ends up reinforcing the division in order to preserve what she understands as a common moral order. On the other hand, Young has moved away from attention to the family to the understanding that the private world of the family will only change when there has been a radical reshaping of the public into a place where heterogeneity and difference are acknowledged. Cahill is speaking out of a church tradition that has always embraced public and private roles, and by highlighting the role of women, she suggests that their concerns should be part of the public advocacy of the church. Welch, on the other hand, moves away from the traditional church to advocate forms of communities that seem to blur church / world, private / public boundaries.

Ultimately, I believe, Elshtain and Cahill illustrate integrative forms of community that hope to transcend conflict through the means of the binding power of norms and traditions. For both of them what is at stake is not capitalism, but liberal individualist ideologies. If the problem is constructed at the level of meaning, the solution will correspondingly stress meaning, to the exclusion of politics and economics. Their concern for harmony leads them to stress partnership, and to avoid any challenges raised by conflict and power, whether these are raised from different versions of white feminism or from nonwhite experiences and traditions.

Welch and Young, on the other hand, are prepared to reject the liberal capitalist (and, in Welch's case, Christian) framework. They seek out issues of power and difference in order to recast civil society in terms of counterhegemonic communities engaged in participatory political struggle against oppressive forms of power. For Young civil society can provide intermediary institutions shaping identity and relation in ways not possible in traditional family and political structures. Accepting the necessity of some form of overarching state, she sees these groups as checks on its power. Welch does not have the same concern about the state and the practicalities of politics, demonstrated by her focus on the ways the advanced capitalist state creates alienation, as opposed to domination. Her sense of communities of resistance seems to be of groups that simultaneously provide identity through participation and work to transform general society. Her major specific example of such communities is the black community, which suggests that she is pointing to identity-based social movements that challenge the status quo. Young, on the other hand, rejects any form of community as a site of exclusion and dominating power. Instead, she establishes a looser structure of groups—which, however, seem to be primarily made up of the same persons found in Welch's communities of resistance, that is, persons with marginalized identities. Young puts these groups within a clearly articulated public order, to check and shape the state.

Both Welch and Young stress discontinuities, seeing any form of continuous tradition as an expression of domination. While both acknowledge the alienation and disintegration surrounding liberal capitalism, they analyze it not only in terms of meaning, but also in terms of power. For Welch, middle class alienation is not due to a loss of meaning-producing institutions, but to a loss of meaningful political participation and to fear rooted in the misuse of privilege. For Young, the issue to be addressed is not alienation, but oppression and suffering. For both the project is not achieving a renewed cohesive morality, but achieving a more just social order. Welch's and Young's commitment to transformation and participation suggests communities no longer focussed on questions of meaning. And their recognition of difference suggests communal forms that do not form their identity on the basis of exclusion. They also demonstrate the difficult problems of tradition, particularly for white women.

Since both completely reject dominant white male traditions, they must seek basepoints elsewhere. As I suggested, Young is unable to resolve tensions around recognition of our given identities in contrast to chosen groups or identities. The groups that she finds foundational have such fluid identities, that they seem to float clear of history. Some of that ambivalence rests, I would suggest, in her location, shared with all of the others considered here, in the white PMC, a class which has lost its roots through upward mobility, and which is involved in the most culturally disorienting aspects of capitalism. That same ambivalence appears in Welch's characterization of the white middle class as being without cultural resources of resistance. Welch cannot find basepoints within the white heritage and looks to the traditions of black women.

Young and Welch are, I believe, interesting complements to one another. Welch, I find, provides some of the specificity of tradition and resistance lacking in Young's work, while Young locates her communal concerns in a far more complex social theory which potentially allows greater discernment of different forms of oppression and exploitation. I appreciate especially the ways in which Welch refuses to separate religion and politics. She insists upon a model of community, including church community, that is shaped around an ongoing commitment to transformative justice, a commitment which provides the normative center for community. The work of both women begins to sketch some important new ways of modeling community.

COMMUNITY APART
African-American Models of Community

Our history joins with that common hopeful element in all histories of human struggle for community and calls each of us to develop our great hidden capacities to dream, to imagine a new American society.

—Vincent Harding[1]

The courage and perseverance of these everyday black women shaped a model of faith and social behavior passed down to generations of women in the community and church.

—Delores Williams[2]

chapter 5

TO TURN to a discussion of some African-American models of community is to face more fully the issues of difference raised in previous chapters. When the experiences of white women enter the discourse on community, questions of family and the relation of private and public spheres previously hidden become highlighted. Similarly, attention to the African-American experience, what Vincent Harding calls the "razor-sharp memories of poverty, joblessness, protest and despair,"[3] highlights the implicit exclusionary assumptions of many models of community and the common good.

In an often quoted passage, W.E.B. Du Bois wrote of the double nature of African-American identity:

the Negro is a sort of seventh son, born with a veil, and gifted with second sight in this American world.... It is a peculiar sensation, this double-consciousness, this sense of always looking at one's self through the eyes of others. … One ever feels his twoness—an American, a Negro; two souls, two thoughts, two unreconciled strivings; two warring ideas in one dark body.[4]

It is, in fact, this double nature (tripled, even quadrupled, nature in the case of black women and black gay / lesbian people) that is at the heart of the strengths and the tensions in black notions of community. As I discussed in chapter 3,[5] Michael Walzer emphasizes the important contribution of the doubled citizenship and ethnic identities of so many Americans. But the connection between citizenship and race has been much harder and more painful. For the first part of their existence on the American continent, blacks were simply African slaves, whose males only counted as 3/5 of a person and whose women did not count at all. Even after emancipation into citizenship, they were only secondclass Americans. Yet on the basis of their shared African identity they developed a unique, strong community that lay outside the gaze of white America. When the Civil Rights movement opened the way to new forms of (selective) inclusion, African-American communities were simultaneously offered new opportunities for advancement *and* broken apart in ways which are only now becoming clear.

Black models of community are a vital part of the discourse of community, both because the heritage of their past offers resources invisible in dominant discussions of community and because the complexities of their present raise challenges avoided by many communitarian models. In this chapter I will first outline some features of the African-American experience that fostered a distinct sense of community. I will show how the complexities of the relation of the "private" public of the African-American world led to two models of its relation to the "public" public of white America: integration and black nationalism. Martin Luther King, Jr. and Malcolm X , the two most famous recent proponents of these contrasting possibilities, faced the changed situation of African-American community in the postsegregation era. I will describe this new context and show how contemporary black intellectuals, such as Glenn Loury, bell hooks, and Cornel West provide revised models of black civil society. Finally, I will point to the distinctive contribution of womanist models of community, highlighting the work of Delores Williams and Emilie Townes.

AFRICAN–AMERICAN COMMUNITY: UNDER SIEGE, UNDER SEPARATION

When the newly enslaved Africans arrived in this land, they brought with them habits and practices of community rooted in a variety of tribal heritages. Although their community life had no legal or political validity, since slaves had no control over conditions of work, family relations, or geographical location, slave culture developed its own forms of connection, resistance, and accommodation, drawing on both African traditions of mutuality and extended community and also visions of equal worth, heavenly care, and future kingdom found through their new contact with Christian biblical teachings.[6] With emancipation, blacks believed that their marginalized community would become a partner of the dominant white community. For example, the Black Convention in Charleston in 1865, organized in response to the growing disappointment at the lack of postwar land redistribution, said to white America, "We would address you—not as Rebels and enemies, but as friends and fellow countrymen, who desire to dwell among you in peace, and whose destinies are interwoven and linked with those of the whole American people."[7] They put forward a claim to be treated as citizens of the community.

Such hope for integration was rejected with the postbellum emergence of segregated Jim Crow society. In their separate and publicly unequal communities, African Americans developed their own forms of community, in continuity with the traditions already cultivated under slavery. "Within dominant white society," says Patricia Hill Collins, "the model of community reflected capitalist market economies of competitive, industrial, and monopoly capitalism.... this model stresses the rights of individuals ... [and] legitimates relations of domination either by denying they exist or by treating them as inevitable but unimportant."[8] Although the labor of African Americans was crucial for the maintenance and reproduction of this community, the actual lives and bodies of African American peoples were excluded from its borders.[9] In their separate communities, African-Americans preserved "[n]otions such as equating family with extended family, of treating community as family, and of seeing dealings with whites as elements of public discourse and dealings with Blacks as part of family business."[10] Their distinctive communal identity arose out of their exclusion from the benefits *and* the costs of expanding industrial capitalism.

Thus, the dual nature of the black community developed the dual identity of African Americans as described by Du Bois. African-Americans lived in their own sphere, with all the appropriate institutions of civil society. All businesses, local political institutions, churches and neighborhood organizations were black. These institutions maintained the "traditions for black surviving and thriving" by "sustain[ing] familial and communal networks of support."[11] The power of these networks was reinforced by a sense of unity against the rejection of the white public "outside": "Under traditional racial segregation, the strict barriers that were established forced a wide variety of professional and social classes into intimate interaction.... The sense of shared suffering and collective cooperation provided the basis for an appreciation of the community's racial identity and heritage."[12] Remembering her childhood under

95

segregation, bell hooks writes of the "innocence" possible for children in that black world, "a world where we had a history … places that honored us." In these communities, black people exercised power, and were supported in their experience of powerlessness in the white world through "the sweetness of our solidarity, the heaviness of our pain and sorrow, the thickness of our joy."[13]

The segregated black communities provided a public where public and private was connected, rather than separate, where the "private" institutions of church and family played much more "public" roles than in the dominant white society. From the eyes of the dominant white public, the black community was hidden, excluded, "private" like the white bourgeois family, with few legal rights and little status for its dependent participants. But from the African-American perspective, it was both a haven from a hostile white world and an arena for agency.[14]

The different shape of the black public is key to comprehend the important role of the black church in segregated black communities. The church was the place where there could be "the exercise of citizenship rights and expression of social dignity," where notions of freedom, justice, and equality not practiced in the larger world could be lived out.[15] It was, says Katie Cannon, "the community's sole institution of power … the only institution totally controlled by Blacks."[16] This heritage, embedded in a different relation of public and private, makes clear why black notions of the proper relation of religion and politics differ radically from dominant white notions. As Manning Marable puts it, "[f]or white Americans, their vision of faith provides an intellectual shield through which the oppressive essence of their economic and political systems are made virtually invisible."[17] In contrast, for black Christians, religion is about liberation of the soul, and, on occasion, also of the body, since "justice is what love sounds like when it speaks in public, civic piety is love's public language, equality its tone of voice, and freedom its constant pitch."[18] For them, religion has an inescapable political role in the promotion of the well-being of black people within society. The black church preserved the idea that God was on the side of the oppressed and provided both the practical and spiritual resources for the black community to make claims upon the common good of American society.

MERGING / SEPARATING:
INTEGRATION AND NATIONALISM AS COMMUNITY MODELS

Up until the Civil Rights movement, the ongoing communal present of the black community included two separate, yet intertwined, visions of the community's future: integration and nationalism. The vision of integration was present in the appeal of the 1865 Black Convention in Charleston quoted above, and, in spite of postbellum rejection by white society, continued to motivate many in the black community, particularly the elites. For leaders such as

Frederick Douglass, the hope of "racial uplift" lay in the acculturation of black persons into the American mainstream.[19] Black middle-class persons "believed that success in education, morality and business would eventually cause whites to accept them as human beings and thus as equal partners."[20] The challenge facing this approach (apart from its rejection by the white majority until the Civil Rights period) was that when a minority assimilates into a majority, the terms of interaction are likely to be those of the more powerful party. In the words of James Cone, "integration, by its very definition, alienated blacks from their cultural history and thereby from those religious values that empowered them.... To be 'free' meant to become *white*."[21]

In contrast, the nationalist stream, responding to white supremacist nationalism, insisted that the improvement of the race could only happen in communities separated from whites. Such separation might be prerequisite to closer relations to white society through economic self-development (Booker T. Washington), or it might be an expression of cultural solidarity (some forms of Afrocentrism), or it might be a permanent political and territorial separation (Marcus Garvey). Nationalism expressed "what it *felt* like to be black in America"[22] and offered important expressions of self-love and self-respect in a culture which offered neither. However, the challenge continuously facing nationalist vision of community has been, as Marable puts it, that "Black Americans are not in the fullest sense a 'nation'."[23] All black nationalist movements have had to struggle with the challenge of forging some sort of relationship with the larger, white-dominated public.

The differing models of community present in these streams can be discerned in the thought of Martin Luther King, Jr., and Malcolm X, who struggled to redefine integration and nationalism when the social circumstances of black community were beginning to change in ways that presented new challenges. Martin Luther King, Jr. was the product of a strong black elite family who were the well-educated leaders of their segregated Southern black community. This background enabled him to forge a vision of community that, while deeply nourished by the "symbol systems" of the black church, also drew on "the iconic structure, symbolic worldview, and heroic values that undergirded much of American society."[24] The "beloved community" King spoke of was the historic dream of integration, "the black vision of a new American community beyond slavery and white superiority"[25] where "all God's children—black men and white men, Jews and Gentiles, Protestants and Catholics—will be able to join hands and sing in the words of the old Negro spiritual, 'Free at last, free at last; thank God Almighty, we are free at last.'"[26] It was a national dream where black identity was completely integrated into a unified (yet plural) American identity.

"At the heart of all that civilization has meant and developed," wrote King, "is 'community'—the mutually cooperative and voluntary venture of man to assume a semblance of responsibility for his brother."[27] Community was, to him, a foundational component of human ontology. By virtue of being human, we are all "caught in an inescapable network of mutuality, tied in a single garment of destiny."[28] Throughout his life, he emphasized themes of forgiveness, reconciliation, hope, and inclusivity which he considered the norms governing our life together at all levels of community, from neighborhood to globe. The church was the community at the heart of the society, serving as its moral custodian, and, at least in the black community, as its moral center.[29] Using the "political language of civil religion,"[30] King brought the black church into the U.S. public sphere.

King defined evil as the forces that broke community: disorder, disruptiveness, intrusion, recalcitrance and destruction. "Through our sin, through our evil, and through our wickedness," he said, "we have broken community."[31] For him, the cross was the ultimate expression of this brokenness, and, simultaneously the sign of the promise that "God is able to conquer the evils of history."[32] Nonviolent action here on earth was carried out on the basis of trust in this promise. Further, the suffering blacks experienced through nonviolent resistance demonstrated, King said, the "virtues" of "humility and self-restraint" necessary for the ultimate reconciliation of social community.

In many ways, King's model of community, with its stress on harmony and integration, resonates with the communitarian models I have criticized. Indeed, Cornel West has pointed out that King's vision of a community of *caritas* is partially "defensive and romantic."[33] But here social location becomes important, since King's dream of a harmonious future was actually aimed at challenging the false harmonies and dominance of the racist present. King's model of community, as West also points out, "did not support and affirm the bland American dream of comfortable living and material prosperity."[34] Its purpose was not domination or exclusion but empowerment, as it assumed black people had "the power to affect their destiny and to exercise transformative moral agency."[35]

For Malcolm X, black community was completely separate from American identity. To state this divide, he believed, was not defining a new relationship between African Americans and white America, but naming the actual historical relationship. Black nationalists, writes James Cone, "define their identity by their resistance to America and their determination to create a society based on their own African history and culture." As Malcolm put it, "I'm not an American. I'm one of the twenty-two million black people who are the victims of Americanism."[36] His vision was shaped by the realities of northern ghetto life, where blacks who had left the tight-knit segregated rural communities of the South found themselves not in a "promised land" of acceptance and job opportunity, but in new, bitter forms of poverty and segregation.

For Malcolm (and for many others), the Nation of Islam modeled a community based on black and Islamic traditions alien to, indeed opposite to, the dominant white Christian community. The Nation of Islam drew on the heritage of black pride and mutual help rooted in slave and reconstructionist traditions but revised in light of newer urban experience. Instead of a community of resistance and hope responding to white laws and restrictions, Malcolm called for a community of chosen separation, based on the strength of black identity: "We want SEPARATION, but not segregation.... Segregation is that which is forced upon inferiors by superiors, but *SEPARATION* IS THAT WHICH IS DONE VOLUNTARILY."[37] The key point that Malcolm continually stressed was the necessity for black people to live as "human beings" that is, as *black* people who had the power and authority to shape their own community and destiny. "Afro-Americans must unite and work together," he said, "We must take pride in the Afro-American community, for it is our home and it is our power.... Our history and our culture were completely destroyed.... We must launch a cultural revolution to unbrainwash an entire people."[38] The focus of this community was the common blackness, distinct from any white identity: "This integrationist Negro is the one who doesn't want to be black—and he knows that he can't be white. So he calls himself a Negro—an American Negro—which means he is neither black nor white."[39]

On the basis of blackness, Malcolm appealed for renewal of the tradition of black pride and memory of black suffering which he believed essential for community identity. The specificity of Malcolm's reappropriated tradition contrasts with King's more general appeal to an entwined white and black heritage. While King suggests that past experiences of suffering are overcome in community reconciliation, Malcolm makes the heritage of black oppression central to black identity. He assumes that disunity in the black community is due to white power, while unity of values is rooted in a common black heritage.

However, after his split with Elijah Muhammad and pilgrimage to Mecca, Malcolm began, just before he died, to reappraise black nationalism. In one of his final interviews, he remarked that while he "used to define black nationalism as the idea that the black man should control the economy of his community, the politics of his community," encounters with Africans were leading him to change his thinking. Now, he acknowledged, he was not sure what he thought was necessary "for the liberation of black people." "Recognition and respect" for black people, were, however, still fundamental.[40]

As James Cone and others have argued,[41] the positions of Malcolm X and Martin Luther King grew closer toward the end of their lives as Malcolm began to put black nationalism in a global context, and King came into contact with the Northern ghettoes and the Vietnam War. While Malcolm began talking about "respect," King began to speak of the urban slums as "domestic colonialism," and saw the need for "temporary segregation" to overcome the

99

real powerlessness of black people.[42] Both of them were beginning to recognize the changes in black experience in the post-Civil Rights era. Desegregation under conditions of advanced capitalism meant challenges for both nationalist and integrationist models of community.

ENTERING THE MARKETPLACE:
THE POST–CIVIL RIGHTS COMMUNITY

The process of desegregation in the context of the overall shifts in the U.S. economy profoundly reshaped the nature of black community in ways which deeply affected black civil society. The first, and most obvious change, was an opening up of possibilities for blacks to enter the middle class. In the pre-Civil Rights era, no more than five percent of the African-American community ever achieved middle-class status. This number has now increased to over twenty-five percent.[43] As Manning Marable wrote in 1990, "Since 1964, the number of black elected officials has increased from barely 100 to 7,000. The number of African Americans enrolled in colleges and universities has quadrupled; the number of black-owned banks and financial institutions has increased tenfold."[44]

Nevertheless, the effects of this shift have been ambiguous. As was the case with many other ethnic groups, middle-class status meant departure from the poor neighborhoods, into more affluent communities.[45] Yet for blacks this departure has been far more problematic than for other ethnic groups. Desegregation may have benefitted certain segments of black communities, but others, left behind in ghetto areas, now comprise what William Julius Wilson has called, "the truly disadvantaged" or the "black underclass."[46] This failure of desegregation to achieve the "racial uplift" so long hoped for by African Americans is partly due to the specific history of U.S. racism and partly to the particular socioeconomic circumstances under which blacks were incorporated more fully into contemporary capitalism.

Whether middle, upper, or lower class, black people are always, through skin color, distinctively black. Considered apart from history (if this was possible), that point is of no significance. But black skin is seen by all U.S. citizens through a conscious or unconscious filter of the specific history of slavery and segregation. In a *Playboy* interview conducted shortly before his death, King, the crusader of integration, said that "Men of the white West, whether or not they like it, have grown up in a racist culture.... They don't really respect anyone who is not white."[47] Much reflection has occurred among the intellectuals of the "assimilated" black middle class over what it means to be middle-class, wondering whether it means losing the heritage of black identity and, even after this heritage is lost, whether white Americans ever see them as anything but black.[48]

Further, the desegregation of the black community occurred during the shifts of capitalism discussed in chapter 2. Thus, a few blacks were given more entree to professional status at a time when, for the larger portion of the black community, the decline in manufacturing and trade, increasing automation, labor market segmentation, and the relocation of industry out of urban centers were all eroding job opportunities and "destroy[ing] the basis of a group to reproduce its life materially."[49] Blue-collar work has been transformed into low-paying service jobs or moved out of the urban areas.[50] Currently, "almost one-half of young black men have had no work experience at all."[51] As middle-class blacks moved to the suburbs, urban tax bases have eroded, weakening education and other public institutions desperately needed for advancement.[52] Simultaneously, desegregation has meant greater access to and interest in black consumer markets on the part of white corporations. One of the most rapidly integrated fields has been consumer advertising as industries, working with complex marketing segmentation, recognized a "black sector" as one of their potential targets. This access not only exposed blacks to new forms of capitalist consumption, but accelerated the disappearance of the traditional forms of black business (local stores and service establishments) that had served to knit together the different classes within the black community.[53]

These structural changes have had what Frank Kirkland calls "an existentially critical impact" on black communities through the "desiccation of ethical life".[54] The combined result of these changes has been the destruction of the institutions of black civil society. Black institutions, no less than white ones, have been subject to the further penetration of advanced capitalism, reshaping families, education, forms of consumption, health care. When Cornel West says that "we have created rootless, dangling people with little link to the supportive networks—family, friends, school—that sustain some sense of purpose in life," he is speaking about all of U.S. society.[55] Yet the effects of this penetration have been shaped by the specific history of racist institutions. The black community experienced the destruction of institutions "that used to serve as the infrastructures for transmitting values and notions of self-respect and self-esteem" at a time when material resources were disappearing.[56]

Thus, for example, the intensification of consumption, while profoundly unsettling throughout U.S. society, has been lethal in poor black urban communities where the drive to consume under conditions devoid of economic resources quickly leads to increased drug traffic, violence, and homicide. And while all family forms have been in transition for the past few decades, black families, more than any other, have been treated as "pathological." Immediately after the legal decree of desegregation, traditional institutions such as the extended black family/community were constructed as aberrations, as, for example, in the Moynihan Report of 1965 which stated that "a community that allows a large number of young men to grow up in broken families, dominated by women, never acquiring any stable relation to male authority, never acquires any set of rational expectations about the future—that community asks for and gets chaos."[57] Now his words are treated as prophetic, while soaring unemployment, depleted urban resources, and drug wars are seen as secondary effects of family decay. The dominant public acknowledgement of the black community occurs through condemnations of black violence or else the community is rendered invisible in a new way through "the prevailing myth of racial history [which] absorbs all racial complexities and contradictions into a narrative of uncomplicated linear progress."[58] And there is no longer even the "will to undo the legacy of past racial injustice" on the part of many whites.[59] In this context, black intellectuals face the challenge of finding positive notions of black community in continuity with African-American history but in contact with contemporary realities.

WHAT IS TO BE DONE?
SOME CONTEMPORARY AFRICAN–AMERICAN RESPONSES

While the black community participates in the general moral and communal crisis that has been the context for this work, the issues it brings to the communal discussion are distinctive. The issue of meaning and the question of moral order in society look different in the context of the history of racism and the current challenge of the black urban poor. To illustrate this point, I will look more closely at the work of a variety of contemporary black intellectuals: Glenn Loury (representing a neoconservative perspective), Cornel West and bell hooks (representing radical democratic perspectives). There are differences in both the presumed sources of crisis in the black community and the proposed solutions.

Until recently, Glenn Loury has been a member of the American Enterprise Institute, proof of his conservative credentials.[60] Loury's emphases on cultural crisis, rather than socioeconomic conditions, and on overall social harmony make his work similar to that of Daniel Bell. However, unlike Bell, Loury speaks with a strong sense of the impact of the history of U.S. racism, a perspective that has deepened in his later work. In one of his more recent essays, he begins "We Americans remain a nation struggling to confront intractable problems of race."[61] However, the "We", as he acknowledges, bears the imprint of Du Bois's notion of "twoness" in the discussion of racism and in his own life. The discourse on race, he says, must be "undertaken openly by the nation as a whole as part of our larger political conversation, but also by and among black Americans as part of a communal deliberation."[62] He himself is talking, he says, "a kind of doublespeak," writing as "a public man, an American" and as "a black, addressing 'my people' about how we (that is, black Americans) should endeavor to make progress."[63] This "doubledness," the sense of participating in two communities, marks Loury's sense of community, viewing the black community as an institution within a larger civil society. He hopes for moral cohesion both within the black community and within the larger civil society of which it is a part.

Loury follows many of Martin Luther King's notions of tradition and community. Like King, he hopes for a common community of persons of all colors. And like King, he sees that community informed by both the mainstream American tradition of "the Founding Fathers" and "the great figures of black American political and cultural history."[64] However, King emphasized the moral and political claims made on the common good by black Americans on the basis of suffering and of justice. Loury, on the other hand, while recognizing these claims, de-emphasizes them in the post-Civil Rights context in favor of a strong emphasis on the responsibilities of the black community itself. Instead of rights, blacks need, he believes, "to deal with issues of dignity, shame, personal responsibility, character and values, and deservingness."[65] The core of the problem is "the values, attitudes and behaviors of individual blacks."[66] Blacks need to "project ... the image of a disciplined, respectable black demeanor.... Discipline, orderliness, and virtue in every aspect of life contribute to the goal of creating an aura of respectability and deservingness."[67]

An emphasis on rights, Loury argues, is part of the weakness of liberalism which has left blacks seeing themselves solely as victims of white racism, has blinded them to pathologies of black behavior, and has censored honest discussion within the black community.[68] By contrast, Loury invokes the self-help and self-improvement heritage of Booker T. Washington as the basis for a reconstitution of black civil society "through the building of constructive, internal institutions."[69] By doing this, Loury believes, the black community will be undertaking "the challenge of taking control of our future by exerting the requisite moral leadership."[70] In his more recent writings, Loury has moved away from an exclusive focus on black self-improvement to articulate a dual responsibility of self-help and public action: "acceptance among blacks of personal responsibility for our actions and acceptance among all Americans of their social responsibility as citizens."[71] To achieve this, blacks must play both an "inside game" of self-help / moral uplift through living out common moral values within the black community and an "outside game" (less well-defined) of appealing for white / public support.

Loury's inside / outsider model of the black community is dualistic—the black community is degraded and in need of moral activity, while the public community (which sometimes Loury assumes includes blacks and sometimes seems white only) is, evidently, morally neutral and the source of programs and funds. This split leaves the morality of the proposed solution as solely the responsibility of the black community while, in order to wean blacks away from their reliance on being "victims", the larger community has little moral role. There is some indication that the moral responsibility blacks must undertake is already possessed by the larger community's "commonly held norms" and "national ideals."[72] Loury never takes into consideration the moral/economic/cultural/social role the capitalist public is *already* playing through removal of funds and jobs, and through the promotion of new patterns of consumption, violence, and sexuality.[73]

By contrast, the models of both Cornel West and bell hooks stress the role of capitalist culture in reshaping the nature of the black community. West names a "threefold" crisis: economic (unemployment and career ceilings), political (relations with the Democratic Party), and spiritual (rising black suicides and homicides).[74] He stresses in his work the connections between the ways in which these forces affect the entire American society and the particular effects they have on the black community. In general there has been a destruction of any notion of public and community, but in particular, there has been the destruction of the old black civil society by "corporate market institutions" which "have helped create a seductive way of life, a culture of consumption."[75] What has been lost is the "buffer" of black families, schools, churches which had protected blacks from white society and nourished their self-development.[76] While agreeing with Loury about the problem of black violence, West does not use the language of violence and degradation, but describes the underclass as nihilistic and says their "behavior is the tragic response of a people bereft of resources in confronting the workings of U.S. capitalist society."[77] Black people, he argues, have lost their tradition, since distance from "those communities and institutions that have played a fundamental role in transmitting to younger generations our values and sensibility, our ways of life and our ways of struggle" has meant distance from "our predecessors" and from "the critical project of Black liberation."[78] Entrance into the mainstream has meant entrance into an individualizing consumer capitalism which has erased the distinctive African–American communal heritage.

Hooks concurs with West's analysis but expresses the situation of the black community in more existential terms. "We act," she writes, "as though we have managed to hold on to traditional black folk experience, with its ethical values system, while we participate wholeheartedly in consumer capitalism. We have been reluctant as a people to say that capitalism possesses a direct threat to the survival of an ethical belief system in black life."[79] Hooks mourns the loss of that "communal ethic of service that was so necessary for survival in traditional Black communities," a communal ethic that she remembers as providing the strong extended community of her childhood. Now, she says, "a certain kind of bourgeois individualism of the mind prevails."[80]

West and hooks both call for a community renewal. For hooks, that renewal occurs in the moral, spiritual, and cultural life of the black community which needs to recover memories of struggle rather than stay in a passive nostalgia.[81] West calls for a revitalization of an economic and social common good, for all Americans including the black community. "*All* of us need," he says, "to *care* about the quality of our lives together."[82] While public policy, the language of the U.S. public sphere, is important, what is lacking is the language of spirituality, which was the language spoken in the old forms of black civil society.[83] Throughout her work, hooks emphasizes a vision of community for persons of all colors, where people retain distinct identities yet share commitment to relational bonds. For black people, "collective self-recovery" is a prerequisite for participating in this common community.[84] Like Loury, hooks and West see themselves as simultaneously addressing the black community and the entire U.S. community (more specifically, nonblack conservatives in Loury's case and nonblack progressives in West's and hooks's cases). However, while Loury's vision of restored black moral community presumes an understood set of common moral values, hooks's and West's overall vision of public community is decidedly pluralistic, similar in many ways to the heterogeneous public, bound in solidarity and struggle, envisioned by Young and Welch.

MAKING A WAY OUT OF NO WAY:
WOMANIST VISIONS OF COMMUNITY

From the slave period onwards, African-American women have played central roles in their communities. Cheryl Townsend Gilkes has argued that slave women brought with them African traditions that "not only accorded women great visibility and autonomy but also contained strong models of female leadership."[85] As slaves, black women strove under conditions of economic, racial, and sexual exploitation to help their extended families stay together and survive. This domestic-focused work, considered inferior in the dominant society, took on special importance as work *for blacks* in a world where all labor was done for whites.[86] It also included work that, in white society, would have been considered men's work. When slavery ended, women still continued to keep family as the central focus in their work inside and outside of their homes. "By placing family, children, education, community at the center of our political activism," Patricia Hill Collins writes, "African-American women draw on Afrocentric conceptualizations of mothering, family, community, and empowerment" which stress shared power and mutual relationships.[87]

The model of family and community implicit in this experience differed from the dominant white bourgeois model in several important ways. First, African-American women never had the chance to be the "angels in the house." Initially, they worked as slaves, then they worked as cotton pickers, domestics, laundry women, cooks, factory laborers, cleaning women.[88] Thus, there was no image of black women as too "delicate" for participation, as Sojourner Truth so eloquently pointed out. Second, the family form of black families was more blended into the general community than separated in a "nuclear family" model. Black women saw work for their communities as intimately connected with work for their families. The prime example of these connections is the role of "othermother" or "community mother" discussed in the work of many black women scholars. Although rooted in shared family responsibilities for child care, the work of othermothers is often for the church and for the entire community. Community mothers are, says Gilkes, "the guardians of community political traditions."[89] They have been leaders of community women's organizations which saw their role as support of domestic activities *and* "the practical encouragement of all efforts ... for the upbuilding, ennobling, and advancement of the race."[90]

Third, black women have understood their domestic work of nurturance in terms of survival in a harsh world. While certainly teaching their children virtues and values, black women understood that the purpose of moral education was for their children to survive and perhaps even thrive in a racist world. Black women novelists such as Zora Neale Hurston and Toni Morrison have portrayed black mothers as being capable of acting harshly towards their children out of the understanding that this training was necessary to survive white power.

All of these differences between black and white family life point to a fourth distinction already noted above. Black women did not see themselves as inhabiting a private world, but a communal public. Yet this public stood, as I have said, in a privatized relationship to the dominant white world which many black women visited daily as laborers. Bell hooks writes of a tension in the lives of black women "between service outside one's home, family, and kin network, service provided to white folks which took time and energy, and the effort of black women to conserve enough of themselves to provide service (care and nurturance) within their own families and communities."[91] Further, in their service to white families, black women participated in the dominant family form, making it possible for the white woman to be the "angel of the house." This model of domesticity represented "success" in the dominant world and, necessarily, influenced the African-American community. Thus black women may be urged to accept male domination in the service of "progress" for their community. Emilie Townes speaks of "the delicate balance between speaking out in the public realm and seeking moral uplift for a whole people" which was generally resolved in favor of a model of women as "moral guarantors of the social order."[92] Yet the fact that the social order and its morality was lived out in a racist context meant African-American women were always different "moral guarantors" than bourgeois white women.

Drawing on these traditions, Emilie Townes and Delores Williams consider the situation of black women today, in the midst of middle-class possibilities and impoverished communities. In *Sisters in the Wilderness*, Williams searches black women's traditions to understand new dimensions of their self and community understanding. She discovers themes within African-American religious life that celebrate the biblical figure of Hagar and her wilderness experience. Hagar's story represents "miraculous 'resisting and rising above'" which "has for generations been many black women's contribution of faith, love, and hope."[93] In Williams's understanding, the core of black women's experience has been "survival struggle and quality of life struggle" for the resources necessary to achieve economic, educational, and political well-being for themselves and their communities.[94] Black women are the central, strong value-transmitters of their communities: "They maintain and transmit values and ideas that support and enrich the black community as a viable unit."[95] These ideas are not just dutifulness and obedience, but defiance, risktaking, independence, and endurance, which are enacted in both the private and public spheres.

In her discussion of the idea of wilderness, Williams notes its development from a journey and encounter outside of slavery to "the wide, wide world (a hostile place) where black women must go to seek a living for their families."[96] It is a powerful symbol, she says, that holds together a number of significant dimensions of the African-American communal tradition: human initiative and endurance, women's leadership, the unity of sacred and secular, and the black community's struggle for creating community in adversity.[97]

Williams seeks, in particular, to renew the black church as the heart of the black community. However, this can only happen, she believes, if current church institutions renounce their oppressive behavior, particularly towards women, and their reliance on white values of individualism, capitalist economy and class differentiation. With the adoption of the nuclear family model as an ideal, there has been a loss of "solidarity" and the "wisdom of the old folks" which had maintained the identity of the black community, enabling survival.[98] The black church needs to remember its true identity as "the heart of hope in the black community's experience of oppression, survival struggle and its historic efforts toward complete liberation."[99] Inside or outside of the church, the renewal of black women's traditions is, Williams believes, essential. The symbols of wilderness and Hagar are components of traditions of endurance, strength, and resilience where "spirituality and politics came together to design resistance strategies benefitting the entire community."[100]

Emilie Townes presents a womanist communal spirituality that seeks to address many of the issues currently pressing the black community: racism, poverty, AIDS, sexism. She sees, as have many of the writers discussed here, the damage wrought on African-Americans by "an individualistic nihilistic morality with no meaning-filled ethical core" which has meant a movement away from the traditional, transclass type of community.[101] "What we have lost," says Townes, "is our sense of community, our sense of family beyond ourselves."[102]

Like Williams, Townes suggests that these nihilistic values are the values of the dominant white world, and what is needed is a revival of the values of the womanist black community, a heritage that includes the work of black women in the home, in the church, and in the community. Central to this spirituality is a reaffirmation of the communal nature of black identity and the particularity of black women's experiences. Values "like hope, virtue, sacrifice, risk, and accountability have had," says Townes, "a different cast in the Black community." The difference lies in the "relational matrix," the "wholeness" at the heart of black community.[103] This wholeness encompasses both the religious and the secular spheres since the world is full of sacred meaning.

Townes takes these old traditions in new directions when she urges that relational responsibility and respect be extended to the "others" within the black community, excluded because of class, gender, and/or sexuality. All blacks should know, she says, that the doctrine of "separate but equal" has always been a cover for exclusion and rejection.[104] Black women need to recover their lived spirituality which "comes out of a community of faith that recognizes and *knows* its story." That story demands responsibility and accountability: "Justice holds us accountable to the demands of living in a community of responsibility and one that fosters self-worth and self-esteem for others and for itself."[105] Townes suggests that, drawing on their past, African-American women can provide a model of a community that embraces justice, equality, and mutuality.

In sharp contrast to many of the models and experiences of community discussed previously, the African-American heritage of community has preserved a sense of wholeness, what Delores Williams refers to as "the holistic philosophy of integrating the spiritual, the carnal, and the political."[106] Emilie Townes writes, "As a people who survived fourteen generations of slavery and seven generations of emancipation, the blending of body and soul is crucial."[107] The "different cast" in values mentioned by Townes is due to a location at the margins of the dominant white world. As a survival tradition, African-American notions of community necessarily stress relation and responsibility, for as isolated individuals, black people could not have endured and resisted.

In the past decades, social and economic changes have profoundly reshaped these traditions of black community. Civil Rights legislation took blacks down the path of integration, but the fruits of that journey have not all been sweet. The crisis in the situation of the black poor has led black intellectual leadership to call for remembrance and renewal of traditions, for some in forms of black nationalism such as the Nation of Islam, for others in forms of renewal within the black church. The partial inclusion of the marginalized "private" public of the traditional African-American community in the white "public" public has meant that the question of "twoness," of doubled community and identity, must be rethought in a new context of capitalism and a renegotiated public sphere.

Like many of the writers discussed and criticized in this work, progressive African-American intellectuals such as West, hooks, Williams, and Townes link the loss and recovery of community with a loss and recovery of meaning. But rather than linking the loss of meaning to abstract concepts such as liberalism or modernist culture, they name specific socioeconomic structures that generate poverty and racism. Rather than turning to a church separate from society, they seek to revitalize a church central to the economic and political struggles of the black community. And rather than evaluating meaningfulness in relation to an abstract transcendent norm, they look to the particulars of African-American history. For them, communal meaning cannot exist without solidarity for justice.

COMMUNITY, CIVIL SOCIETY, AND SOLIDARITY
Some Concluding Comments

The overall impact of postmodernism is that many other
groups now share with black folks a sense of deep alienation,
despair, uncertainty, loss of sense of grounding, even if it is
not informed by shared circumstance. Radical postmodernism calls attention to those shared sensibilities which cross
the boundaries of class, gender, race, etc., that could be fertile
ground for the construction of empathy—ties that would
promote recognition of common commitments, and serve as
a base for solidarity and coalition.

—bell hooks[1]

chapter 6

THE "SENSE of deep alienation, despair, uncertainty" which hooks names is a
response to the dissolution of a particular conjunction of politics, culture and
economics that has controlled the modern existence of most Western countries. In my work, I have connected the crisis of this conjunction—liberal
capitalist modernity—with the emergence of a new concern for, and discourses about, community. I have argued that the unprecedented depth and
breadth of current capitalism have created conditions of fragmentation and
alienation where it is difficult to develop stable relational identities. "In the
increasingly individualized and differentiated modern world," Elizabeth
Frazer and Nicola Lacey write, "the question of how to generate a degree of
social integration adequate to sustain peaceable and mutually supportive
coexistence without unduly curtailing hallowed individual freedom has
become a central political concern,"[2] since the institutions of civil society

that have provided such integration can no longer do so—at least under previous political and cultural conditions. The profound reshaping of the conjunction of public and private spheres within civil society has thrown into question the relation of national and particular identities in ways that leave persons struggling to make sense of the different pieces of their lives.

I am convinced that the communitarian emphasis on historical particularity and relations is a comprehensible and valuable reaction to the destructive heritage of liberal capitalism. Yet the ethnic-based, seemingly intractable conflagrations in such places as Bosnia, Armenia, Israel/Palestine, India, and Germany, vividly suggest the dangers inherent in prioritizing communal tradition and ethnic identity. The challenge is to maintain particular identity within democratic polity, a challenge which no modern nation state has yet solved.

In the postmodern context, our social relations are changing rapidly in ways that compel reformation of civil society. We live, as it is often said, in an interdependent world where we are aware of and connected in a variety of ways to vast numbers of people far different than ourselves. Such a time holds great possibilities and great dangers as we search for social forms that can enable us to manage these new realities. The choice may not be, as Martin Luther King, Jr. put it, "chaos or community," but "exclusion or connection," between simplicity bought at the price of avoidance or relations painfully shaped out of our complex social world.

A few years ago, commuters in New York's Grand Central Station were polled as to whether the homeless should be "removed" from the station. The majority (mostly white) were delighted, saying it bothered them to have to look at "those people" (many black and Hispanic) every day as they traveled between work and home. None of them asked what conditions led to large number of visible homeless. And none asked where the people would actually go, when removed from the station.

The attitudes demonstrated by these ordinary citizens represent the dangers inherent in the current discussion of community. As people become weary of the instability and confusion of their lives, they become eager for the certain answer, the solid tie, the reassurance of security. As I have suggested, I believe this is a particular challenge for white persons (both of the working class and the PMC) fully incorporated into capitalist institutions who have generally lost the older ethnic connections. While all of us need some measure of stability, the question is whether our stability is bought at the price of someone else's instability and suffering. Stability bought at this price ultimately erodes the moral empathy crucial for enduring social bonds. Often the appeal to community combines power, ethnicity and a tacit acceptance of the inequalities and exploitation of advanced capitalism, allowing whites to enjoy communal connection while avoiding conflict and accountability.

The only counter to this appeal is, I believe, the development of communal

forms based upon participatory forms of democracy that seek to negotiate justice for different identities and heritages in ways requiring both interaction
and cooperation. There are also possibilities present of tolerance rooted in
understanding, not apathy, and of relationships that span divides of space, race,
gender, and class. The sphere of our society that can offer both connection and
challenge is the sphere of civil society. All of the writers studied here understand that a renewed civil society, a set of institutions mediating between the
individual and the state, is important for the revitalization of society and, ultimately for any kind of common morality. The question pursued here has been
what the conditions might be for such a renewal. I will review some of the
key features of the proposals and possibilities, then suggest some specific challenges for liberal Protestantism, and, finally, point to solidarity as a central
norm for renewed community/civil society.

FORMS OF HEGEMONY, FORMS OF RESISTANCE

Throughout my discussion of different approaches to community and civil
society, I have used criteria for evaluation derived from marxist ideological critique, seeking to distinguish neohegemonic dimensions, reestablishing dominant forms of power, from counterhegemonic dimensions, pointing to new
possibilities. These criteria lead me to highlight the following points in the discussion of community:

Where's the Economy?

113

One of the key indication of a neohegemonic approach to community is
avoidance of the role of capitalism in the "loss" of community. Common to
both communitarian and liberal thought is an avoidance of the economic
dimension of both politics and culture. This is a signal of common hegemonic
interests, as it suggests that both ideologies wish to assume ongoing capitalist
economic relations of exploitation and domination. For communitarian thought,
this avoidance places a contradiction in the center of the critique of liberalism, since it displaces the effects of capitalism onto liberal politics and morality, leaving untouched the economic processes that have led to the very rationalization and alienation it seeks to transform. While purporting to oppose the
dominant modernist/liberal world view, it tacitly supports the economic and
state rationalization that is the foundation of liberal modernity, because neo-
conservatives still benefit and hope to continue to benefit from the dominant
economic and state power.

Neoconservatism thus exemplifies a neohegemonic development, that seeks
to relegitimize the state in ways that maintain traditional forms of power and
yet, simultaneously, address the lifeworld pathologies which it recognizes as
threatening the legitimacy of the social order. It does this by rigidly dividing
economics, culture, morality, and politics, ignoring the complex interconnections

in favor of its theses that cultural narcissism, permissive individualism and politicization have damaged the vital, normative traditions required for maintenance of the social order.

In contrast, I suggest that a transformative, counterhegemonic form of community will acknowledge the material conditions of our society and the ways in which these affect culture and social formation. Modernity and postmodernity need to be represented as not only cultural or philosophical movements, but as socioeconomic forces.

A Monolithic Culture

A hallmark of a variety of communal theories is an appeal to particular historical traditions. The ideological nature of definitions of community becomes clear when one realizes that these called upon vital historical traditions no longer exist—or at least do not exist in the ways implied by neohegemonic or neoconservative movements. These traditions are invented/reinvented in response to new situations and in order to serve needs of particular groups.[3] Under cover of what professes to be a new turn to history, actual historical change and conflict are concealed. Or a reconfiguration of power is concealed in an appeal to community which presumes a fundamental commonality as ultimate reality or goal. The image of unity as starting or endpoint is contrasted as "good" to the "bad" present conflict, which then leads to the conclusion that what is needed is elimination of the "bad."

Even when difference is acknowledged as "pluralism" in society, there is still an effort to fit all groups within a uniform framework. The neohegemonic task is to "control both the present and the future by redefining and mastering the dominant, collectively shared sense of the historical past,"[4] as foundation for a homogeneous, exclusive community which will rejoin personal and national/social identity into one "membership-citizenship." This culture is considered "as noncontradictory, as isolated from questions of history, and as a storehouse of unchanging facts, behaviors, and practices."[5] And the repository of that culture is a community whose relations are "integrated," that is, "naturally" harmonious, where tradition is authoritative, and where membership determines one's personal and social identity.

Privatized individuated culture is, necessarily, pluralized. However, it is important to distinguish between two different forms of pluralization which often become blurred in communitarian discussions. On the one hand, there is a pluralization of institutions, that is, the increasing complexity and differentiation of spheres that has occurred in modern societies. On the other hand, there is also, in the liberal model, a pluralization of values. But this plurality is not on structured on the basis of any kind of historically-based differences, but is envisioned as a collection of individual preferences, each uniform in the lack of impact outside the self. "Difference," as Chandra Talpede Mohanty puts it, is "seen as benign variation (diversity), rather than as conflict, struggle, or the threat of disruption ... [it] bypasses power as well as history, to suggest a harmonious, empty pluralism."[6] Thus, the existence of different, and generally marginalized, communal ways of life is never acknowledged.

Neohegemonic communal theories have difficulty engaging both institutional and normative pluralism. While they generally accept institutional differentiation, they seek to contain or control it through the bonds of unified meaning. And they reject the individualized form of plurality as exemplifying the very fragmentation they seek to challenge, the self "separated from family, religion, and calling as sources of authority ... autonomously pursuing happiness and satisfying its wants."[7] These communal theories find themselves, however, in greater difficulties when confronting marginalized cultures, which may exemplify the very kind of traditional communities and embedded selves they claim to seek, since such communities challenge the desired security of homogeneity. The marginalized communities may then be rejected as politicized, i.e., challenging the moral harmony, or they may be subsumed within the larger organic whole. This desire for community, as Iris Young puts it, "relies on the same desire for social wholeness and identification that underlies racial and ethnic chauvinism on the one hand, and political sectarianism on the other ... [it] totalizes and detemporalizes ... social life by setting up an opposition between authentic and inauthentic social relations."[8] Further, since there is no possibility of reaching such a unity in multicultural U.S. society, communitarians either have to imagine a society that simply breaks sharply with current social relations or retreat into a despairing pessimism.[9]

Communal proposals with counterhegemonic possibilities will assume that there is no pure tradition or identity which can support an ideal, harmonious community.[10] They point to subversive, politicized memories, "that remembering that serves to illuminate and transform the present."[11] And they assume that any democratic polity will require recognition of difference achieved through a process enabling the real participation of all concerned.[12]

Justice as a Family Value

Family becomes a special symbol of the types of changes being opposed and the kinds of community being sought. Here again communitarianism follows liberalism's description of the family as a set of "natural" relations, but, rather than practicing the benign neglect of liberalism, it makes the family a central concern of its cultural renewal program. Communitarians recognize that the family is one of the key institutions of reproduction of moral values, and thus its stability is key to their vision of renewed social order. Here the kind of norms implicit in the communitarian argument become clear. If family, and, especially, *women* in the family, operates on a more participatory basis, then, in their eyes, the foundation of our society is undermined. Clearly, participation is not a normative basepoint for their model of the social order. Further, to acknowledge the unequal status of women within the family seriously calls into question the possibility of common moral culture which is critical to their enterprise. Even the less conservative communitarians face difficulties combining a call for renewal of traditional communal relations with any changed role for women within the family.

In their criticisms of liberal individualism, many communal theorists tend to dismiss claims of justice as examples of atomized self-interest or politicized group-interest which threaten the cohesion of society around a particular moral conception of the common good. The problem, as Frazer and Lacey put it, is to counter our fragmented postmodern reality "in ways which do not ... repress difference or seek stability via the institutionalization of unjust inequality."[13] Admittedly, these liberal concepts have been truncated by a restriction of justice to issues of distributions of goods and by an individualist (patriarchal and racist) anthropology. Nevertheless they still provide grounds for individuals and communities to criticize the existing structures in the name of human dignity and a variety of entitlements.[14] Unless community and tradition are corrected by these norms, old forms of hierarchy and exclusion may be perpetuated.

Public vs. Private, Politics vs. Culture

Underlying almost all of the issues raised here is a fundamental question concerning the relation between public and private spheres. As I have argued, the entrance of new participants (minority men and women of all colors) into the liberal public occurs simultaneously with the reconfiguring of these spheres by the entrance of capitalism into previously "private" areas of the lifeworld. The ambiguity surrounding the postmodern condition is particularly evident here. On the one hand, "private" worlds become exposed to new forms of bureaucratization and commodification and public issues run the risk of privatization. Yet, on the other hand, public norms can be used to judge previously "private" issues, such as domestic violence; and marginalized ways of life, such as African-American values of endurance or bourgeois female forms of caring, can become public.

In liberal theory, culture has been defined as the privatized desires and interests of the individual, while politics has been the public procedural regulation of the interaction of those individuals as they seek to realize these interests. Although some form of difference and particularity is assumed on the private level, on the public level, persons are interchangeable, as citizens, on the basis of a common rationality underlying the procedural relations of the social contract. For liberalism, as Nancy Fraser says, "the problem of democracy becomes the problem of how to insulate political processes from what are considered to be nonpolitical or prepolitical processes."[15]

As I pointed out in chapter 2,[16] the viability of this division depended upon the ongoing existence of socializing institutions of community/civil society which continued to shape common moralities that linked persons with each other, and linked culture and politics, private and public.[17] The crisis of civil society thus enures a moral crisis involving moral formation in both public and private spheres.[18]

Neohegemonic communitarian theories, while claiming to reject liberalism, actually reproduce the liberal ideology of the division of culture and politics, but seek to "renew" privatized culture, not through participation, but through a reaffirmation of a unified authoritative tradition governing a common set of norms. The problematic relationship of communal membership and citizenship is merged into a single identity, or else the communal identities are written off as troublesome group-based contestations.

The static notion of culture, the rejection of social differentiation, and the rejection of diversity are all dimensions of the rejection of politics. In neohegemonic communal theories there is not even affirmation of liberal interest-based politics, but simply a rejection of any kind of political interaction. Politics is considered an example of our moral disintegration, instead of a process in which we negotiate and form our identities through participation.

Politics are central to all transformative notions of community, not politics as interest-group bargaining, but participatory politics which "challenges, redefines, and renegotiates the divisions between the good and the just, the moral and the legal, the private and the public."[19] Such politics are foundational for the renewal of social morality as they produce vital public spheres which "are not only arenas for the formation of discursive opinion" but also "arenas for the formation and enactment of social identities."[20] These spheres can help us renegotiate the division of private and public both by bringing traditionally private issues such as sexuality and religion into public discourse and by subjecting the state and the economy to moral critique.[21] Some possibilities are already available to us in the histories of "subaltern counterpublics" such as the African-American community, which have a history of forming moralities and identities of resistance, endurance, and responsibility. These counterpublics are currently, as I have argued, under stress, but there is potential for them to function as "spaces of withdrawal and regroupment" and "bases and training grounds for agitational activities directed toward wider publics."[22]

Liberal Protestantism: Not Custodian, but Companion

Although this conversation has been wide-ranging, I am convinced that it is a necessary prologomenon to any serious discussion of the possibility of a renewed liberal Protestant public ethics. The reality that "all the modern institutions which at first tended to exercise some of the public functions traditionally performed by religious institutions abandoned their public normative roles: academic philosophy, the specialized social sciences, the universities, the press, politicians, intellectuals" may suggest the potential for new public religious roles.[23] However, liberal Protestantism, struggling with dwindling memberships and resources and with its captivity to liberalism, has been at a loss.

I hope that I have demonstrated the dangerous appeal of communal-based ethics for a liberal Protestantism in search of a direction. At a time of dislocation and alienation, there is enormous attraction in theories that affirm an unambiguous identity, offer supportive community, and require little to no public participation with its accompanying confrontation with others different than one's self. Vestiges of liberal Protestantism's privileged status can be maintained by simply screening out the challenges and preserving the white church's "shield" against acknowledging their participation in exploitative economic and political systems.[24]

Richard Neuhaus and Stanley Hauerwas are good examples of these attractive communal "shields." Both men, in their criticism of liberalism, throw out valuable parts of the liberal Protestant heritage: commitments to public participation, justice, and critical reflection on inherited traditions.[25] Of the two, Hauerwas, I believe, is the more appealing because the political dimensions of his agenda are hidden in his emphases on narrative, community and history.

I do believe that liberal Protestant churches need to attend to the call to community. But these communities should be modeled not around a unified, unchanging appropriation of Christian tradition, but around a notion of tradition as a rich and diverse heritage, open to a variety of competing appropriations. In his discussion of contemporary forms of Christianity, José Casanova has sketched some intriguing possibilities for "deprivatized" religions. He suggests that religious institutions are entering the public sphere to: (1) defend the lifeworld against penetration by bureaucratic and market rationality (U.S. Right to Life movements); (2) "question and contest the claims of the two major societal systems, states and markets, to function according to their own intrinsic functionalist norms without regard to extrinsic traditional moral norms" (U.S. Catholic pastorals on nuclear war and the economy); (3) bring into the public sphere issues which liberal theories have decreed as private, thereby highlighting the necessary intersubjective and interpersonal nature of morality. Through these actions, religious institutions question the authority of the liberal division of private and public spheres, by "abandon[ing] [their] assigned place in the private sphere and enter[ing] the undifferentiated public sphere of civil society to take part in the ongoing process of contestation, discursive legitimation, and redrawing of boundaries."[26]

Like Larry Rasmussen, Casanova is suggesting the church can operate as one of the integrating institutions of civil society. But the integration that they

118

and Sharon Welch imagine is not a neohegemonic unity, but a process of contestations and participation. Possibilities 2 and 3 suggest ways that Protestant churches can help foster a rich, participatory morality that can challenge the status quo. What is required is an exploration of new forms of Christian citizenship, emphasizing our responsibilities to the entire community, nation and world, and the necessity of our acting humbly as one among many to bring about changes in this world community. As such, liberal Protestantism can serve as a "subaltern counterpublic" offering, as Rasmussen suggested, a haven, a safe place, not for retreat but for engaging in responsibilities to others, often very different others, in our world.

Hope and Solidarity

"Listen. For survival and transcendence. I must assume that you know that there can be no twenty-first century definition of the public good that does not find some way to include the reality of our interdependent relationships with the life forms around us—whose health and well-being we need at least as much as they need ours."[27]

In this statement, Vincent Harding states an obvious truth that almost all people in U.S. society find hard to recognize. Whether the "life forms" are human, animal, or vegetable, we are relational beings in a relational universe that continuously calls us to responsibility. Yet much of the discourse of community is conducted by those who long for the connections, but are frightened of the challenges and responsibilities.

Is it possible to envision a society where strong communal ties are maintained, along with the cherishing of the modern normative commitment to equality, participation and critical questioning?[28] I believe many of the figures discussed here (Walzer, Rasmussen, Young, Welch, West, hooks, Williams, and Townes) make suggestions leading toward this type of model. Walzer tries to combine a strong commitment to common national membership, with recognition of a plurality of communities within that nation, although, as I have pointed out, the priority he gives to a pre-given shared meaning damages his attempt. Rasmussen presumes an inescapable givenness of connection and points to a pluralized civil society and a diverse church community as ways of living out the relationships necessary for our collective survival.

Young recasts the good life in terms of justice and participation, writing that the good life can be expressed as two general democratic values, "1) developing and exercising one's capacities and expressing one's experience, and 2) participating in determining one's action and the condition of one's action."[29] This good life requires not a progressive inclusion into a homogeneous public, the model behind the "melting pot," but a heterogeneous public where different groups with different experiences can participate in the policies affecting their lives.

119

Yet, as I have argued, I am not sure that Young gives enough weight to the power of ongoing traditions, which is where I find Welch's example of black communal traditions helpful. Welch begins to model a possibility of society where different communities not only negotiate with one another, but listen so deeply to another's narrative that their own narrative is changed.[30] Welch's response to black women's narratives suggests this kind of transformation, although, as I have noted, I am troubled by her presumption that white PMC like herself have no positive narrative of their own, and that whiteness is a category that does not include some complexity of narratives, such as those due to class differences.[31]

While I have only begun to learn from African-American discussions of community, I recognize that their contribution to the dialogue over community and civil society is vital. The type of solidarity and interdependence that we need requires learning from the multiple traditions that are part of the U.S. heritage, hearing their stories of struggle, achievement, loss, and alienation. And it means supporting the efforts of these traditions to maintain the best of their "subaltern counterpublics" in the midst of capitalist postmodernity. Whatever transformations of capitalism are possible (an uncertain question in our post-Cold War world), they will rest upon the collective work of those whom capitalism has diminished, disenfranchised, and disenchanted.

What I am tentatively sketching here is a model of complex, diverse, plural, and participatory society, still able to substantively interact on grounds of a practice of solidarity, which means, says Ada María Isasi-Díaz, "mov[ing] away from the false notion of disinterest, of doing for others in an altruistic fashion" and moving towards "common responsibilities and interests which necessarily arouse shared feelings and lead to joint action." It is a *committed* "praxis of mutuality."[32]

NOTES

NOTES TO CHAPTER I

1. Adrienne Rich, *An Atlas of the Difficult World: Poems 1988–91* (New York: W. W. Norton & Co., 1991), 6.

2. Martin Luther King, Jr., *Where Do We Go From Here: Chaos or Community?* (New York: Harper & Row, 1967); cited in *A Testament of Hope: The Essential Writings of Martin Luther King, Jr.*, ed. J. M. Washington (San Francisco: Harper & Row, Publishers, 1986), 617.

3. John Keane, *Democracy and Civil Society: On the Predicaments of European Socialism, the Prospects for Democracy and the Problems of Controlling Social and Political Power* (New York: Verso Books, 1988), 21.

4. It is a heritage in Western culture which comes into its first self-consciousness with the questions asked by Aristotle and others about the nature of the Ancient Greek *polis*. Raymond Williams dates the presence

of the word in the English language from the fourteenth century. He notes that "unlike all other terms of social organization (*state, nation, society*, etc.) it seems never to be used unfavorably." Raymond Williams, *Keywords: A Vocabulary of Culture and Society* (New York: Oxford University Press, 1976), 65–6. For an interesting description of the use of "community" and "communitarian," along with a skeptical account of the historical nature of communities, see Derek L. Phillips, *Looking Backward: A Critical Appraisal of Communitarian Thought* (Princeton: Princeton University Press, 1993).

5. Each of these terms points to a different political tradition of interpretation. "The end of liberalism" and "the crisis of modernity" are terms emphasizing problems of meaning and politics which tend to be used by more mainstream critics, including many of the communitarian writers to be discussed below. "The crisis of capitalism" is a term emphasizing problems of economics which comes out of the tradition of western marxism. It has been recast by Jürgen Habermas as a "legitimation crisis," a phrase that tries to combine the economic, political, and cultural dimensions of the situation.

6. Elizabeth Fox-Genovese, *Feminism Without Illusions: A Critique of Individualism* (Chapel Hill: The University of North Carolina Press, 1991), 54.

7. Liberalism and modernity are the cultural and political philosophies/ideologies of capitalism. As David Harvey puts it, "It is precisely in such a context [capitalism] that possessive individualism and creative enterprise, innovation and speculation, can flourish, even although this also means a proliferating fragmentation of tasks and responsibilities, and a necessary transformation of social relations to the point where producers are forced to view others in purely instrumental terms." David Harvey, *The Condition of Postmodernity* (Oxford: Basil Blackwell, 1989), 103.

8. Antonio Gramsci, *Selections from the Prison Notebooks*, ed. and trans. Q. Hoare and G. Nowell Smith (New York: International Publishers, 1971), 377.

9. Michele Barrett, *Women's Oppression Today: Problems in Marxist Feminist Analysis* (London: Verso, 1984), 97.

10. T.H. Marshall, as cited by George Armstrong Kelly, "Faith, Freedom and Disenchantment: Politics and the American Religious Consciousness," in *Religion and America: Spiritual Life in a Secular Age*, eds. M. Douglas and S. Tipton (Boston: Beacon Press, 1983), 220.

11. Harvey, *Condition*, 277. Harvey here is describing the emergence of Nazism as a cautionary tale for postmodernity.

12. While I discuss here a specific debate within political philosophy, I generally will use the term "communitarian" to refer to a broader group of intellectuals critical of liberal modernity.

13. See, for example, Charles Taylor's discussion of the communal theories of Rousseau and Hegel in *Multiculturalism and "The Politics of Recognition"*, ed. A. Gutman (Princeton, NJ: Princeton University Press, 1992), 50. In this history, its political location has varied from radical (guild socialism, for example), to conservative (Burkean organic communities, for example), but the attack on liberalism has been constant. Michael Walzer has suggested that we should view these discussions as a continuing "communitarian correction" within the liberal tradition (Michael Walzer, "The Communitarian Critique of Liberalism," *Political Theory* 18/1 [February 1990]:15).

14. Nancy Rosenblum, "Introduction," *Liberalism and the Moral Life*, ed. N. Rosenblum (Cambridge, MA: Harvard University Press, 1989), 2.

15. I am summarizing Will Kymlicka's discussion in *Contemporary Political Philosophy: An Introduction* (Oxford: Oxford University Press, 1990), 199–237. Major expressions of these arguments are found in Michael Sandel, *Liberalism and the Limits of Justice* (Cambridge: Cambridge University Press, 1982); and, Charles Taylor, *Philosophy and the Human Sciences: Philosophical Papers*, vol. 2 (Cambridge: Cambridge University Press, 1985).

16. See Seyla Benhabib, "In the Shadow of Aristotle and Hegel: Communicative Ethics and Current Controversies in Practical Philosophy," in *Hermeneutics and Critical Theory in Ethics and Politics*, ed. M. Kelly (Cambridge, MA: The MIT Press, 1990), 3.

123

17. Nancy Rosenblum, *Another Liberalism: Romanticism and the Reconstruction of Liberal Thought* (Cambridge, MA: Harvard University Press, 1987), 154.

18. Jose Casanova, *Public Religions in the Modern World* (Chicago: University of Chicago Press, 1994), 40.

19. Casanova makes a helpful distinction about the processes of differentiation, decline and privatization contained (and usually conflated) within theories of secularization. He points out that while the first is essential, the second is correct and the third is an historical option, rather than a necessity. His point is that theories of secularization were really prescribing, rather than describing. Casanova, *Religions*, 211–15.

20. Michael Dyson, *Making Malcolm: The Myth and Meaning of Malcolm X* (New York: Oxford University Press, 1995), 164.

21. In this work, "nonreligious" intellectuals does not suggest, as will be shown, the actual faith commitment or atheism of the individual. The distinction is based on whether or not the intellectual writes as a person of faith to an audience within a faith community.

22. In discussing religion as a "sacred canopy," Peter Berger describes it as "the human enterprise by which a sacred cosmos is established…. By sacred is meant here a quality of mysterious and awesome power, other than man,

and yet related to him." He remarks that "religion has been the histori-
cally most widespread and effective instrument of legitimation" (Peter
Berger, *The Sacred Canopy* [Garden City, NY: Doubleday and Co., Inc.,
Anchor Books, 1969], 25, 32).

23. Steven Tipton, "The Moral Logic of Alternative Religion," in *Religion and
America*, ed. Douglas and Tipton, 105.

24. There are many problems with the classification of religion into these
basically Christian forms. However, there is no room here to discuss this
issue further.

25. Thus, some scholars have argued, the "return of the sacred" indicates the
ways in which persons are searching for meaning, community and relationship. See, for example, Daniel Bell, "The Return of the Sacred?", in
The Winding Passage: Essays and Sociological Journeys 1960–1980 (Cambridge,
MA: ABT Books, 1980, 324–54.

26. See, for example, the U.S. Bishops' pastoral on the economy, *Economic
Justice for All: Catholic Social Teachings and the U.S. Economy* (Washington,
D.C.: U.S. Catholic Conference, 1986). In this vein, it is striking that José
Casanova in his discussion of the deprivatization of religion includes case
studies of U.S. Protestant fundamentalism and U.S. Catholicism, but says
nothing of U.S. liberal Protestants (Casanova, *Religions*).

27. As John Simmons puts it, "If liberal Protestantism has engaged in the most
intense bargaining with modernity, it seems quite understandable that
during modernity's 'identity crisis,' liberal Protestantism would exhibit
more internal upheaval, more identity problems" (John K. Simmons,
"Complementism: Liberal Protestant Potential Within a Fully Realized
Pluralistic Cultural Environment," in *Liberal Protestantism: Realities and
Possibilities*, ed. R. Michaelsen and W. Roof [New York: Pilgrim Press,
1986], 176).

28. The professional-managerial class (PMC) is the location of the majority of
U.S. professional intellectuals, both in education and media. Barbara and
John Ehrenreich define this group as "salaried mental workers who do
not own the means of production and whose major function in the social
division of labor may be described broadly as the reproduction of capi-
talist culture and capitalist class relations" (Barbara and John Ehrenreich,
"The Professional-Managerial Class," in *Between Labor and Capital*, ed. P.
Walker [Boston: South End Press, 1979], 12).

29. In discussing the problems of the middle class, Harvey remarks that this
group has no clear moral tradition and thus "either become 'value para-
sites'—drawing their consciousness from association with one or other of
the dominant classes in society—or cultivate all manner of fictitious
marks of their own identity" (Harvey, *Condition*, 347).

30. My usage of "we" here locates me specifically within the white PMC.

31. Rosemary Hennessy, *Materialist Feminism and the Politics of Discourse* (New York: Routledge, 1993), 15.

32. John Keane, *Democracy*, 14; Jean Cohen and Andrew Arato, *Civil Society and Political Theory* (Cambridge: the MIT Press, 1992), ix.

33. The definitions of civil society are varied. From a liberal perspective, the one constant feature is an opposition to the sphere of the state. For a good overview, see Keane, *Democracy*, 31–63.

34. Alan Wolfe, *Whose Keeper? Social Science and Moral Obligations* (Berkeley: University of California Press, 1989), 191.

35. Cohen and Arato, *Civil Society*, 427–33. See also Jean Cohen and Andrew Arato, "Politics and the Reconstruction of the Concept of Civil Society," in *Zwischenbetractungen im Prozess der Aufklärung*, ed. A. Hönneth, et al. (Frankfurt: Suhrkamp Verlag, 1989), 482–503. I note that Habermas himself does not always seem to accept this correspondence since he writes that lifeworld cannot necessarily be identified with society as it is more abstract than any given social structure. For him, it is always essential to distinguish between the abstract systemic level and the historical forms in which these systemic imperatives have been realized (Jürgen Habermas, *The Theory of Communicative Action, Vol. 2: Lifeworld and System: A Critique of Functionalist Reason*, translated by T. McCarthy [Boston: Beacon Press, 1987], 148, 339–440). Although the question about the ontological status of the lifeworld is beyond the scope of this discussion, I suggest that we can understand civil society as the realization of the lifeworld in this historical period—an understanding that Cohen and Arato believe Habermas himself shares. The problems inherent in the question of ontological status are nicely demonstrated in Nancy Fraser's discussion of the ways in which these "deep–seated structures" render women invisible. She suggests that it is best to consider the division a "pragmatic-contextual" distinction, rather than a "natural kinds" distinction which, for example, would absolutely separate meaning production and reproductive labor from economic production. That is, it is important *not* to view it as a division found "naturally" throughout all societies, but a division analytically useful for illuminating our particular social order. See Nancy Fraser, *Unruly Practices: Power, Discourse, and Gender in Contemporary Social Theory* (Minneapolis: University of Minnesota Press, 1989), 113–43.

36. Habermas, *Lifeworld*, 125. This division is a good example of the abstraction of Habermas's work which requires critical correction. Habermas says he proceeds "reconstructively" to describe "anthropologically deep-seated structures ... found in the intuitive knowledge of competent members of modern societies" (*Lifeworld*, 383). But it is sometimes difficult to locate these structures.

37. Habermas, *Lifeworld*, 125–6.

38. Habermas, *Lifeworld*, 137.

39. Cohen and Arato, *Civil Society*, 411.

40. Jürgen Habermas, "Modernity—An Incomplete Project," in *The Anti-Aesthetic: Essays on Postmodern Culture*, ed. H. Foster (Port Townsend, WA: Bay Press, 1983), 8. See also Habermas, *Lifeworld*, 179–87.

41. The limitations of Habermas's assumptions of a model of a liberal bourgeois sphere are discussed in Nancy Fraser, "Rethinking the Public Sphere: A Contribution to the Critique of Actually Existing Democracy," in *Habermas and the Public Sphere*, ed. Craig Calhoun (Cambridge: The MIT Press, 1992), 114; Cohen and Arato, *Civil*, 431; Geoff Eley, "Nations, Publics, and Political Cultures: Placing Habermas in the Nineteenth Century," in *Habermas and the Public*, ed. Calhoun, 303–6. All, however, stress the usefulness of the concept.

42. Speaking of the division between public and private, Frazer and Lacey remark, "There have been many shifts over time: in the nineteenth century, *laissez-faire* liberalism constructed the economic market as private; in the late twentieth century, mixed economic liberalism has shifted this boundary, and the quintessentially private sphere is seen as being constituted by the family and sexual relations.... The revival of free-market ideology has begun to push economic relations back into the 'private' sphere" (Elizabeth Frazer and Nicola Lacey, *The Politics of Community: A Feminist Critique of the Liberal-Communitarian Debate* [Toronto: University of Toronto Press, 1993], 72).

43. Nancy Fraser uses the phrase "subaltern counterpublics" to describe "arenas where members of subordinated social groups invent and circulate counterdiscourses to formulate oppositional interpretations of their identities, interests, and needs." She says she has coined the phrase from Gayatri Spivak's notion of "subaltern" and Rita Felski's notion of "counterpublic." Fraser, "Rethinking," 123, 140 n.21.

44. Fraser, "Rethinking," 121.

45. See Frazer and Lacey, *Politics of Community*, 76.

46. Seyla Benhabib, "Models of Public Space: Hannah Arendt, the Liberal Tradition, and Jürgen Habermas," in *Habermas and the Public*, ed. Calhoun, 84.

47. Eley, "Nations," 306; Fraser, "Rethinking," 125.

48. Marshall Berman, *All That Is Solid Melts Into Air* (New York: Simon and Schuster, 1982), 345.

49. Seyla Benhabib writes, "Communitarians argue that the liberal conception of historical progress is illusory and that history has brought with it irretrievable losses, e.g., of a coherent sense of community and a moral vocabulary that was part of a shared social universe. In a similar vein, postmodernists argue that there is no 'meta-narrative' of history which

recounts the tale of *Geist* or of the proletariat, of freedom and continuous human emancipation. Not only has Marxism failed to appreciate irreversibility in history ... it has been complicitous in the destruction of traditional communities and the lives of premodern peoples." Seyla Benhabib, "Autonomy, Modernity, and Community," in *Zwischenbetrachtungen*, ed. Hönneth, 374.

50. Cohen and Arato, *Civil Society*, 295, 461.

51. Charles Taylor, *Sources of the Self: The Making of the Modern Identity* (Cambridge, MA: Harvard University Press, 1989), 623.

52. Edward Shils, *Tradition* (Chicago: University of Chicago Press, 1981), 324.

53. As Bruce Lawrence suggests, technology has delivered the (material) goods to back up its claims for dominance: "Modernity ... depends upon the enormous prestige of EuroAmerican and now Asian technologies .... No one wants to grant [technology] ultimate power, but neither does anyone want to be bereft of its instrumental benefits" (Bruce Lawrence, *Defenders of God: The Fundamentalist Revolt Against the Modern Age* [San Francisco: Harper and Row, Publishers, 1989], 41).

54. As I have noted, Habermas's pioneering work on the public sphere does not recognize this process, idealizing the bourgeois public that emerged in early modernity. For criticisms, see Fraser, "Rethinking," Cohen and Arato, *Civil Society*, and Eley, "Nations."

55. John Keane, *Public Life and Late Capitalism: Toward a Theory of Socialist Democracy* (New York: Cambridge University Press, 1984), 228.

56. Ruth Smith, "Relationality and the Ordering of Difference," *Journal of Feminist Studies in Religion* 9 1/2 (Spring/Fall 1993): 208.

57. Eley, "Nations," 307.

58. Carole Pateman, *The Disorder of Women* (Stanford, CA: Stanford University Press, 1989), 121, 43; Carole Pateman, "Equality, Difference, Subordination: the Politics of Motherhood and Women's Citizenship" in *Beyond Equality and Difference*, eds. G. Bock and S. James (New York: Routledge, 1992), 18–19.

59. Ralph Ellison, "What America Would Be Like Without Blacks," quoted in Cornel West, *Race Matters* (Boston: Beacon Press, 1993), 1.

60. The previously dominant term, "mainline," is no longer accurate to describe the increasingly sidelined liberal Protestant churches. "Oldline" is, at this point, a more exact term.

61. Gail Gehrig, *American Civil Religion: An Assessment*, Society for the Scientific Study of Religion, Monograph Series #3 (Storrs, CN: University of Connecticut Press, 1981), 108. Bellah's classic essay, "Civil Religion in America" is reprinted in Robert Bellah, *Beyond Belief: Essays on Religion in a Post-Traditional World* (New York: Harper and Row, 1970).

62. Bellah, *Beyond Belief*, 171–186; Will Herberg, *Protestant, Catholic, Jew* (New York: Anchor Books, Doubleday and Co., Inc., 1960).

63. Wade Clark Roof, "America's Voluntary Establishment: Mainline Religion in Transition," in *Religion and America*, eds. Douglas and Tipton, 138.

64. Leonard Sweet cites statistics from 1967–84 showing 40% decrease in the membership of the Christian Church (Disciples of Christ), 27% in the Presbyterian Church (U.S.A.), 19% in the Episcopal Church, 17% in the United Church of Christ, 16% in the United Methodist Church and 8% in the Lutheran Church in America. Leonard Sweet, "The Modernization of Protestant Religion in America," in *Altered Landscapes: Christianity in America 1935–1985*, ed. D. Lotz, et al. (Grand Rapids, MI: Eerdmans, 1989), 38. A recent study noted that the overall percentage of white adults with membership in oldline Protestant churches has declined from 41% in 1960 to 22% in 1992 (and a large proportion of this smaller percentage do not describe themselves as active members of their churches). Thomas B. Edsall, "Religion playing a bigger role in politics, studies show," *Roanoke Times and World News*, 14 January 1994, C9.

65. R. Michaelsen and W. Roof, "Introduction," in *Liberal Protestantism*, eds. Michaelsen and Roof, 10.

66. This division is an underlying assumption of most Protestant churches. An example is the shock that many of my Protestant students express when they realize that churches do not only speak about private issues, such as abortion and sexuality, but may speak about public issues as well, such as economics and war.

67. Beverly Harrison, *Making the Connections: Essays in Feminist Social Ethics*, ed. C. Robb (Boston: Beacon Press, 1985), 59.

68. Jeffrey Stout, *Ethics After Babel: The Languages of Morals and Their Discontents* (Boston: Beacon Press, 1988), 183–4.

69. Philip Hammond, "The Extravasation of the Sacred and the Crisis in Liberal Protestantism," in *Liberal Protestantism*, ed. Michaelsen and Roof, 63. George Armstrong Kelly describes civil religion as the nostalgia of the knowledge class (Kelly, "Faith, Freedom,") 223.

70. Harrison, *Connections*, 56.

71. Bruce Birch and Larry L. Rasmussen, *Bible & Ethics in the Christian Life*. rev. ed. (Minneapolis: Augsburg Fortress, 1989), 38.

72. Wolfe, *Whose Keeper*, 220.

73. Alasdair MacIntyre, *After Virtue: A Study in Moral Theory* (Notre Dame, IN: University of Notre Dame Press, 1981), 201.

74. Benhabib, "In the Shadow of Aristotle and Hegel," 27.

75. Beverly Harrison, "The Fate of the Middle 'Class' in Late Capitalism," in *God and Capitalism: A Prophetic Critique of Market Economy*, ed. J. Mark Thomas and V. Visick (Madison: A-R Editions, Inc., 1991), 55.

76. See Dennis P. McCann, *Christian Realism and Liberation Theology* (Maryknoll, NY: Orbis Books, 1981). Similarly, Schubert Ogden says that liberation theologies merely rationalize positions already taken for nonreligious reasons. See Schubert Ogden, *Faith and Freedom: Toward a Theology of Liberation* (Nashville: Abingdon Press, 1979).

77. Harrison, *Connections*, 22.

78. Juan Luis Segundo, *The Liberation of Theology* (Maryknoll, NY, 1981), 97–124. See also Pablo Richard, "The Church, the Authoritarian State, and Social Classes in Latin America," *Lucha/Struggle* 9/1 and 9/2 (1985):35–9 and 29–39.

79. Michel Foucault, *Power/Knowledge: Selected Interviews and Other Writings: 1972–77*, trans. Colin Gordon et al. (New York: Pantheon, 1980), 98.

80. Hennessy, *Materialist Feminism*, 18.

81. Michel Foucault, *The Use of Pleasure*, vol. 2 of *The History of Sexuality*, trans. Robert Hurley (New York: Vintage, 1983), 335.

82. The reality that the proletariat was often not revolutionary in its activities and organization was recognized by early twentieth century marxists such as Lukacs, Gramsci and the Frankfurt School. The question was revived with the 60s protest movements in Europe and the United States. Out of this context, many Western marxists, such as Andre Gorz (*Farewell to the Working Class: An Essay on Post-Industrial Socialism*, translated by Michael Sonenscher [Boston: South End Press, 1982]) and Stanley Aronowitz (*The Crisis of Historical Materialism: Class, Politics, and Culture in Marxist Theory* [New York: Praeger, A J.F. Bergin Publishers Book, 1982]), did, indeed, say "farewell" to this key marxist presupposition.

83. Here I follow the twentieth century revisions of marxism, primarily those of the Frankfurt School and those of Gramsci and Williams, which describe the relations between economic and social/cultural forces as far more complex than a simple determinism. For overviews of this development, see Perry Anderson, *Considerations on Western Marxism* (London: Verso, 1976) and Martin Jay, *Marxism and Totality* (Berkeley: University of California Press, 1984). For more specific discussion of the Frankfurt School, see Martin Jay, *The Dialectical Imagination: A History of the Frankfurt School and the Institute for Social Research, 1923–1950* (Boston: Little, Brown, and Co., 1973) and Andrew Arato and Eike Gebhardt, eds. *The Essential Frankfurt School Reader* (New York: Continuum, 1982). For discussion of Gramsci, see Chantal Mouffe, ed. *Gramsci and Marxist Theory* (Boston: Routledge and Kegan Paul, 1979). Habermas's model of system and life-world, described more fully in the following chapter would be one example of a heavily revised marxist model of ideology. Stanley Aronowitz has argued that Habermas is no longer a marxist, but Habermas continues to place himself in this tradition (at a conference in 1989, he remarked "I

mostly feel that I am the last Marxist") ["Concluding Remarks," in *Habermas and the Public*, ed. Calhoun, 469]. The important work of Chantal Mouffe and Ernesto Laclau argues for a relationship of overdetermination among the spheres. Ernesto Laclau and Chantal Mouffe, *Hegemony and Socialist Strategy* (London: Verso, 1985).

84. Part of the difficulty underlying the discourse vs. ideology question is the fact that most U.S. academics do not share the philosophical and political heritage of marxism that is part of the landscape for most of their European counterparts. Deconstructionist/post-structuralist theory is, in its origins, a response to the collapse of marxist political possibilities, "the experience of nihilism in the immediate wake of the historical *depassement* of Marxism," as Fraser describes the work of Derrida (Fraser, *Unruly*, 81). As such, it must be read in conjunction with marxist traditions. In one of his early works, Fredric Jameson speaks of "a real problem about the importation and translation of theoretical polemics which have a quite different semantic content in the national situation in which they originate." For example, there is an important difference between a critique of totalization in the context of "the historic weight of French centralization" and in the United States "where it is precisely that intensity of social fragmentation ... that has made it historically difficult to unify Left or any 'antisystemic' forces." "[T]he attack on the concept of 'totality' in the American framework," he claims, "means the undermining and repudiation of the only realistic perspective in which a genuine Left could come into being" in the United States. Fredric Jameson, *The Political Unconscious: Narrative as a Socially Symbolic Act* (Ithaca: Cornell University Press, 1981), 54 n.31. Given the lack of a marxist heritage, it is easy for U.S. postmodernists to avoid any consideration of forces of power and domination inherent in the socioeconomic context.

85. Describing the work of Mouffe and Laclau, Hennessy remarks that "the aim of that effort [to challenge reductive identification between agents and classes] is to do away once and for all with the function of economic forces in the shaping of social identities," Hennessy, *Materialist Feminism*, 22.

86. This point is made by Cohen and Arato in their critique of Foucault's model of civil society. Cohen and Arato, *Civil Society*, 270–2.

87. Harvey, *Condition*, 117; see Nancy Hartsock, "Foucault on Power: A Theory for Women?" in *Feminism/Postmodernism*, ed. Linda Nicholson (New York: Routledge, 1990), 157–75; Nancy Fraser, *Unruly*, 17–34; Cohen and Arato, *Civil Society*, 270–2.

88. See Kumkum Sangari, "The Politics of the Possible," *Cultural Critique* 7 (Fall 1987): 157–86; Nancy Hartsock, "Rethinking Modernism: Minority

vs. Majority Theories," *Cultural Critique* 7 (Fall 1987): 187–206. For general discussions on the issues of the relations between feminist and postmodernist theories, see Linda Nicholson and Nancy Fraser, "Social Theory Without Philosophy," in *Feminism/Postmodernism*, ed. L. Nicholson, 19–38; Seyla Benhabib, *Situating the Self: Gender, Community and Postmodernism in Contemporary Ethics* (New York: Routledge, 1992), 203–41.

89. Hennessy, *Materialist Feminism*, 14; see also David Tracy, *Plurality and Ambiguity* (San Francisco: Harper and Row, Publishers, 1987), 77.

90. Keane, *Democracy*, 214.

91. Gerald Fourez, *Liberation Ethics* (Philadelphia: Temple University Press, 1982), 33.

92. Since Gramsci did not work out his theories systematically, his definition of civil society is not completely clear. As Cohen and Arato put it, "Gramsci's conception is presented in a notoriously confusing terminology." They argue that he was unwilling to work through the challenge to marxist orthodoxy implied by his hypothesis of a civil society differentiated from both state and economy. See Cohen and Arato, *Civil Society*, 142–59.

93. Gramsci, *Selections*, 349.

94. Gramsci, *Selections*, 60–1.

95. Raymond Williams, *Marxism and Literature* (Oxford: Oxford University Press, 1978), 110.

96. It is important to emphasize the possibilities inherent in the uneven and contradictory nature of ideological processes in contrast to the tendencies in the pessimistic later writings of the Frankfurt School (Horkheimer, Adorno and Marcuse) and in the structuralist interpretations of Althusser. For them the ideological power of capitalism is so massive that resistance is at best futile, at worst nonexistent.

97. Jim Merod, *The Political Responsibility of the Critic* (Ithaca, NY: Cornell University Press, 1987), 14.

98. Laclau and Mouffe's Lacanian-influenced model calls these areas "the original lack" (Laclau and Mouffe, *Hegemony*, 88 n.1).

99. Williams, *Marxism*, 122–3. See also Raymond Williams, *The Sociology of Culture* (New York: Schocken Books, 1982), 204. These categories are derived from Gramsci's writings. One of the examples of his framework Williams offers is particularly pertinent to this discussion: "the idea of rural community is predominantly residual, but is in some limited respects alternative or oppositional to urban industrial capitalism, though for the most part it is incorporated, as idealization or fantasy, or as an exotic—residential or escape—leisure function of the dominant order itself" (Williams, *Marxism*, 122).

100. Cornel West, *Prophesy Deliverance! An Afro-American Revolutionary Christianity* (Philadelphia: Westminster Press, 1982), 118–121.

101. Elements of a prehegemonic communitarianism can be found in the works of conservative thinkers Leo Strauss, Robert Nisbet, and Alan Bloom who see no positive possibilities in modernity and democracy in relation to premodern hierarchical societies.

102. Craig Owens, "Feminists and Postmodernism," in *The Anti-Aesthetic*, ed. Hal Foster, 58.

103. Michael Ryan, *Marxism and Deconstruction* (Baltimore: Johns Hopkins Press, 1982), 119.

104. Benhabib, *Self*, 77, 81 (Benhabib's emphasis).

105. Such an assumption has been extremely evident in the tradition of sociological discussion of community, a tradition influential for many of the figures here. As sociology emerged among intellectuals who themselves were the production of mobility and urban dislocation, it sought to answer the question, "How can the moral order of society be maintained and the integrity of its members achieved within a highly differentiated and technological social structure?" (Claude S. Fisher, "The Study of Urban Community and Personality," *Annual Review of Sociology* 1975). The concern for moral order was expressed as a concern for community, which was generally defined in Ferdinand Toennies's terms of *Gemeinschaft* and *Gesellschaft*. *Gemeinschaft* was a natural group solidarity of family, kinship groups, friendship networks, and neighborhoods. In contrast, *Gesellschaft* was defined in relation to the city as an "artificial construction of an aggregate of human beings," characterized by competition and impersonality. In *Gemeinschaft*, people "remain essentially united in spite of all separating factors, whereas in *Gesellschaft*, they are essentially separate in spite of all uniting factors." (F. Toennies, *Community and Society*, trans. C.P. Loomis [New York: Harper and Row, Inc., 1963], 33, 64, 65).

106. Martin Marty, "Religion in America since Mid-century," in *Religion and America*, ed. M. Douglas and S. Tipton, 283.

107. See also the conservative account of tradition offered by Edward Shils which assumes a smooth "handing down" rather than a process ruptured by conflict and struggle as different interpretations, embodied in different groups of people, work to maintain and reproduce their way of life (Shils, *Tradition*).

108. Thomas Bender, *Community and Social Change in America* (New Brunswick, NJ: Rutgers University Press, 1978), 9. Toennies's model for *Gemeinschaft* was marriage, "a perfect unity of human wills."

109. Arlene Skolnick, *Embattled Paradise: The American Family in an Age of Uncertainty* (New York: Basic Books, Harper Collins Publishers, 1991), 5.

110. Susan Moller Okin, "Humanist Liberalism," in *Liberalism and the Moral Life*, ed. N. Rosenblum, 48.

111. Iris Young, *Justice and the Politics of Difference* (Princeton, NJ: Princeton University Press, 1990), 227.

112. See Harrison, *Connections*, 66.

113. Ruth Smith, "Feminism and the Moral Subject," in *Women's Consciousness/Women's Conscience*, ed. B. Andolsen, et al. (San Francisco: Harper and Row, Publishers, 1985), 249–50.

114. Although white women and their work are somewhat more frequently drawn upon, it is still astonishing how frequently liberal white academics omit any engagement with the issues and experiences of persons of color.

115. Dyson, *Making Malcolm*, 148.

116. Richard John Neuhaus has now, of course, converted from Lutheranism to Catholicism, but the works considered here date from his Protestant days.

117. Beverly Harrison points to this tension when she remarks that "our present political economy places unprecedented moral, social, and economic demands on women, while at the same time weakening the social bonds of women's culture…" (Harrison, *Connections*, 33).

118. Cahill is the one Catholic among the liberal Protestants studied here. I was unable to find a Protestant woman writer who simultaneously showed feminist sympathies, was concerned about community, and was neither radical nor socialist.

NOTES TO CHAPTER 2

1. Marx and Engels, "Manifesto of the Communist Party," in *The Marx-Engels Reader*, 2d ed., ed. R. C. Tucker (New York and London: W. W. Norton & Company, 1978), 476.

2. David Harvey, *The Condition of Postmodernity* (Oxford: Basil Blackwell, 1989), 106.

3. John Keane, *Public Life and Late Capitalism: Toward a Theory of Socialist Democracy* (New York: Cambridge University Press, 1984), 77. Keane is summarizing Habermas's analyses which are applicable only to advanced capitalist countries.

4. Perry Anderson writes that the modern "sensibility dates, in its initial manifestations, from the advent of the world market itself—1500 or thereabouts" (Perry Anderson, "Modernity and Revolution," in *Marxism and the Interpretation of Culture*, ed. C. Nelson and L. Grossberg [Urbana: University of Illinois Press, 1988], 319).

5. A phrase used by Islamicist Marshall Hodgson, as cited in Bruce Lawrence, *Defenders of God* (San Francisco: Harper and Row, Publishers, 1989), 48. Perry Anderson remarks that it was only after 1790 that there was a "common vocabulary" for modernity (Anderson, "Modernity and Revolution," 319). It is important to emphasize that what is being dis-

cussed here is the particular western development of modernity. One feature of the heritage of western power is the presentation of western models of modernity as acultural or universal requirements of modernity. Although my own language here is somewhat general and ahistorical, my discussion is exclusively of western modernity. See Charles Taylor's remarks about "cultural" and "acultural" models in "Inwardness and the Culture of Modernity," in *Zwischenbetrachtungen Im Prozess der Aufklärung*, ed. A. Hoenneth, et al. (Frankfurt: Suhrkamp Verlag, 1989), 601–23.

6. Lawrence, *Defenders*, 52.

7. Jürgen Habermas, *The Philosophical Discourse of Modernity: Twelve Lectures*, trans. F. Lawrence (Cambridge, MA: The MIT Press, 1987), 2.

8. Jürgen Habermas, *Toward a Rational Society: Student Protest, Science and Politics*, trans. J. Shapiro (Boston: Beacon Press, 1970), 92–3. Habermas's more recent, more complex development of this analysis can be found in his critique of Weber in Jürgen Habermas, *The Theory of Communicative Action, Vol. 2: Lifeworld and System: A Critique of Functionalist Reason*, trans. T. McCarthy (Boston: Beacon Press, 1987), 303–31.

9. Habermas, *Lifeworld*, 146. One critical comment to be offered here is Habermas's troubling use of the word "primitive" that points to an elitism which is an unfortunate heritage of the Frankfurt School tradition. For further discussion of this problem, see Anthony Giddens's remarks on Habermas's attitude towards oral cultures in Anthony Giddens, "Reason without Revolution?" in *Habermas and Modernity*, ed. R. Bernstein (Cambridge, MA: The MIT Press, 1985), 118–9.

10. Habermas, *Lifeworld*, 385.

11. Habermas, *Lifeworld*, 77. Habermas draws here primarily on Weber, Durkheim and Mead. José Casanova sums up the process of secularization in these categories: 1) the decline of religion; 2) shift from other-worldly to this-worldly orientation; 3) disengagement of society from religion; 4) transposition of beliefs and activities from a divine to a secular point of reference; and, 5) disenchantment of the world. See José Casanova, "The Politics of the Religious Revival," *Telos* 59 (1984), 4, n. 7.

12. Keane, *Public Life*, 169.

13. To put it in Habermas's words, the increased complexity and differentiation of modern societies "shifts the burden of social integration more and more from religiously anchored consensus to processes of consensus formation in language … laws need to be intersubjectively recognized by citizens.… This leaves culture with the task of supplying reasons why an existing political order deserves to be recognized" (Habermas, *Lifeworld*, 180, 188).

14. Benedict Anderson, *Imagined Communities* (New York: Verso, 1983), 31.

15. Habermas, *Lifeworld*, 170.

134

16. By "natural," I do not mean biologically given or historically unchanging. Rather I use the term to designate the subject's perspective, to point to assumed social relations and characteristics which are perceived as unchosen and thus "natural."

17. Alan Wolfe, *Whose Keeper? Social Science and Moral Obligations* (Berkeley: University of California Press, 1989), 128.

18. Jon P. Gunnemann, "A Theological Defense of the Brute: The Christian Stake in Political Liberalism" (photocopy), 58.

19. Rogers Smith, "'One United People': Second-Class Female Citizenship and the American Quest for Community," *Yale Journal of Law and Humanities* 1/2 (May 1989): 232.

20. Ruth Smith and Deborah Valenze, "Mutuality and Marginality: Liberal Moral Theory and Working Class Women in Nineteenth-Century England," *Signs* 13/2 (Winter 1988): 278.

21. Taylor, "Inwardness," 613.

22. Keane, *Public Life*, 235.

23. I follow Taylor's use of the male pronoun, because as feminist analysis has shown, the rational modern individual was constructed as male. See Carole Pateman, *The Sexual Contract* (Stanford, CA: Stanford University Press, 1988).

24. Habermas, *Modernity*, 5.

25. As Ruth Smith and Deborah Valenze put it, "how, under the terms of liberal theory, does one express or explain the moral life at all?" (Smith and Valenze, "Mutuality and Marginality," 280).

26. Wolfe, *Whose Keeper*, 108.

27. As Dick Anthony and Thomas Robbins put it, civil religion was "a dominant American politico-moral ideology" which "combined three key elements into a consistent world view: (1) stringent moral absolutism reflecting both the Puritan covenantal traditions and subsequent evangelical awakenings; (2) a fervent belief in laissez-faire and competitive individualism in the economic realm; and (3) messianic conceptions of America as an instrument of Divine Providence and an exemplary utopia" (Anthony and Robbins, "Spiritual Innovation and the Crisis of American Civil Religion," in *Religion and America: Spiritual Life in a Secular Age*, ed. M. Douglas and S. Tipton [Boston: Beacon Press, 1983], 244).

28. Cited in Robert Bellah, *Beyond Belief: Essays on Religion in a Post-Traditional World* (New York: Harper and Row, Publishers, 1970), 174.

29. Peter Berger, *The Sacred Canopy* (Garden City, NY: Doubleday and Co., Inc., Anchor Books, 1969), 159.

30. A phrase found in a 1929 work, quoted by Christopher Lasch in *The True and Only Heaven: Progress and Its Critics* (New York: W.W. Norton and Co., 1991), 47. Bruce Lawrence remarks that "without the presuppositions of a nation-state powerful enough to elicit the loyalty of its citizens, a power

vastly increased by the instrumentalities of modern-day technology and communications, civil religion would be jejune" (Lawrence, *Defenders*, 94).

31. Carole Pateman, *The Disorder of Women* (Stanford, CA: Stanford University Press, 1989), 43.

32. Pateman, *Disorder*, 21.

33. Craig Calhoun, "Introduction," in *Habermas and the Public Sphere*, ed. C. Calhoun (Cambridge: The MIT Press, 1992), 10.

34. Elizabeth Fox-Genovese, *Feminism Without Illusions: A Critique of Individualism* (Chapel Hill: The University of North Carolina Press, 1991), 121.

35. Jürgen Habermas, *The Structural Transformation of the Public Sphere*, trans. T. Burger and F. Lawrence (Cambridge: The MIT Press, 1989), 55, 48.

36. Patricia Hill Collins, *Black Feminist Thought* (London: Harper Collins, 1991), 53.

37. Harvey, *Condition*, 103.

38. Gunnemann, "Brute," 14. Habermas says that "the bourgeois state accelerated the dissolution of this [lifeworld] substratum on which it tacitly fed" (Habermas, *Lifeworld*, 359).

39. For example, there are interesting analogies between the ways young female labor was incorporated as capitalism developed in the nineteenth-century United States and as it is now developing in countries such as Malaysia, Korea, or Mexico. However, there are also key differences due to different cultures and traditions and due to the differing stages of development of global capitalism. Thus, Malaysian young women may, like the young women in nineteenth-century United States, have found themselves the mostly likely to be hired in the new industries and thus most able to bring in the newly-required cash income to support their families. However, women in nineteenth-century Massachusetts textile firms were not part of a global industrial complex, which has shaped not only their labor but also their self-understanding. For an excellent account of nineteenth century U.S. female labor, see Thomas Dublin, *Women at Work: The Transformation of Work and Community in Lowell, Mass., 1826–60* (New York: Columbia University Press, 1979). For some accounts of the situation of Third World women's labor, see K. Young, et al., eds. *Of Marriage and the Market* (London: CSE Books, 1981), Aihwa Ong, *Spirits of Resistance and Capitalist Discipline: Factory Women in Malaysia* (Albany: SUNY Press, 1987), and Haleh Afshar, *Women, Work and Ideology in the Third World* (London: Tavistock Publications, 1985).

40. Under this rubric I would classify conservative theorists such as Burke, *gemeinschaft* theorists such as Toennies and the sociological traditions derived from his work, and progressive visionaries such as William Morris and Jane Addams.

41. In other words, the crisis of modernity was sooner apparent at the philosophical/intellectual level than at the level of everyday life. For discussions of community persisting in marginalized cultures see Ruth Smith and Deborah Valenze, "Mutuality and Marginality"; Jane Humphries, "Class Struggle and the Persistence of the Working-Class Family," *Cambridge Journal of Economics* 1 (1977): 241–58; Mina Davis Caulfield, "Imperialism, the Family, and Cultures of Resistance," *Socialist Revolution* 4/2 (October 1974): 67–85; Bonnie Thornton Dill, "Our Mothers' Grief," *Journal of Family History* 13 (1988): 415–31; and, Collins, *Black Feminist*, 115–38.

42. David Harvey describes the postwar boom built on a Fordist/Keynesian model of capitalist accumulation in Harvey, *Condition*, 124–40.

43. Anderson, *Imagined*, 327. David Harvey describes this development as the dominance of "Fordism," i.e., a structuring of work and life according to the rhythm and organization of the assembly line (see Harvey, *Condition*, 135). Speaking of religion in this period, Peter Berger writes, "Probably for the first time in history, the religious legitimations of the world have lost their plausibility not only for a few individuals, but for the broad masses of entire societies" (Berger, *Canopy*, 124).

44. Harvey, *Condition*, 137.

45. Harvey, *Condition*, 134.

46. Or "the functional necessities of systemically integrated domains of action shall be met, if need be, even at the cost of *technicizing* the lifeworld" (Habermas, *Lifeworld*, 345). It is important to note that Habermas does not consider the technological rationality of the system spheres of economy and bureaucracy to be in itself a problem. Habermas is careful to distinguish between what could be called the "good" rationalization of the lifeworld in contrast to the "bad." Thus he critiques Weber's view of the "iron cage" of modern rationality as mistakenly collapsing these two forms. In his view, the "dying out of vital traditions" to be replaced by "communicatively secured" consensus would not be a problem for legitimation if it was not accompanied by "one-sided rationalization" penetrating the lifeworld (see Habermas, *Lifeworld*, 327). The issue is the movement of this form of rationality into the lifeworld. Cohen and Arato suggest that this question goes back to the problem of the ontological status of Habermas's framework, that is, whether the system consists of the *actual* institutions of economy and state, or, the underlying *logic* of these historical institutions. They assert that it is important both to distinguish between economy and state *and* to offer critiques of the actual reification of these institutions as they exist embedded in the lifeworld (see Cohen and Arato, *Civil Society*, 495–6). It is also important, as Nancy Fraser points out, to avoid seeing (as Habermas apparently does) the "penetration" as a one-way action. The incorporation of "lifeworld" gender roles into the structures of economy

137

and state suggest, she says, a more complicated interaction (see Fraser, *Unruly*, 134). Anthony Giddens points out how Habermas's language of "systems" and their "steering mechanisms" does "scant justice" to "the active struggles of individuals and groups" (Anthony Giddens, "Reason," 119). I stress that I am using Habermas's framework heuristically, in terms of Fraser's "pragmatic-contextual" interpretation.

47. Habermas, *Lifeworld*, 325. Habermas has developed a four-sphere model of society in which the system is differentiated into an economic sphere (private, persons constructed as workers) and a state sphere (public, persons constructed as clients) while the lifeworld is differentiated into a domestic sphere (private, persons constructed as consumers) and a public sphere (public, persons constructed as citizens) (see Habermas, *Lifeworld*, 320 for a diagram of the model, and see discussion by Fraser, *Unruly*, 123–4).

48. Habermas, *Lifeworld*, 363.

49. Thomas Bender, *Community and Social Change in America* (New Brunswick, NJ: Rutgers University Press, 1978), 40.

50. Harvey, *Condition*, 137–40.

51. David Harvey notes that while the half-life of an average product was 5–7 years under older Fordist forms of capital production, under the new, postmodern, conditions of flexible accumulation, a product half-life is often 18 months. Harvey, *Condition*, 141–72.

52. Fredric Jameson sees postmodernism emerging in the sixties in response to the "institutionalization of the modern" by the late fifties. David Harvey discusses a "sea change" occurring in the global development of capitalism between 1968 and 1972, while Cornel West points to the monetary crisis of 1973, the start of the eclipse of the U.S. economy and military, as a significant transition. See Fredric Jameson, "Postmodernism or the Cultural Logic of Late Capitalism," *New Left Review* 146 (July–August 1984):56; Harvey, *Condition*, 38–9; and Cornel West, "Demystifying the New Black Conservatism," *Praxis International* 7/2 (July 1987):145.

53. Jameson, "Postmodernism," 78.

54. Harvey, *Condition*, 171.

55. Jameson sums up the postmodern as depthlessness, "a whole new culture of the image or the simulacrum; a consequent weakening of historicity, both in our relationship to public History and in the new forms of our private temporality ... the bewildering new world space of late multinational capital" (Jameson, "Postmodernism," 58).

56. Harvey, *Condition*, 344.

57. Harvey discusses the "restorations" of areas such as the Baltimore Harbor or the New York South Street Seaport as examples of the repackaging of history. The various constructed and planned Disneyworlds are ongoing

examples of the ways in which historical and cultural differences are commodified for profitable consumer consumption. Harvey, *Condition*, 66–98.

58. Harvey, *Condition*, 301. See Jameson's use of Lacan's notion of schizophrenia, Jameson, "Postmodernism," 71–2.

59. Habermas, *Lifeworld*, 395.

60. Habermas, *Lifeworld*, 386, 392; and Harvey, *Condition*, 238. It is important to emphasize here the broadest possible interpretation of Habermas's term "ways of life." It is easy to read him as speaking only about meaning at an abstract, nonsocial level (an interpretation aided by the overwhelmingly abstract—if not abstruse—character of his writing). Yet I would argue that, unlike some of the figures to be considered here, Habermas always seeks to ground the issue of meaning within a framework of the problems of advanced capitalism. The places where I find Habermas most vulnerable to the charge of mystifying abstraction arise in his positive project of communicatively-based action as the solution for/response to reification. These areas of his work seem to me to preserve a Kantian idealism that emphasizes an excessively sanitized form of meaning at the expense of the other dimensions of lived experience. Keane discusses the problem of the formalism of Habermas's theory of universal pragmatics and its privileging of abstract, consensual action (Keane, *Public Life*, 147–89). Giddens remarks that communicative rationality "is not enough to secure emancipation" (Giddens, "Reason," 131). As I have stressed, I attempt here to draw on Habermas's critical, rather than constructive contributions.

61. Habermas, *Lifeworld*, 327. Writing of the new social movements, David Harvey says, "the capacity of most social movements to command place [particular locality] better than space [geographic power] puts a strong emphasis upon the potential connection between place and social identity." Harvey, *Condition*, 302, additions mine.

62. Keane, *Public Life*, 88.

63. Anthony and Robbins, "Spiritual," 232.

64. Harvey, *Condition*, 48.

65. Manning Marable, "The Rhetoric of Racial Harmony," *Sojourners* (August–September 1990): 16.

66. Ruth Frankenberg, *White Women, Race Matters: The Social Construction of Whiteness* (Minneapolis: The University of Minnesota Press, 1993), 202–3.

67. Harvey, *Condition*, 192, 329–35. See also Barbara Ehrenreich, *Fear of Falling: The Inner Life of the Middle Class* (New York: Pantheon Books, 1989).

68. Habermas, *Lifeworld*, 395. Habermas specifies only communities of resistance / withdrawal while I am drawing equal attention to communities of resistance / transformation.

69. Although it is important to remember that almost any resistance movement can be incorporated into state capitalist culture. One example is rap music, which began as a protest by young ghetto males, and is now an accepted part of mainstream youth culture.

70. See Ehrenreich, *Falling*.

71. Stanley Aronowitz, "On Intellectuals," in *Intellectuals: Aesthetics, Politics, Academics*, ed. B. Robbins (Minneapolis: University of Minnesota Press, 1990), 13.

72. Barbara Ehrenreich writes, "The university is ... the core institution of the PMC—the employer of its intellectual elite and producer of the next generation of middle-class professional personnel" (Ehrenreich, *Falling*, 58).

73. Harvey, *Condition*, 160. In their article introducing the concept of the PMC, Barbara and John Ehrenreich discuss the ways in which universities in the 50s and 60s began to play a more direct role in the functioning of the state (Barbara Ehrenreich and John Ehrenreich, "The Professional-Managerial Class," in *Between Labor and Capital*, P. Walker [Boston: South End Press, 1979], 34–40). Following up on this work, Barbara Ehrenreich describes how by the 80s universities were the place for the production of "corporate cadres" (Ehrenreich, *Falling*, 199).

74. A subject who "is better equipped for the heightened alienation of capitalism's refined divisions of labor, more readily disciplined by a pandemic corporate state and more available to a broad nexus of ideological controls" (Rosemary Hennessy, *Materialist Feminism and the Politics of Discourse* [New York: Routledge, 1993], 9).

75. William Dean, *The Religious Critic in American Culture* (Albany: SUNY Press, 1994), xiv. Edward Farley describes a similar process in the theological education system in *Theologia: The Fragmentation and Unity of Theological Education* (Philadelphia: Fortress Press, 1983). This separation is less possible for female and black academics, revealing some of the impact of differing social locations.

76. Dorothy Bass, following Robert Handy, argues that while Protestantism was legally disestablished by 1833, it experienced a second disestablishment in the 1930s when the religious consensus was broadened to include Catholics and Jews. Dorothy Bass, "The American Religious Landscape: Relocating 'Mainline' Protestantism," unpub ms., 4. José Casanova, on the other hand, dates a second cultural disestablishment in the post-Civil War and Reconstruction era as higher educational institutions became secularized. The Scopes trial in the 1920s marked the disestablishment of evangelicals and fundamentals from the "mainline" Protestants and the complete disestablishment of Protestantism from

higher education and scholarship (José Casanova, *Public Religions in the Modern World* [Chicago: University of Chicago Press, 1994], 137–40). Philip Hammond sees the second disestablishment as the loss of Protestant dominance in civil society after World War II. Philip Hammond, *Religion and Personal Autonomy* (Columbia: the University of South Carolina Press, 1992).

77. As Leonard Sweet puts it, "there is general agreement that, from 1935 onward, Protestantism has been set upon by troublesome forces." Leonard Sweet, "The Modernization of Protestant Religion in America," in *Altered Landscapes: Christianity in America 1936–85*, ed. David Lotz (Grand Rapids: Eerdmans, 1989), 19.

78. Casanova, *Religions*, 144.

79. Bass, "Landscape," 12–13.

80. For a fascinating study of the implications of these changes in middle- to lower-class white families, see Judith Stacey, *Brave New Families: Stories of Domestic Upheaval in Late Twentieth Century America* (New York: Harper Collins/Basic Books, 1991).

81. Fox–Genovese, *Illusions*, 54.

82. Fox–Genovese, *Illusions*, 54.

83. Chandra Talpade Mohanty, "Feminist Encounters: Locating the Politics of Experience," *Copyright* 1 (1987): 38.

84. As Elizabeth V. Spelman puts it, "Have white women ever asked themselves to distinguish between being white and being a woman?" (Elizabeth V. Spelman, *Inessential Woman: Problems of Exclusion in Feminist Thought* [Boston: Beacon Press, 1988], 76).

85. Manning Marable, *How Capitalism Underdeveloped Black America* (Boston: South End Press, 1983), 67. For an account of the major role black women played in creating and maintaining these institutions, see Carol B. Stack, *All Our Kin: Strategies for Survival in a Black Community* (New York: Harper and Row, Publishers, 1974).

86. William Julius Wilson, "The Political Economy and Urban Racial Tensions," *The American Economist* 39/1 (Spring 1995): 8.

87. Marable, *Underdeveloped*, 64.

88. Cornel West, *Race Matters* (Boston: Beacon Press, 1993), 16, 15.

89. Here I am slightly rewriting Anthony's and Robbins's definition of a "civil religion sect" to encompass positions that are broader than sectarian (see Anthony and Robbins, "Spiritual," 235).

90. I am aware that Stanley Hauerwas's appeal to a Christian sectarian community against a sinful state might make him appear as an exception here. Yet, as I will show in the next chapter, his discussion of highly contested public issues and "the Christian position" on these issues suggests that his proclaimed sectarianism cannot avoid assumptions about civil society.

NOTES TO CHAPTER 3

1. Stephen Holmes, "The Permanent Structure of Antiliberal Thought," in *Liberalism and the Moral Life*, ed. N. Rosenblum (Cambridge, MA: Harvard University Press, 1989), 230.

2. Ernst Troeltsch, *The Social Teaching of the Christian Churches*, vol. 1, trans. O. Wyon (Chicago: University of Chicago Press, Phoenix Edition, 1981), 32.

3. Joseph Hough, "The Loss of Optimism as a Problem for Liberal Christian Faith," in *Liberal Protestantism: Realities and Possibilities*, ed. R. Michaelsen and W. Roof (New York: Pilgrim Press, 1986), 159.

4. Daniel Bell, *The Cultural Contradictions of Capitalism* (New York: Basic Books, Inc., 1976), 25.

5. Bell, *Cultural*, 170–1.

6. Bell, *Cultural*, 157–8. In his essay, "The Return of the Sacred?," Bell calls the changes "profanation" which he describes as: "1. The growth of the idea of a radical individualism ... 2. The crossover from religion to the expressive arts ... 3. The decline of the belief in Heaven and Hell, and the rise in fear of nothingness" (Daniel Bell, "The Return of the Sacred?" in *The Winding Passage: Essays and Sociological Journeys 1960–1980* [Cambridge, MA: ABT Books, 1980], 334–5).

7. Bell, *Cultural*, 155.

8. For example, Bell characterizes the modernist work of Virginia Woolf as representing "centrifugal aesthetic forces" released by the loss of a "unified cosmology" which no longer provides common symbols. Bell, *Cultural*, 86, 95.

9. Bell, *Cultural*, 245.

10. "A moral order," Bell writes, "has to transcend the parochialism of interests." Daniel Bell, "The End of Ideology Revisited (Part II)," *Government and Opposition* 23/3 (Summer 1988): 331.

11. Bell argues that knowledge (rather than labor) is the "axial principle" of post-industrial society. Thus, those with knowledge, that is the experts or the "Knowledge class" are those who should have the political decision-making power.

12. Bell has said that the general question of authority in our culture spreads from the changing role of women ("the oldest form of social authority").

13. Bell, *Cultural*, 252, 282.

14. Jürgen Habermas, "Modernity—An Incomplete Project" in *The Anti-Aesthetic: Essays on Postmodern Culture*, ed. H. Foster (Port Townsend, WA: Bay Press, 1983), 7.

15. Steinfels, *The Neo-Conservatives* (New York: Simon and Schuster, 1979), 180.

16. Christopher Lasch, *The World of Nations* (New York: Vintage Books, Random House, 1974), 27.

17. Christopher Lasch, *The Minimal Self* (New York: W. W. Norton and Co., Inc., 1984), 193.

18. Christopher Lasch, *The Culture of Narcissism* (New York: Warner Books, 1979), 393.

19. Christopher Lasch, "Popular Culture and the Illusion of Choice," *democracy* 2/2 (April 1982): 89.

20. Lasch, *Minimal*, 18, 254.

21. Christopher Lasch, *The True and Only Heaven: Progress and Its Critics* (New York: W. W. Norton and Co., 1991), 36.

22. Lasch sees a "weakening of the capacity for independent judgment, initiative, and self-discipline, on which democracy has always been understood to depend." Lasch, *Heaven*, 31.

23. Lasch, *Minimal*, 259. It is significant that all of Lasch's appropriation of Freud follows him in assuming the *male* as the model of psychological development.

24. Lasch, *Minimal*, 184.

25. Lasch, *Minimal*, 185.

26. Lasch, *Minimal*, 206.

27. Lasch, *Minimal*, 20; see also 258.

28. Lasch, *Heaven*, 15–6.

29. Lasch, *Heaven*, 530.

30. Lasch, *Heaven*, 487, 170.

31. Lasch, *Heaven*, 50.

32. Some of Lasch's earliest historical essays (in, for example, *The World of Nations*) discussed the dilemmas of early feminists caught between advocating entry into the world of men and defending the "superior" and special morality of women (a debate that has by no means ended). Lasch was extremely perceptive about how shifts in capitalism affected the terms in which this debate was conducted and notes that the new egalitarian model of the family has done little to strengthen the position of women and children in the world *outside* the family (Lasch, *Minimal*, 186). However in his later work Lasch states that women's desire for equality, realized in relation to the shifts in other institutions, "would undermine equally important [as women's equality] values associated with the family" and disregard "the needs of future generations." What is needed, he argues, is a redefinition of work "which becomes itself another aspect of nurture," so that women do not have to choose between their interests and those of their children. (Christopher Lasch, *Haven in a Heartless World: The Family Besieged* [New York: Basic Books, Inc., 1979], xvi). This is evidently not a choice that should trouble men. For a more sympathetic reading of Lasch, which promotes more egalitarian family models for the recovery of conscience, see Guyton B. Hammond, *Conscience and Its*

Recovery: From the Frankfurt School to Feminism (Charlottesville: University Press of Virginia, 1993).

33. Christopher Lasch, "The Communitarian Critique of Liberalism," *Soundings* 69/1–2 (Spring–Summer 1986): 67.

34. Lasch, *Heaven*, 50.

35. These works include: *Obligations: Essays in Disobedience, War, and Citizenship*; *The Revolution of the Saints*; *Just and Unjust Wars*; *Spheres of Justice*; *Exodus and Revolution*; *Interpretation and Social Criticism*; and *The Company of Critics*.

36. The duality of Walzer's purpose has put him on the list of both communitarian and liberal thinkers. Although Gilbert Meilaender has described this duality as contradictory, it is, on the contrary, central to Walzer's project (Gilbert Meilaender, "A View from Somewhere: The Political Thought of Michael Walzer," *Religious Studies Review* 16/3 [July 1990]: 199).

37. Michael Walzer, *Spheres of Justice: A Defense of Pluralism and Equality* (New York: Basic Books, Inc., 1983), 319.

38. Walzer, *Spheres*, 50n.

39. Michael Walzer, "The Communitarian Critique of Liberalism," *Political Theory* 18/1 (February 1990): 21.

40. Walzer, "Communitarian," 12.

41. Walzer, *Spheres*, 254.

42. Michael Walzer, *Interpretation and Social Criticism* (Cambridge, MA: Harvard University Press, 1987), 16.

43. Walzer, "Communitarian," 15.

44. Walzer, *Spheres*, 29.

45. Thus Walzer is subject to criticism from a liberal Augustinian like Meilaender for his refusal to accept the givenness of "the people given to me" and from a liberal feminist like Okin for acceptance of givenness which Okin sees as reproducing domination. Recently, he has sought to distinguish himself more clearly from communitarians, saying, for example, that "communitarianism … doesn't reach to our complexity" (Michael Walzer, *What It Means to be an American* [New York: Marsilio, 1992], 47).

46. *Spheres*, 62.

47. For example, all of the critics Walzer discusses in *The Company of Critics* are critics of their *nation* (Michael Walzer, *The Company of Critics: Social Criticism and Political Commitment in the Twentieth Century* [New York: Basic Books, Inc., 1988]).

48. Consequently, it is obvious why, in *Exodus*, Walzer stresses the Sinai interpretation of the covenant as representing the choice of the Jews, rather than the more authoritarian Abrahamic or Davidic account (Michael Walzer, *Exodus and Revolution* [New York: Basic Books, 1985], 79).

49. Walzer, "Communitarian," 15, 22.

50. Michael Walzer, *What Kind of a State is a Jewish State?*, The Shalom Hartman Institute, Center for Jewish Political Thought (New Jersey: Friends of SHI, 1989), 12.

51. Walzer, *American*, 8.

52. Walzer, "Communitarian," 16.

53. Walzer, *State*, 12; Walzer, *American*, 26.

54. Walzer, *Spheres*, 61.

55. Walzer, *Spheres*, 28.

56. Walzer, *Spheres*, 314.

57. Walzer, *Interpretation*, 22.

58. Walzer, *Spheres*, 10.

59. Walzer, *Spheres*, 320–1.

60. In his set of recommendations for a vital U.S. society, Walzer writes, "Don't shut the gates. This is not Europe; we are a society of immigrants … the flow of people, the material base of multiculturalism, should not be cut off" (Walzer, *American*, 17).

61. Walzer, *Company*, 112.

62. Walzer, *Spheres*, 320.

63. Walzer, *Spheres*, 232.

64. Walzer, *Spheres*, 240.

65. See, for example, works by Linda Nicholson, Michèle Barrett, Christine Delphy. See in particular Nancy Fraser's analysis of the division of spheres in the model of Jürgen Habermas which she argues serves to hide the place of gender so that the particular oppression of women simply disappears (Fraser, *Unruly*, 113–43).

66. Walzer, *State*, 18.

67. Walzer, *State*, 18, 20.

68. Walzer, *American*, 17.

69. Walzer, *American*, 46.

70. Walzer, *Exodus*, 142.

71. See, for example, Delores Williams's discussion of the androcentric bias of the Exodus "liberation tradition," in contrast with the womanist heritage of the "survival tradition" rooted in the story of Hagar (Delores Williams, *Sisters in the Wilderness: The Challenge of Womanist Godtalk* [Maryknoll: Orbis Books, 1993]). See also Robert Warrior's discussion of the impact of the Exodus story on Native Americans (Robert Warrior, "Canaanites and Conquerors," *Christianity and Crisis* 49/12 [September 11 1989]: 261–64). Walzer has, recently, discussed these problems, remarking that "the conquest of Canaan, with all its attendant slaughter, is the most problematic moment in the history of ancient Israel" and suggesting that "[h]oly community and holy war are related ideas" (Michael Walzer, "The Idea of Holy War in Ancient Israel," *Journal of Religious Ethics* 20/2 [Fall 1992]: 215, 225).

72. Susan Moller Okin, *Justice, Gender, and the Family* (New York: Basic Books, Inc., 1989), 62–8. Okin suggests the limitations of Walzer's perspective when she points out that of the eleven intellectuals chosen for *The Company of Critics*, only one, Simone de Beauvoir, is a woman. Okin does not point out the equally obvious fact that all of them are of white, Western origin. The issue again is which voices Walzer may assume are inside his community.

73. Michael Walzer, "A Critique of Philosophical Conversation," in *Hermeneutics and Critical Theory in Ethics and Politics*, ed. M. Kelly (Cambridge, MA: The MIT Press, 1990), 192.

74. Walzer, *Spheres*, 314.

75. And, as he also remarks, it "is a bit surprising ... how little is said about this principle [of respecting creations] which apparently is accorded universal validity" (Stephen White, "Justice and the Postmodern Problematic," *Praxis International* 7/3–4 [Winter 1987/8]:315, 313).

76. Seyla Benhabib, *Situating the Self: Gender, Community and Postmodernism in Contemporary Ethics* (New York: Routledge, 1992), 79.

77. Sheila Briggs, "The Politics of Identity and the Politics of Interpretation," *USQR* 43/1–4 (1989):178.

78. Richard Fox, "The Niebuhrs and the Liberal Protestant Heritage," in *Religion and Twentieth-Century American Intellectual Life*, ed. M. J. Lacey (New York: Woodrow Wilson International Center for Scholars and Cambridge University Press, 1991), 98.

79. Stanley Hauerwas, *After Christendom?* (Nashville: Abingdon Press, 1991), 25.

80. Reinhold Niebuhr, *Moral Man and Immoral Society* (New York: Charles Scribner's Sons, 1932), 19, 21.

81. Ernst Troeltsch, "The Dogmatics of the '*Religionsgeschichtliche Schule*'," *The American Journal of Theology* 17/1 (January 1913):12.

82. Ernst Troeltsch, *The Social Teaching of the Christian Churches*, Vol. 2, trans. O. Wyon (Chicago: University of Chicago Press, Phoenix Edition, 1981), 796.

83. Ernst Troeltsch, *Protestantism and Progress: The Significance of Protestantism for the Rise of Modern World* (Philadelphia: Fortress Press, 1986), 92.

84. Troeltsch, *Teaching*, vol. 2, 743. He also wrote of "the events of history leading us to God" that "without these sources of power and centers of concentration, personal piety would be impoverished and crippled, and the religious community would possess no center" (Troeltsch, "Dogmatics," 14–5).

85. Troeltsch, *Teaching*, vol. 1, 32.

86. Troeltsch, *Teaching*, vol. 2, 618.

87. Troeltsch, *Teaching*, vol. 2, 1010.

88. Troeltsch, "Dogmatics," 15, 16, 10. Underneath his proposal for a practical dogmatics lies some hints that he may have wondered whether the only

guarantee of harmony was a nondemocratic solution. He suggested frequently in his writings that force may be necessary to maintain a unified Christian culture and community. As he put it, "in the last resort no sociological cohesion can possibly exist permanently without some method of compulsion. This is a fact of life…" Troeltsch, *Teaching*, vol. 2, 492.

89. H. Richard Niebuhr, *The Social Sources of Denominationalism* (New York: Henry Holt and Co., 1929), 11.

90. Niebuhr, *The Meaning of Revelation* (New York: The Macmillan Co., 1960), 5, 112.

91. Niebuhr, *Meaning*, 78, 115.

92. Niebuhr, *Meaning*, 80; H. Richard Niebuhr, *The Responsible Self: An Essay in Christian Moral Philosophy* (New York: Harper and Row, Publishers, 1963), 123.

93. Niebuhr, *Responsible*, 94.

94. Benhabib, *Self*, 159. Benhabib's distinction between the "generalized" and the "concrete" other involves a slightly different definition of generalized other derived from the works of Rawls and Kohlberg, but the point of her criticism is still relevant.

95. Yoder remarks that Niebuhr measures each of the proposed positions in *Christ and Culture* "according to the *consistency* with which it responds to the entire realm of values called 'the world' or 'culture.'" See John Howard Yoder, "'Christ and Culture': A Critique of H. Richard Niebuhr," unpub. ms.

96. Darryl Trimiew, *Voices of the Silenced: The Responsible Self in a Marginalized Community* (Cleveland: Pilgrim Press, 1993), 4.

97. Trimiew, *Voices*, 90.

98. Reinhold Niebuhr, *The Nature and Destiny of Man: A Christian Interpretation; Volume Two: Human Destiny* (New York: Charles Scribner's Sons, 1943), 249, 257.

99. Ruth Smith, "Reinhold Niebuhr and History: The Elusive Liberal Critique," unpub. ms., 8.

100. Reinhold Niebuhr, *The Self and the Dramas of History* (New York: Charles Scribner's Sons, 1955), 37.

101. Niebuhr, *Destiny*, 308.

102. Niebuhr, *Destiny*, 93.

103. Reinhold Niebuhr, *An Interpretation of Christian Ethics* (New York: The Seabury Press, 1979), 100.

104. Philip E. Hammond, "The Extravasation of the Sacred and the Crisis in Liberal Protestantism," in *Liberal Protestantism*, eds. R. Michaelsen and W. Roof, 58.

105. Neuhaus has written of the events and experiences "that made it increasingly problematic to call myself simply a liberal." These include coming

147

to believe that the War on Poverty would only result in the "corruption and degradation of the poor," reaction to the rise of "black power" and "the fashionable angers of separatism, victimization and ideological resentment" (particularly present, Neuhaus likes to emphasize, in the women's movement), reaction to the pro-choice movement and disillusionment with the results of U.S. withdrawal from Vietnam. These developments have linked him to the company of capitalist-affirming neoconservatives such as Michael Novak, and, most recently, have steered him out of the Evangelical Lutheran Church in America and into the Catholic Church. See Richard Neuhaus, "Religion and Public Life: The Continuing Conversation," *The Christian Century* 107/21 (July 11–18 1990):669 ff.

106. Neuhaus, "Religion and Public," 669.

107. Neuhaus himself does not label this change as a turn to neoconservatism, but to "conservative liberalism" (Neuhaus, "Religion and Public," 669). This strikes me as a spurious distinction as most neo-conservatives are, like Neuhaus, former liberals who focus on what they perceive as the disintegration of morality and culture and who tacitly assume the system of laissez-faire capitalism.

108. Neuhaus, "Religion and Public," 671.

109. Richard J. Neuhaus, *The Naked Public Square: Religion and Democracy in America* (Grand Rapids, MI: William B. Eerdmans Publishing Company, 1984), vii.

110. Neuhaus, *Naked*, 154.

111. Neuhaus, *Naked*, 74–5.

112. Neuhaus, *Naked*, 138.

113. The source of disorder, in fact, is the professional liberal culture producers or "the New Class"—that is, the very Professional-Managerial class to which Neuhaus himself belongs. The fingering of a "New Class" which mysteriously does not include themselves has been a typical strategy of neoconservative intellectuals.

114. "Sacred canopy" is a term of Peter Berger's which Neuhaus appropriates.

115. The only difference which Neuhaus takes seriously is Judaism. He frequently warns the church about the legacy of anti-semitism.

116. Neuhaus, *Naked*, 260, 123.

117. Neuhaus, *Naked*, 63.

118. Neuhaus, *Naked*, 144.

119. Richard J. Neuhaus, *America Against Itself: Moral Vision and the Public Order* (Notre Dame, IN: University of Notre Dame Press, 1992), 174.

120. Neuhaus, *Naked*, 84, 111, 76.

121. Disagreement arises only when persons smuggle in "political," non-Christian positions.

122. In other words, Neuhaus has joined the conservative, anti-modern wing of the Catholic church.

123. Stanley M. Hauerwas, *Christian Existence Today: Essays on Church, World and Living In Between* (Durham, N.C.: The Labyrinth Press, 1988), 2.

124. Stanley Hauerwas, *A Community of Character: Toward a Constructive Christian Social Ethic* (Notre Dame, IN: University of Notre Dame Press, 1981), 78.

125. Hauerwas, *Community*, 61.

126. Hauerwas, *Community*, 60. Hauerwas's implicit reference here is to a Hobbesian idea that the coercive power of the state is necessary to restrain the innate conflict of human beings. In this view, authority is an unavoidable externally-imposed force.

127. Hauerwas, *Existence*, 29.

128. Stanley Hauerwas, *The Peaceable Kingdom* (Notre Dame, IN: The University of Notre Dame Press, 1983), 15.

129. Hauerwas, *Christendom*, 27.

130. Hauerwas, *Community*, 110.

131. Hauerwas, *Christendom*, 48.

132. Hauerwas, *Christendom*, 70.

133. In his early work Hauerwas affirmed the traditional family. However, in his more recent writings, he makes a stronger distinction between church community and family, remarking on the necessity of an "eschatological ambivalence" towards the family which means that "the first enemy of the family is the church" (Hauerwas, *Christendom*, 128, 127). Indeed, he says, both liberalism and the church are "at war against the family," that is, attacking the power of familial ties. Yet, while the liberal polity seeks to make family ties voluntary, the church seeks to assert the priority of community in shaping personal relations. Thus, "we do not love because we are married, but because we are Christians" (Hauerwas, *Christendom*, 127). These Christian relationships are the necessary foundation for non-hierarchical sexual and familial relations because God's kingdom "challenges the forms of domination that we exercise over others that we all too willingly accept in the name of 'relationships'"(*Christendom*, 131).

134. Stanley Hauerwas, *Dispatches from the Front: Theological Engagements with the Secular* (Durham: Duke University Press, 1994), 8.

135. *Dispatches*, 173.

136. Hauerwas, *Dispatches*, 104–5.

137. Hauerwas, *Kingdom*, 103.

138. Hauerwas, *Kingdom*, 46.

139. Hauerwas, *Community*, 85.

140. Hauerwas, *Christendom*, 91, 108; Hauerwas, *Community*, 30.

141. *Community*, 222

142. *Christendom,* 127

143. *Community,* 252; *Existence,* 37, 38; *Kingdom,* 100.

144. At the end of *After Christendom?*, Hauerwas struggles again with these questions, engaging with T. Todorov's statement, "is there not already a violence in the conviction that one possesses the truth oneself, whereas this is not the case for others, and that one must therefore impose that truth on those others." He responds, "We recoil at this suggestion. If it is true, it seems we are simply silenced ... it seems to imply the very histories that we teach our children as Christians ... are narratives that continue to legitimate the coercive imposition of Christianity." While posing the challenge, reaffirmed in a letter about Christian violence towards native Americans printed in an appendix, Hauerwas cannot really answer it. In his text, he turns again to the inherent violence in Enlightenment assumptions about universality and objectivity and counterposes the Christian activity of embodying the "counterstory" through "witness." The assumption is that the Christian community *only* participates in domination when assimilated to the previously dominant liberal paradigm. Hauerwas, *Christendom,* 140.

145. Gloria H. Albrecht, "Myself and Other Characters: A Feminist Liberationist Critique of Hauerwas's Ethics of Christian Character," *The Annual of the Society of Christian Ethics* (1992): 111.

146. Michael Dyson, *Reflecting Black: African-American Cultural Criticism* (Minneapolis: University of Minnesota Press, 1993), 287.

147. I imagine that Hauerwas sees the reconstructed liberal Protestant church as continuing some of its social involvements, but in relation to the "Jesus story," rather than the "liberal story." But since he is so opaque about what these involvements might be, this is only an hypothesis.

148. Larry Rasmussen, *Moral Fragments and Moral Community: A Proposal for Church in Society* (Minneapolis: Fortress Press, 1993), 38, 11.

149. Rasmussen, *Fragments,* 38.

150. Rasmussen, *Fragments,* 11.

151. Rasmussen, *Fragments,* 72.

152. Rasmussen, *Fragments,* 48.

153. Rasmussen, *Fragments,* 65.

154. Rasmussen, *Fragments,* 70.

155. Rasmussen, *Fragments,* 154.

156. Rasmussen, *Fragments,* 62, 120–1. Rasmussen is drawing on Philip Selznick, *The Moral Commonwealth: Social Theory and the Promise of Community* (Berkeley: University of California Press, 1992).

157. Rasmussen, *Fragments,* 107.

158. Rasmussen, *Fragments,* 146.

159. Rasmussen, *Fragments,* 86.

160. Rasmussen, *Fragments*, 109.

161. Rasmussen, *Fragments*, 152.

162. Rasmussen, *Fragments*, 169.

163. Rasmussen, *Fragments*, 17.

164. Rasmussen, *Fragments*, 18.

165. Rasmussen, *Fragments*, 148, 149.

NOTES TO CHAPTER 4

1. Marilyn Friedman, "Community and Modern Friendship," in *Feminist Ethics*, ed. E. Cole and S. Coultrap-McQuin (Bloomington: Indiana University Press, 1992), 95.

2. Jean Bethke Elshtain, *Power Trips and Other Journeys: Essays in Feminism as Civic Discourse* (Madison: University of Wisconsin, 1990),144.

3. "As women" in this discussion means as white women. The point of this chapter is not to discuss the ways communitarian issues involve *women* but the ways they involve *white middle-class women*. Only with this specificity can I avoid the essentialism and exclusion criticized by Elizabeth Spelman in *Inessential Woman: Problems of Exclusion in Feminist Thought* (Boston: Beacon Press, 1988).

4. Sharon Welch, *Communities of Resistance and Solidarity: A Feminist Theology of Liberation* (Maryknoll, NY: Orbis Books, 1985), ix. Welch is one example of the many white feminists who are struggling to express the moral and political ambiguities of this status. See, for example, the rich autobiographical account by Minnie Bruce Pratt in E. Bulkin et al., *Yours in Struggle* (Brooklyn: Long Haul Press, 1984), 9–64. Theoretical discussions can be found in Spelman, *Inessential Woman*; and, Susan B. Thistlethwaite, *Sex, Race, and God: Christian Feminism in Black and White* (New York: Crossroad, 1989).

5. Mary Daly, *Gyn/Ecology: The Metaethics of Radical Feminism* (Boston: Beacon Press, 1978), 390; and, Sarah Lucia Hoagland, *Lesbian Ethics* (Palo Alto: Institute of Lesbian Study, 1988). A tradition of separate community runs from Daly's radical feminism to Hoagland's lesbian feminism and connected cultural feminist movements. For discussion of radical feminism, see Alison Jaggar, *Feminist Politics and Human Nature* (Totowa, NJ: Rowman and Allanheld, Publishers, 1983); for cultural feminism, see Linda Alcoff's critical account, "Cultural Feminism versus Post-Structuralism: The Identity Crisis in Feminist Theory," *Signs* 13/3 (1988):402–36.

6. A good summary of these criticisms can be found in Elizabeth Frazer and Nicola Lacey, *The Politics of Community: A Feminist Critique of the Liberal-Communitarian Debate* (Toronto: University of Toronto Press, 1993), 41–100.

7. Friedman, "Community and Modern Friendship," 89.

151

8. Elizabeth Fox-Genovese, *Feminism without Illusions: A Critique of Individualism* (Chapel Hill: University of North Carolina Press, 1991), 45.

9. Carole Pateman, *The Disorder of Women* (Stanford, CA: Stanford University Press, 1989), 20.

10. Ruth Smith argues that liberal theory constructed white, bourgeois women and the private sphere as either a threat to morality or naturally moral. See Ruth Smith, "Moral Transcendence and Moral Space in the Historical Experience of Women," *Journal of Feminist Studies in Religion* 4/2 (Fall 1988):21–37; and, "Relationality and the Ordering of Difference in Feminist Ethics" *Journal of Feminist Studies in Religion* 9/1–2 (Spring/Fall 1993): 199–214.

11. Fox-Genovese, *Illusions*, 37.

12. As Fox-Genovese puts it, "The logic of individualism offered no grounds for excluding women from its benefits, but in practice the subordination of women anchored individualism." There was an "unacknowledged recognition that pure individualism could not anchor social cohesion, much less foster nonmarket values" (Fox-Genovese, *Illusions*, 130).

13. Fox-Genovese, *Illusions*, 11, 45.

14. See Nancy Fraser's discussion of the complex ways women are constructed as clients within the welfare state (Nancy Fraser, *Unruly Practices* [Minneapolis: University of Minnesota Press, 1989], 144–60).

15. Nora's famous self-description at the end of Ibsen's play, *A Doll's House* (Henrik Ibsen, *Four Major Plays*, Vol. 1, rev. ed., trans. R. Fjelde [New York: Signet Classics, Penguin Books, 1992], 109).

16. For discussion of some of these issues, see Patricia Hill Collins, *Black Feminist Thought* (London: Harper Collins, 1991); Bonnie Thornton Dill, "Our Mothers' Grief," *Journal of Family History* 13 (1988):415–31; Carol B. Stack, *All Our Kin: Strategies for Survival in a Black Community* (New York: Harper and Row, Publishers/Harper Torchbooks, 1974); Jane Humphries, "The Working Class Family, Women's Liberation and Class Struggle: The Case of Nineteenth Century British History," *Review of Radical Political Economics* 9/3 (1977):25–41; Ruth Smith and Deborah Valenze, "Mutuality and Marginality: Liberal Moral Theory and Working-Class Women in Nineteenth-Century England," *Signs* 13/2 (Winter 1988):277–98; and, Susan Estabrook Kennedy, *If All We Did Was to Weep at Home: A History of White Working-Class Women in America* (Bloomington: Indiana University Press, 1979).

17. Spelman, *Inessential Woman*, 139.

18. One communitarian forum where she is particularly visible is her participation as editor in *The Responsive Community*, a journal and institute run by Amitai Etzioni, that claims to represent the "communitarian movement" which seeks a new path, neither liberal nor conservative, balancing

rights and responsibilities in relation to the common good. The circle around *The Responsive Community* attained new political visibility with the Clinton Administration, since the vice president, Al Gore, has, on occasion, participated in some of their events and an editor, William Galston, has been a policy advisor.

19. Jean Bethke Elshtain, "The Liberal Captivity of Feminism: A Critical Appraisal of (Some) Feminist Answers," in *The Liberal Future in America: Essays in Renewal*, ed. P. Abbott and M. B. Levy (Westport, CT: Greenwood Press, 1985), 65.

20. Elshtain, *Trips*, 92–3.

21. Jean Bethke Elshtain, *Democracy on Trial* (New York: Basic Books, 1995), 41.

22. Elshtain, *Trips*, 48, 120.

23. Elshtain, *Trips*, 53.

24. Elshtain, *Trips*, 143.

25. Elshtain, *Democracy*, 38.

26. Elshtain, *Democracy*, 44.

27. Jean Bethke Elshtain, "Feminism, Family, and Community," *Dissent* (Fall 1982): 444.

28. Elshtain, "Captivity," 77.

29. Elshtain, *Trips*, 48.

30. Elshtain, *Trips*, 49.

31. Elshtain, *Trips*, 54.

32. Elshtain, *Trips*, 48, 58, 79.

33. "Modern parental authority is shared by mother and father…" (Elshtain, *Trips*, 54). In marriage, she says, men and women are to be equals and helpmates.

34. Elshtain, "Feminism, Family, and Community," 448.

35. Jean Bethke Elshtain, "Antigone's Daughters," *Democracy* (April 1982):47.

36. Elshtain, *Trips*, 141.

37. Elshtain, "Captivity," 71; and Elshtain, "Daughters," 49.

38. Elshtain, "Daughters," 46.

39. Elshtain, *Trips*, 138.

40. Elshtain, *Trips*, 104. Two key examples of state power are, for Elshtain, wage issues and day care. She argues that the focus of debate should not be equal opportunities and pay (although she does not discount these demands), but a family wage which would allow proper care for children. Similarly, women should not be demanding day care, because, again, children would be harmed, this time by state control of their nurture. Elshtain says that the family wage should be open to men and women, but her position has some important ambiguities. If women are the ones with the socialized nurturing capacities, are they not likely to be the ones staying at home? Elshtain

might respond that the issue is to revalue these capacities so that they would be qualities valued in both men and women. But if women are not supposed to be participating in the "hard-nosed" discussions of power, how are these changes to be brought about? By their superior moral influence?

41. Elshtain, *Trips*, 144.

42. Elshtain, "Daughters," 59; Jean Bethke Elshtain, "On Feminism, Family, and Community—A Response to Barbara Ehrenreich," *Dissent* (Winter 1983):108.

43. Elshtain, *Democracy*, 53.

44. Interestingly, Elshtain sounds here quite similar to Daniel Bell. As with Bell, no specific groups are named, nor are their platforms detailed. Radical feminists have left women with a "perfervid ideology of victimization," while gay activists have "flaunt[ed] [their] most intimate self," "breaching the boundary of shame."

45. Elshtain, *Democracy*, 47, 32.

46. Elshtain, *Democracy*, 67.

47. Elshtain, *Trips*, 79, 136.

48. Elshtain, "Captivity," 75.

49. Elshtain, *Democracy*, 38.

50. Mary Dietz, "Citizenship with a Feminist Face: The Problems with Maternal Thinking," *Political Theory* 13/1 (February 1985):25.

51. Lisa Sowle Cahill, *Women and Sexuality* (New York: Paulist Press, 1992), 1–2.

52. Lisa Sowle Cahill, *Between the Sexes: Foundations for a Christian Ethics of Sexuality* (Philadelphia and New York: Fortress Press and Paulist Press, 1985), 140.

53. Cahill, *Sexes*, 141.

54. Cahill criticizes John Courtney Murray and Jacques Maritain on this point in "The Catholic Tradition: Religion, Morality, and the Common Good," *The Journal of Law and Religion* 5 (1987):84.

55. Lisa Sowle Cahill, "Notes on Moral Theology: 1989, Feminist Ethics," *Theological Studies* 51 (1990):57–8.

56. Cahill, *Women*, 54.

57. Lisa Sowle Cahill, "Is Catholic Ethics Biblical? The Example of Sex and Gender," Warren Lecture Series in Catholic Studies, no. 20, Public Lecture, the University of Tulsa, March 15, 1992, 14.

58. Cahill, *Sexes*, 150.

59. Cahill, "Biblical," 14.

60. Cahill, *Women*, 45.

61. See Cahill, *Sexes*, 26–30.

62. Cahill avoids in general language of conflict, preferring to discuss perspectives that are in tension, but which always prove, in the end, to be complementary.

63. Cahill, *Sexes*, 148.

64. Iris Marion Young, "Beyond the Unhappy Marriage: A Critique of Dual Systems Theory," in *Women and Revolution*, ed. L. Sargent (Boston: South End Press, 1981), 43–70.

65. Iris Marion Young, *Throwing Like a Girl and Other Essays in Feminist Philosophy and Social Theory* (Bloomington: Indiana University Press, 1990), 5.

66. As Young discusses, the work of John Rawls is a preeminent example. Although there is much value in Rawls's efforts to justify the least possible inequalities in distribution, there is no place in his method that permits critique of the institutional structures actually producing, distributing, and consuming goods. See Iris Marion Young, *Justice and the Politics of Difference* (Princeton, NJ: Princeton University Press, 1990), 16–21. See also John Rawls, *A Theory of Justice* (Cambridge: Harvard University Press, 1971).

67. Young, *Justice*, 35. Nancy Fraser has described Young's theory of justice as "bifocal," seeking to combine a socialist interest in exploitation with a cultural emphasis on identity and recognition. Nancy Fraser, "Debate: Recognition or Redistribution? A Critical Reading of Iris Young's Justice and the Politics of Difference," *The Journal of Political Philosophy* 3/2 (1995): 166–80.

68. Young, *Justice*, 73.

69. Young, *Justice*, 72.

70. Young, *Throwing*, 98–9.

71. Young, *Justice*, 97.

72. Young, *Justice*, 98–105. Young points to Rousseau and Hegel as the main sources for this theory.

73. Young, *Justice*, 112.

74. Young, *Throwing*, 101.

75. Iris Marion Young, "Mothers, Citizenship, and Independence: A Critique of Pure Family Values," *Ethics* 105 (April 1995): 549.

76. Young discusses these issues in *Justice*, 114–5. I have slightly expanded the implications of her discussion.

77. Iris Marion Young, "The Ideal of Community and the Politics of Difference," in *Feminism/Postmodernism*, ed. L. Nicholson (New York: Routledge, 1990), 307.

78. There is, says Young, "an element of opacity of the other, whom we will never fully know" (Young, "Community," 313).

79. Young, *Justice*, 234.

80. "[A] group," Young writes, "exists only in relation to at least one other group." Young, *Justice*, 43.

81. Young, *Justice*, 46.

82. Young, *Justice*, 46–7, 172.

83. Young, *Throwing*, 128.

84. This is also Chantal Mouffe's conclusion; however, she criticizes Young from an even deeper deconstructionist perspective. See Chantal Mouffe, "Feminism, Citizenship, and Radical Democratic Politics," in *Feminists Theorize the Political*, ed. J. Butler and J. Scott (New York: Routledge, 1992), 369–82.

85. Nancy Fraser, "Debate," 180.

86. Young defines the public as what is open and accessible (at all levels, including linguistic-cultural) and the private in liberal terms as "that aspect of his or her life and activity that any individual has a right to exclude others from" (Young, *Throwing*, 108).

87. Welch, *Communities*, ix. It is interesting that Welch, an academic, never names the academy as a community.

88. Welch, *Communities*, 13.

89. Welch, *Communities*, 87.

90. Welch, *Communities*, 45.

91. Welch, *Communities*, 66.

92. Fraser, *Unruly*, 53. See also Nancy Hartsock, "Postmodernism and Political Change: Issues for Feminist Theory," *Cultural Critique* (Winter 1989–90):22. As Linda Alcoff puts it, the result of feminist theory following Foucault is a wholly negative feminism with no project of social transformation (Alcoff, "Cultural Feminism versus Post-Structuralism," 418). Welch's skepticism towards post-structuralism is shown in her article, "Sporting Power: American Feminism, French Feminisms, and an Ethic of Conflict," in which she criticizes the nonmaterial (if not elitist) sense of representation found in the works of Irigaray and Cixous (Sharon Welch, "Sporting Power: American Feminism, French Feminism, and an Ethic of Conflict," in *Transfigurations: Theology and French Feminists*, ed. M. Kim, et. al. [Minneapolis: Fortress Press, 1993], 193–7).

93. Most recently, Welch has named pragmatism as a matrix, remarking that the debate over foundations is "irrelevant." Sharon Welch, "'Dreams of the Good': From the Analytics of Oppression to the Politics of Transformation," in *New Visions for the Americas: Religious Engagement and Social Transformation*, ed. David Batstone (Minneapolis: Augsburg Fortress Press, 1993), 184–8.

94. Sharon Welch, *A Feminist Ethic of Risk* (Minneapolis: Fortress Press, 1990), 37.

95. Welch, *Risk*, 21.

96. Welch, *Risk*, 6.

97. Welch, *Risk*, 124.

98. Welch, *Risk*, 133.

99. Welch, "Sporting," 181.

100. Welch, "Dreams," 188.
101. Welch, *Risk*, 140.
102. Welch, "Dreams," 188.

NOTES TO CHAPTER 5

1. Vincent Harding, *There Is a River: The Black Struggle for Freedom in America* (San Diego: Harvest/HBJ Book, Harcourt Brace Jovanovich Publishers, 1981/92), xxv.

2. Delores Williams, *Sisters in the Wilderness* (Maryknoll: Orbis Books, 1993), xi.

3. Vincent Harding, "Toward a Darkly Radiant Vision of America's Truth," *Cross Currents* 37/1 (Spring 1987): 13.

4. W.E.B. DuBois, *The Souls of Black Folk* (Greenwich, CT: Fawcett Publications, Inc., 1961), 16–17.

5. See above, p. 53.

6. African-American scholars differ over the relative roles of these two streams of tradition. For example, Cheryl Townsend Gilkes stresses the Afrocentric heritage of the black community (Cheryl Townsend Gilkes, "'Mother to the Motherless, Father to the Fatherless': Power, Gender, and Community in an Afrocentric Biblical Tradition," *Semeia* 47 [1989]: 57–85), while Delores Williams emphasizes the creativity of the American slave experience of wilderness and survival (Williams, *Sisters*, 192).

7. Quoted in Harding, *River*, 326–7.

8. Patricia Hill Collins, *Black Feminist Thought: Knowledge, Consciousness, and the Politics of Empowerment* (London: Harper Collins Academic, 1990), 52.

9. Manning Marable defines a racist social order as comprising: 1) white expropriation of the surplus value of black workers; 2) systemic physical isolation, exclusion and (often) extermination; 3) the ideological hegemony of white racism; 4) close relations between black people and the coercive apparatus of the state; 5) the dominant definition of "blackness" always in relation to "whiteness"; 6) an emphasis on the sexual "threat" of blacks. Manning Marable, *Blackwater: Historical Studies in Race, Class Consciousness, and Revolution* (Dayton: Black Praxis Press, 1981), 73–5.

10. Collins, *Black Feminist*, 53.

11. Cornel West, *Race Matters* (Boston: Beacon Press, 1993), 15.

12. Manning Marable, "The Rhetoric of Racial Harmony," *Sojourners* (August–September 1990), 17.

13. Bell hooks, *Yearning: Race, Gender, and Cultural Politics* (Boston: South End Press, 1990), 34, 35.

14. Probably the best recreations of this world can be found in the work of black women novelists such as Zora Neale Hurston, Alice Walker, and Toni Morrison.

15. Michael Dyson, *Making Malcolm: The Myth and Meaning of Malcolm X* (New York: Oxford University Press, 1995), 36.

16. Katie Cannon, *Black Womanist Ethics* (Atlanta: Scholars Press, 1988), 19.

17. Marable, *Blackwater*, 40.

18. Michael Dyson, *Reflecting Black: African-American Cultural Criticism* (Minneapolis: University of Minnesota Press, 1993), 365.

19. See, for example, Frederick Douglass, "The Present and Future of the Colored Race in America" (1863), in *Negro Social and Political Thought, 1850–1920*, ed. H. Brotz (New York: Basic Books, 1966), 37–101.

20. James Cone, *Malcolm and Martin and America: A Dream or Nightmare?* (Maryknoll, NY: Orbis Press, 1991), 21.

21. Cone, *Malcolm and Martin*, 149.

22. Cone, *Malcolm and Martin*, 16.

23. Manning Marable, *Black American Politics: From the Washington Marches to Jesse Jackson* (London: Verso, 1985), 66.

24. Dyson, *Reflecting*, 223.

25. Harding, *River*, xxiv.

26. Martin Luther King, Jr., "I Have a Dream," in *A Testament of Hope: the Essential Writings of Martin Luther King, Jr.*, ed. J. Washington (San Francisco: Harper and Row, Publishers, 1986), 220.

27. Martin Luther King, Jr., "The Ethical Demand for Integration," in *Testament*, ed. Washington, 122.

28. King, "Ethical," 122.

29. Thus, in "Letter from Birmingham City Jail," King criticizes the white churches for "standing as a taillight ... rather than as a headlight leading men to higher levels of justice." Martin Luther King, Jr., "Letter from Birmingham City Jail," in *Testament*, ed. Washington, 299.

30. Dyson, *Malcolm*, 103.

31. From a sermon by Martin Luther King, Jr., cited in Cone, *Malcolm and Martin*, 127.

32. Martin Luther King, Jr., *The Strength to Love*, excerpted in *Testament*, ed. Washington, 507.

33. Cornel West, *Prophesy Deliverance! An Afro-American Revolutionary Christianity* (Philadelphia: Westminster Press, 1982), 74–5.

34. Cornel West, *Prophetic Fragments* (Grand Rapids, MI: William B. Eerdmans Publishing Co., 1988), 11.

35. Dyson, *Reflecting*, 233.

36. Quoted in Cone, *Malcolm and Martin*, 1.

37. Quoted in Cone, *Malcolm and Martin*, 110. Emphasis in text.

38. Malcolm X, *By Any Means Necessary* (New York: Pathfinder, 1970), 53, 54.

39. Malcolm X, *The End of World Supremacy: Four Speeches*, ed. and intro. B. Karim (New York: Arcade Publishing/ Little, Brown and Company, 1971), 91.

40. Malcolm X, *By Any Means*, 159, 160.

41. Cone, *Malcolm and Martin*, 244–71.

42. As quoted in Cone, *Malcolm and Martin*, 256.

43. West, *Matters*, 35.

44. Marable, "Rhetoric," 14.

45. William Julius Wilson notes that the suburbs now contain nearly half of the nation's population. William Julius Wilson, "The Political Economy and Urban Racial Tensions, *The American Economist* 39/1 (Spring 1995): 3.

46. This term has developed complex ideological ramifications, to the point that Wilson himself has said that he is no longer sure he wishes to use it. William Julius Wilson, "Studying Inner-City Dislocation: The Challenge of Public Agenda Research," *American Sociological Review* 56 (February 1991): 1–14.

47. King, "A Testament of Hope," in *Testament*, ed. Washington, 318.

48. An artistic rendition of this struggle can be found in one of the "portraits" in George C. Wolfe's play, *The Colored Museum*, where a middle-class black man tries, unsuccessfully, to kill symbolically his black self by throwing out all his black cultural objects.

49. Frank M. Kirkland, "Social Policy, Ethical Life, and the Urban Underclass," in *The Underclass Question*, ed. Bill E. Lawson (Philadelphia: Temple University Press, 1992), 161.

50. Wilson's study of urban Chicago shows that "57 percent of Chicago's employed inner-city black fathers (aged 15 and over and without bachelor degrees) who were born between 1950 and 1955 worked in manufacturing industries in 1974. By 1987 that figure fell to 27 percent." Wilson, "Racial Tensions," 8.

51. Dyson, *Reflecting*, 184.

52. Shown, for example, by the growth in high school drop outs in urban black communities.

53. Manning Marable writes that "the Civil Rights movement and desegregation permitted the white private sector to develop a variety of advertising strategies to extract billions in profits and Black consumers, all in the name of 'equality.' The net result was the increased marginalization of the Black entrepreneur, the manipulation of Black culture and social habits by white corporations, and a new kind of economic underdevelopment for all Blacks at all income levels." Manning Marable, *How Capitalism Underdeveloped Black America* (Boston: South End Press, 1983), 164.

54. Kirkland, "Social Policy," 161.

55. West, *Matters*, 5.

56. Cornel West, "Philosophy and the Urban Underclass," in *Underclass*, ed. Lawson, 195.

57. Quoted in Glenn C. Loury, *One by One from the Inside Out: Essays and Reviews on Race and Responsibility in America* (New York: The Free Press, 1995), 266.

58. Dyson, *Reflecting*, 152.

59. Dyson, *Malcolm*, 153.

60. Loury has, however, recently resigned from the AEI in protest over the work of another member, Dinesh d'Souza. D'Souza's book, *The End of Racism*, argues that slavery was not a racist institution and that the current problems of poor blacks are due to intellectual inadequacy.

61. Loury, *One by One*, 63.

62. Loury, *One by One*, 63.

63. Loury, *One by One*, 64.

64. Loury, *One by One*, 13.

65. Loury, *One by One*, 72.

66. Glenn C. Loury, "The Moral Quandary of the Black Community," *The Public Interest* 79 (Spring 1985): 10.

67. Loury, *One by One*, 77.

68. West, *Matters*, 50.

69. Loury, "Quandary," 22.

70. Loury, *One by One*, 21.

71. Loury, *One by One*, 29.

72. Loury, *One by One*, 80, 81.

73. See West, *Matters*, 56.

74. West, *Fragments*, 35.

75. West, *Matters*, 16.

76. Bell hooks and Cornel West, *Breaking Bread: Insurgent Black Intellectual Life* (Boston: South End Press, 1991), 97.

77. West, *Matters*, 16.

78. Hooks and West, *Breaking*, 10.

79. Hooks and West, *Breaking*, 95.

80. Hooks and West, *Breaking*, 15.

81. Hooks, *Yearning*, 40, 147.

82. West, *Matters*, 6.

83. Hooks and West, *Breaking*, 102.

84. Hooks, *Yearning*, 35, 40.

85. Gilkes, "Motherless," 75.

86. Cheryl Townsend Gilkes, "From Slavery to Social Welfare: Racism and the Control of Black Women," in *Class, Race, and Sex: The Dynamics of Control*, eds. H. Lessinger and A. Swerdlow (New York: G.K. Hall, Publishers, 1983), 290–1.

87. Collins, *Black Feminist*, 151.

88. Manning Marable cites statistics to show that in 1930, 39% of black women worked outside the home, in contrast to 20% of white women (Marable, *Underdeveloped*, 81).

89. Cheryl Townsend Gilkes, "The Roles of Church and Community Mothers:

Ambivalent American Sexism or Fragmented African Familyhood?" *Journal of Feminist Studies in Religion* 2/2 (Fall 1986): 48.

90. From an 1895 agenda of the National Federation of African American Women, quoted in Emilie M. Townes, *In a Blaze of Glory: Womanist Spirituality as Social Witness* (Nashville: Abingdon Press, 1995), 40.

91. Hooks, *Yearning*, 42.

92. Townes, *Blaze*, 37.

93. Williams, *Sisters*, x.

94. Williams, *Sisters*, 240 n.6.

95. Williams, *Sisters*, 50.

96. Williams, *Sisters*, 116.

97. Williams, *Sisters*, 160–1.

98. Williams, *Sisters*, 209–10.

99. Williams, *Sisters*, 205.

100. Williams, *Sisters*, 235.

101. Townes, *Blaze*, 66.

102. Townes, *Blaze*, 142.

103. Townes, *Blaze*, 66, 49.

104. Townes, *Blaze*, 85.

105. Townes, *Blaze*, 118, 86.

106. Williams, *Sisters*, 211.

107. Townes, *Blaze*, 66.

NOTES TO CHAPTER 6

1. Bell hooks, *Yearning: Race, Gender, and Cultural Politics* (Boston: South End Press, 1990), 27.

2. Elizabeth Frazer and Nicola Lacey, *The Politics of Community: A Feminist Critique of the Liberal-Communitarian Debate* (Toronto: University of Toronto Press, 1993), 135.

3. Eric Hobsbawm writes that the invention of tradition occurs "more frequently when a rapid transformation of society weakens or destroys the social patterns for which 'old' traditions had been designed, producing new ones for which they were not applicable, or when such old traditions and their institutional carriers and promulgators no longer prove sufficiently adaptable and flexible, or are otherwise eliminated..." ("Introduction: Inventing Traditions," in *The Invention of Tradition*, ed. E. Hobsbawm and T. Ranger [Cambridge: Cambridge University Press, 1983], 4–5).

4. John Keane, *Democracy and Civil Society: On the Predicaments of European Socialism, the Prospects for Democracy and the Problems of Controlling Social and Political Power* (New York: Verso Books, 1988), 10.

5. Chandra Talpede Mohanty, "On Race and Voice: Challenges for Liberal Education in the 1990s," *Cultural Critique* (Winter 1989–90):201.

6. Mohanty, "On Race," 181.

7. Robert Bellah et al., *Habits of the Heart: Individualism and Commitment in American Life* (New York: Harper and Row, Inc., 1985), 79.

8. Iris Young, "The Ideal of Community and the Politics of Difference," in *Feminism/Postmodernism*, ed. L. Nicholson (New York: Routledge, 1990), 302.

9. David Hollenbach points out that since the communitarians Alasdair MacIntyre and Michael Sandel argue "that the ability of people to iden-tify just what is 'good' or 'noble' is dependent on their being part of a community with a shared tradition ... [which] is just what we do not have in contemporary society," they end up with a stark and pessimistic analysis. See David Hollenbach, "The Common Good Revisited," *Theological Studies* 50 (1989): 77. MacIntyre's famous gloomy prediction comes at the end of *After Virtue*: "the barbarians are not waiting beyond the frontiers; they have already been governing us for quite some time" (Alasdair MacIntyre, *After Virtue: A Study in Moral Theory* [Notre Dame, IN: University of Notre Dame Press, 1981], 245).

10. One of the troubling legacies of the left is an on-going effort to discover such an ideal community. Marx, for example, believed that when the differences between social and political power had been annulled with the triumph of the working class, the state would crumble away in favor of a communal equilibrium (see Keane, *Democracy*, 52). Although the left no longer sees the working class as the "pure" group, it now has a tendency to identify areas of the third world (or the third world within the first world) as ideal communities. For a good example of this romanticization, see Fredric Jameson, "Third-World Literature in the Era of Multinational Capitalism", *Social Text* 5/3 [Fall 1986]: 65–8. This is, of course, the ten-dency identified earlier in Sharon Welch's book, *A Feminist Ethic of Risk*, which she has corrected in her most recent writing.

11. Hooks, *Yearning*, 147.

12. Nancy Hartsock argues that marginalization works against the desire for what she terms a "totalizing discourse," which, I assert, includes a total-ized model of community. She remarks that "marginalized groups are far less likely to mistake themselves for the universal 'man'" (Nancy Hartsock, "Rethinking Modernism: Minority vs. Majority Theories," *Cultural Critique* 7 [Fall 1987]: 205).

13. Frazer and Lacey, *Politics*, 200.

14. The classic account of liberal justice remains John Rawls, *A Theory of Justice* (Cambridge: Harvard University Press, 1973). The liberal notion of justice as the distribution of goods is criticized by Iris Young, *Justice and the Politics of Difference* (Princeton, NJ: Princeton University Press, 1990), 15–42. Rawls himself has, since the publication of *Theory*, been steadily revising his position to a more pragmatist account of how in pluralist

modern political societies we settle upon various principles and institutions. These essays are collected in John Rawls, *Political Liberalism* (New York: Columbia University Press, 1993).

15. Nancy Fraser, "Rethinking the Public Sphere: A Contribution to the Critique of Actually Existing Democracy," in *Habermas and the Public Sphere*, ed. C. Calhoun (Cambridge, MA: The MIT Press, 1992), 121.

16. See pp. 32–3.

17. Thus, for example, any study of nineteenth and early twentieth century working-class life in Europe or America reveals vital working-class cultures whose cultural practices were intimately involved with their political practices. Studies of the English working class demonstrating these connections are E. P. Thompson, *The Making of the English Working Class* (New York: Random House/Vintage Books, 1963), and the works of Raymond Williams. Comparable studies of the American working class are Herbert Gutman, *Work, Culture and Society in Industrializing America: Essays in American Working-Class and Social History* (New York: Alfred A. Knopf, 1976), and Stanley Aronowitz, *False Promises: The Shaping of Working Class Consciousness* (New York: McGraw-Hill Book Company, 1973).

18. Jean Cohen and Andrew Arato, *Civil Society and Political Theory* (Cambridge, MA: The MIT Press, 1992), 411.

19. Seyla Benhabib, "Models of Public Space: Hannah Arendt, the Liberal Tradition, and Juergen Habermas," in *Habermas and the Public*, ed. Calhoun, 83.

20. Fraser, "Rethinking," 125.

21. Benhabib, "Models," 94.

22. Fraser, "Rethinking," 124.

23. José Casanova, *Public Religions in the Modern World* (Chicago: University of Chicago Press, 1994), 205.

24. Manning Marable, *Blackwater: Historical Studies in Race, Class Consciouness, and Revolution* (Dayton: Black Praxis Press, 1981), 40.

25. I am indebted to Barbara Wheeler for suggesting how following Hauerwas's model will eliminate the critical political possibilities of the Reformed Christian heritage.

26. Casanova, *Religions*, 228, 65.

27. Vincent Harding, "Toward a Darkly Radiant Vision of America's Truth," *Crosscurrents* (Spring 1987): 15.

28. Elaborating on Habermas's evaluation of modernity, Benhabib writes of the threefold possibility of modernity, stressing the critical, participatory capacities of this heritage: "1) in the realm of institutions, the consensual generation of norms of action through practical discourse becomes a possibility; 2) in the realm of personality, the formation of individual identities becomes increasingly reflexive, that is less and less dependent upon

accepted conventions and roles; and 3) the appropriation of tradition is also rendered more fluid and more dependent upon the creative hermeneutics of contemporary interpreters" (Seyla Benhabib, "Autonomy, Modernity, and Community: Communitarianism and Critical Social Theory in Dialogue," in *Zwischenbetrachtungen im Prozess der Aufklärung*, eds. A. Hönneth et al. [Frankfurt: Suhrkamp Verlag, 1989], 391).

29. Young, *Justice*, 37.

30. This emphasis on the importance of listening as a prerequisite to deep transformative interaction has been evident in feminist work over the past decade.

31. The same kind of transformative encounter is sketched in Ann Russo, "We Cannot Live without Our Lives," in *Third World Women and the Politics of Feminism*, ed. C. Mohanty, et al. (Bloomington: Indiana University Press, 1991), 297–313. Russo speaks of the encounter with women of other races and the need to give up power and privilege, an act I would describe as altering the narrative of one's life. However, like Welch, she seems also to want to make whiteness a homogeneous category when she writes that white women maintain loyalty to "a common historical and cultural heritage" with white men. While we cannot (and should not) lose our white identity, she says, we should change our accountabilities and loyalties. To me, some loyalty to the pain of white men, especially working-class men, remains central to who I am, and I see no reason not to balance the difficulties of doubled loyalty as I see black, Latina, Asian and indigenous feminists doing.

32. Ada María Isasi-Díaz, "Solidarity: Love of Neighbor in the 1980s," in *Lift Every Voice: Constructing Christian Theologies from the Underside*, ed. S. Thistlethwaite and M. P. Engel (San Francisco: Harper and Row, Publishers, 1990), 33, 39.

BIBLIOGRAPHY

Afshar, Haleh. *Women, Work and Ideology in the Third World*. London: Tavistock Publications, 1985.

Albrecht, Gloria H. "Myself and Other Characters: A Feminist Liberationist Critique of Hauerwas's Ethics of Christian Character." *The Annual of the Society of Christian Ethics* (1992):97–114.

Alcoff, Linda. "Cultural Feminism versus Post-Structuralism: The Identity Crisis in Feminist Theory." *Signs* 13/3 (1988):402–36.

Anderson, Benedict. *Imagined Communities*. New York: Verso, 1983.

Anderson, Perry. *Considerations on Western Marxism*. London: Verso, 1976.

Anderson, Perry. "Modernity and Revolution." In *Marxism and the Interpretation of Culture*, pp. 317–38. Edited by C. Nelson and L. Grossberg. Urbana: University of Illinois Press, 1988.

Anthony, Dick, and Robbins, Thomas. "Spiritual Innovation and the Crisis of American Civil Religion." In *Religion and America: Spiritual Life in a Secular*

Age, pp. 229–48. Edited by M. Douglas and S. Tipton. Boston: Beacon Press, 1983.

Arato, Andrew, and Gebhardt, Eike, eds. *The Essential Frankfurt School Reader.* New York: Continuum, 1982.

Aronowitz, Stanley. *The Crisis in Historical Materialism: Class, Politics and Culture in Marxist Theory.* New York: Praeger, A J.F. Bergin Publishers Book, 1982.

Aronowitz, Stanley. *False Promises: The Shaping of Working Class Consciousness.* New York: McGraw-Hill Book Company, 1973.

Aronowitz, Stanley. "On Intellectuals." In *Intellectuals: Aesthetics, Politics, Academics*, pp. 3–56. Edited by Bruce Robbins. Minneapolis: University of Minnesota Press, 1990.

Barrett, Michèle. *Women's Oppression Today: Problems in Marxist Feminist Analysis.* London: Verso, 1984.

Barrett, Michèle, and McIntosh, Mary. *The Anti-Social Family.* London: Verso, 1982.

Bass, Dorothy. "The American Religious Landscape: Relocating 'Mainline' Protestantism." Unpublished manuscript.

Bell, Daniel. *The Coming of Post-Industrial Society: A Venture in Social Forecasting.* New York: Basic Books, Inc., 1976.

Bell, Daniel. *The Cultural Contradictions of Late Capitalism.* New York: Basic Books, 1976.

Bell, Daniel. "The End of Ideology Revisited (Part II)." *Government and Opposition* 23/3 (Summer 1988): 321–31.

Bell, Daniel. "The Return of the Sacred?" In *The Winding Passage: Essays and Sociological Journeys 1960–1980*, pp. 324–54. Cambridge, MA: ABT Books, 1980.

Bellah, Robert N. *Beyond Belief: Essays on Religion in a Post-Traditional World.* New York: Harper and Row, Publishers, 1970.

Bender, Thomas. *Community and Social Change in America.* New Brunswick, NJ: Rutgers University Press, 1978.

Benhabib, Seyla. "Autonomy, Modernity, and Community: Communitarianism and Critical Social Theory in Dialogue." In *Zwischenbetrachtungen im Prozess der Aufklärung*, pp. 373–91. Edited by A. Hönneth et al. Frankfurt: Suhrkamp Verlag, 1989.

Benhabib, Seyla. "In the Shadow of Aristotle and Hegel: Communicative Ethics and Current Controversies in Practical Philosophy." In *Hermeneutics and Critical Theory in Ethics and Politics*, pp. 1–31. Edited by M. Kelly. Cambridge, MA: The MIT Press, 1990.

Benhabib, Seyla. "Models of Public Space: Hannah Arendt, the Liberal Tradition, and Jürgen Habermas." In *Habermas and the Public Sphere*, pp. 73–98. Edited by Craig Calhoun. Cambridge: The MIT Press, 1992.

Benhabib, Seyla. *Situating the Self: Gender, Community and Postmodernism in Contemporary Ethics.* New York: Routledge, 1992.

Berger, Peter. *The Heretical Imperative*. Garden City, NY: Anchor Press/Doubleday, 1979.

Berger, Peter. *The Sacred Canopy*. Garden City, NY: Doubleday and Co., Inc., Anchor Books, 1969.

Berman, Marshall. *All That is Solid Melts into Air: The Experience of Modernity*. New York: Simon and Schuster, 1982.

Birch, Bruce C., and Rasmussen, Larry L. *Bible & Ethics in the Christian Life*, rev. ed. Minneapolis: Augsburg Fortress, 1989.

Briggs, Sheila. "The Politics of Identity and the Politics of Interpretation." *USQR* 43/1–4 (1989):163–80.

Cahill, Lisa Sowle. *Between the Sexes: Foundations for a Christian Ethics of Sexuality*. Philadelphia and New York: Fortress Press and Paulist Press, 1985.

Cahill, Lisa Sowle. "The Catholic Tradition: Religion, Morality, and the Common Good." *The Journal of Law and Religion* 5 (1987):75–94.

Cahill, Lisa Sowle. "Is Catholic Ethics Biblical? The Example of Sex and Gender." Warren Lecture Series in Catholic Studies, no. 20, Public Lecture, the University of Tulsa, March 15, 1992.

Cahill, Lisa Sowle. "Notes on Moral Theology: 1989, Feminist Ethics." *Theological Studies* 51 (1990):49–64.

Cahill, Lisa Sowle. *Women and Sexuality*. New York: Paulist Press, 1992.

Calhoun, Craig, ed. *Habermas and the Public Sphere*. Cambridge: The MIT Press, 1992.

Cannon, Katie. *Black Womanist Ethics*. Atlanta: Scholars Press, 1988.

Casanova, José. "The Politics of the Religious Revival." *Telos* 59 (1984):3–33.

Casanova, José. *Public Religions in the Modern World*. Chicago: University of Chicago Press, 1994.

Caulfield, Mina Davis. "Imperialism, the Family, and Cultures of Resistance." *Socialist Revolution* 4/2 (October 1974):67–85.

Cohen Jean, and Arato, Andrew. *Civil Society and Political Theory*. Cambridge: The MIT Press, 1992.

Cohen, Jean, and Arato, Andrew. "Politics and the Reconstruction of the Concept of Civil Society." In *Zwischenbetrachtungen im Prozess der Aufklärung*, pp. 482–503. Edited by A. Hönneth et al. Frankfurt: Suhrkamp Verlag, 1989.

Collins, Patricia Hill. *Black Feminist Thought: Knowledge, Consciousness, and the Politics of Empowerment*. London: Harper Collins, 1991.

Cone, James. *Malcolm and Martin and America: A Dream or Nightmare?* Maryknoll, NY: Orbis Press, 1991.

Cone, James H. "Martin Luther King, Jr., Black Theology—Black Church." *Theology Today* 40/4 (January 1984):409–20.

Daly, Mary. *Gyn/Ecology: The Metaethics of Radical Feminism*. Boston: Beacon Press, 1978.

Dean, William. *The Religious Critic in American Culture*. Albany: SUNY Press, 1994.

167

Derrida, Jacques. "Limited Inc abc." *Glyph 2: Johns Hopkins Textual Studies*. Baltimore: Johns Hopkins University Press, 1977.

Dietz, Mary. "Citizenship with a Feminist Face: The Problems with Maternal Thinking." *Political Theory* 13/1 (February 1985):19–34.

Dill, Bonnie Thornton. "Our Mothers' Grief." *Journal of Family History* 13 (1988):415–31.

Douglas, Mary, and Tipton, Steven, eds. *Religion and America: Spirituality in a Secular Age*. Boston: Beacon Press, 1983.

Douglass, Frederick. "The Present and Future of the Colored Race in America" (1863). In *Negro Social and Political Thought, 1850–1920*, pp. 37–101. Edited by H. Brotz. New York: Basic Books, 1966.

Dublin, Thomas. *Women at Work: The Transformation of Work and Community in Lowell, Mass., 1826–60*. New York: Columbia University Press, 1979.

DuBois, W. E. B. *The Souls of Black Folk*. Greenwich, CT: Fawcett Publications, Inc., 1961.

Dworkin, Ronald. "To Each His Own." *The New York Review of Books* (April 13, 1983): 4–6.

Dyson, Michael. *Making Malcolm: The Myth and Meaning of Malcolm X*. New York: Oxford University Press, 1995.

Dyson, Michael. *Reflecting Black: African-American Cultural Criticism*. Minneapolis: University of Minnesota Press, 1993.

Edsall, Thomas B. "Religion playing a bigger role in politics, studies show." *Roanoke Times and World News*, 14 January 1994, C9.

Ehrenreich, Barbara. *Fear of Falling: The Inner Life of the Middle Class*. New York: Pantheon Books, 1989.

Ehrenreich, Barbara, and Ehrenreich, John. "The Professional-Managerial Class." In *Between Labor and Capital*, pp. 5–45. Edited by P. Walker. Boston: South End Press, 1979.

Eley, Geoff. "Nations, Publics, and Political Cultures: Placing Habermas in the Nineteenth Century." In *Habermas and the Public Sphere*, pp. 289–339. Edited by Craig Calhoun. Cambridge: The MIT Press, 1992.

Elshtain, Jean Bethke. "Antigone's Daughters." *Democracy* (April 1982):46–59.

Elshtain, Jean Bethke. *Democracy on Trial*. New York: Basic Books, 1995.

Elshtain, Jean Bethke. "Feminism, Family, and Community." *Dissent* (Fall 1982): 442–9.

Elshtain, Jean Bethke. "The Liberal Captivity of Feminism: A Critical Appraisal of (Some) Feminist Answers." In *The Liberal Future in America: Essays in Renewal*, pp. 63–84. Edited by P. Abbott and M. B. Levy. Westport, CT: Greenwood Press, 1985.

Elshtain, Jean Bethke. "On Feminism, Family, and Community—A Response to Barbara Ehrenreich." *Dissent* (Winter 1983):106–9.

Elshtain, Jean Bethke. *Power Trips and Other Journeys: Essays in Feminism as Civic Discourse*. Madison: University of Wisconsin, 1990.

Etzioni, Amitai. "To Stay the Communitarian Course." *The Responsive Community* 3/1 (Winter 1992/3):4–6.

Farley, Edward. *Theologia: The Fragmentation and Unity of Theological Education.* Philadelphia: Fortress Press, 1983.

Foucault, Michel. *The History of Sexuality.* Vol. 2, *The Use of Pleasure.* Translated by Robert Hurley. New York: Vintage, 1983.

Foucault, Michel. *Power/Knowledge: Selected Interviews and Other Writings: 1972–77.* Translated by Colin Gordon, Leo Marshall, John Mepham and Kate Soper. New York: Pantheon, 1980.

Fourez, Gerald. *Liberation Ethics.* Philadelphia: Temple University Press, 1982.

Fox, Richard. "The Niebuhrs and the Liberal Protestant Heritage." In *Religion and Twentieth-Century American Intellectual Life,* pp. 94–115. Edited by M. J. Lacey. New York: Woodrow Wilson International Center for Scholars and Cambridge University Press, 1991.

Fox, Richard. *Reinhold Niebuhr: A Biography.* New York: Harper and Row Publishers, 1987.

Fox-Genovese, Elizabeth. *Feminism Without Illusions: A Critique of Individualism.* Chapel Hill: The University of North Carolina Press, 1991.

Frankenberg, Ruth. *White Women, Race Matters: The Social Construction of Whiteness.* Minneapolis: The University of Minnesota Press, 1993.

Fraser, Nancy. "Debate: Recognition or Redistribution? A Critical Reading of Iris Young's Justice and the Politics of Difference." *The Journal of Political Philosophy* 3/2 (1995): 166–80.

Fraser, Nancy. "Rethinking the Public Sphere: A Contribution to the Critique of Actually Existing Democracy." In *Habermas and the Public Sphere,* pp. 109–42. Edited by Craig Calhoun. Cambridge: The MIT Press, 1992.

Fraser, Nancy. *Unruly Practices: Power, Discourse, and Gender in Contemporary Social Theory.* Minneapolis: University of Minnesota Press, 1989.

Frazer, Elizabeth and Lacey, Nicola. *The Politics of Community: A Feminist Critique of the Liberal-Communitarian Debate.* Toronto: University of Toronto Press, 1993.

Friedman, Marilyn. "Community and Modern Friendship." In *Feminist Ethics,* pp. 89–97. Edited by E. Cole and S. Coultrap-McQuin. Bloomington: Indiana University Press, 1992.

Galston, William. "Community, Democracy, Philosophy: The Political Theory of Michael Walzer." *Political Theory* 17/1 (February 1989): 119–30.

Gehrig, Gail. *American Civil Religion: An Assessment.* Society for the Scientific Study of Religion, Monograph Series #3. Storrs, CT: University of Connecticut Press, 1981.

Giddens, Anthony. "Reason without Revolution? Habermas's *Theorie des kommunikativen Handelns*" In *Habermas and Modernity,* pp. 95–121. Edited by R. Bernstein. Cambridge, MA: The MIT Press, 1985.

169

Gilkes, Cheryl Townsend. "From Slavery to Social Welfare: Racism and the Control of Black Women." In *Class, Race, and Sex: the Dynamics of Control*, pp. 288–300. Edited by H. Lessinger and A. Swerdlow. New York: G.K. Hall, Publishers, 1983.

Gilkes, Cheryl Townsend. "'Mother to the Motherless, Father to the Fatherless': Power, Gender, and Community in an Afrocentric Biblical Tradition." *Semeia* 47 (1989): 57–85.

Gilkes, Cheryl Townsend. "The Roles of Church and Community Mothers: Ambivalent American Sexism or Fragmented African Familyhood?" *Journal of Feminist Studies in Religion* 2/2 (Fall 1986): 41–59.

Gorz, André. *Farewell to the Working Class: An Essay on Post-Industrial Socialism*. Translated by Michael Sonenscher. Boston: South End Press, 1982.

Gramsci, Antonio. *Selections from the Prison Notebooks*. Edited and translated by Q. Hoare and G. Nowell Smith. New York: International Publishers, 1971.

Gudorf, Christine. "Parenting, Mutual Love, and Sacrifice." In *Women's Consciousness, Women's Conscience: A Reader in Feminist Ethics*, pp. 175–191. Edited by B. H. Andolsen, C. E. Gudorf, and M. D. Pellauer. San Francisco: Harper and Row, Publishers, 1985.

Gunnemann, Jon P. "A Theological Defense of the Brute: The Christian Stake in Political Liberalism." Unpublished manuscript.

Gutman, Herbert. *Work, Culture, and Society in Industrializing America: Essays in American Working-Class and Social History*. New York: Alfred A. Knopf, 1976.

Habermas, Jürgen. "Modernity—An Incomplete Project." In *The Anti-Aesthetic: Essays on Postmodern Culture*, pp. 3–15. Edited by H. Foster. Port Townsend, WA: Bay Press, 1983.

Habermas, Jürgen. "Neoconservative Culture Criticism in the United States and West Germany: An Intellectual Movement in Two Political Cultures." In *Habermas and Modernity*, pp. 78–94. Edited by R. J. Bernstein. Cambridge, MA: The MIT Press, 1985.

Habermas, Jürgen. *The Philosophical Discourse of Modernity: Twelve Lectures*. Translated by F. Lawrence. Cambridge, MA: The MIT Press, 1987.

Habermas, Jürgen. *The Structural Transformation of the Public Sphere*. Translated by T. Burger and F. Lawrence. Cambridge: The MIT Press, 1989.

Habermas, Jürgen. *The Theory of Communicative Action, Vol. 2: Lifeworld and System: A Critique of Functionalist Reason*. Translated by T. McCarthy. Boston: Beacon Press, 1987.

Habermas, Jürgen. *Toward a Rational Society: Student Protest, Science, and Politics*. Translated by J. Shapiro. Boston: Beacon Press, 1970.

Hammond, Guyton B. *Conscience and Its Recovery: From the Frankfurt School to Feminism*. Charlottesville: University Press of Virginia, 1993

Hammond, Philip E. "The Extravasation of the Sacred and the Crisis in Liberal Protestantism." In *Liberal Protestantism: Realities and Possibilities*, pp.

51–64. Edited by R. S. Michaelsen and W. C. Roof. New York: Pilgrim Press, 1986.

Hammond, Philip E. *Religion and Personal Autonomy*. Columbia: the University of South Carolina Press, 1992.

Harding, Vincent. *There Is a River: The Black Struggle for Freedom in America*. San Diego: Harvest/HBJ Book, Harcourt Brace Jovanovich Publishers, 1981/92.

Harding, Vincent. "Toward a Darkly Radiant Vision of America's Truth." *Cross Currents* 37/1 (Spring 1987):1–15.

Harrison, Beverly. "The Fate of the Middle 'Class' in Late Capitalism." In *God and Capitalism: A Prophetic Critique of Market Economy*, pp. 53–71. Edited by J. M. Thomas and V. Visick. Madison: A-R Editions, Inc., 1991.

Harrison, Beverly. *Making the Connections: Essays in Feminist Social Ethics*. Edited by C. Robb. Boston: Beacon Press, 1985.

Hartsock, Nancy. "Foucault on Power: A Theory for Women?" In *Feminism / Postmodernism*, pp. 157–75. Edited by Linda Nicholson. New York: Routledge, 1990.

Hartsock, Nancy. "Postmodernism and Political Change: Issues for Feminist Theory." *Cultural Critique* (Winter 1989–90):15–33.

Hartsock, Nancy. "Rethinking Modernism: Minority vs. Majority Theories." *Cultural Critique* 7 (Fall 1987):187–206.

Harvey, David. *The Condition of Postmodernity*. Oxford: Basil Blackwell, 1989.

Hauerwas, Stanley M. *After Christendom? How the Church Is to Behave If Freedom, Justice, and a Christian Nation Are Bad Ideas*. Nashville: Abingdon Press, 1991.

Hauerwas, Stanley M. *Christian Existence Today: Essays on Church, World and Living In Between*. Durham, NC: The Labyrinth Press, 1988.

Hauerwas, Stanley M. *A Community of Character: Toward a Constructive Christian Social Ethic*. Notre Dame, IN: University of Notre Dame Press, 1981.

Hauerwas, Stanley M. *Dispatches from the Front: Theological Engagements with the Secular*. Durham, NC: Duke University Press, 1994.

Hauerwas, Stanley M. *The Peaceable Kingdom: A Primer in Christian Ethics*. Notre Dame, IN: The University of Notre Dame Press, 1983.

Hauerwas, Stanley M. "The Testament of Friends." *The Christian Century* 107/8 (28 February 1990):212–16.

Hennessy, Rosemary. *Materialist Feminism and the Politics of Discourse*. New York: Routledge, 1993.

Herberg, Will. *Protestant, Catholic, Jew*. New York: Anchor Books, Doubleday and Co., Inc., 1960.

Hoagland, Sarah Lucia. *Lesbian Ethics*. Palo Alto, CA: Institute of Lesbian Study, 1988.

Hobsbawm, Eric. "Introduction: Inventing Traditions." In *The Invention of Tradition*, pp. 1–14. Edited by E. Hobsbawm and T. Ranger. Cambridge: Cambridge University Press, 1983.

171

Hollenbach, David. "The Common Good Revisited." *Theological Studies* 50 (1989):70–94.

Holmes, Stephen. "The Permanent Structure of Antiliberal Thought." In *Liberalism and the Moral Life*, pp. 227–253. Edited by N. Rosenblum. Cambridge, MA: Harvard University Press, 1989.

Hooks, bell. *Yearning: Race, Gender, and Cultural Politics*. Boston: South End Press, 1990.

Hooks, bell and Cornel West. *Breaking Bread: Insurgent Black Intellectual Life*. Boston: South End Press, 1991.

Hough, Joseph. "The Loss of Optimism as a Problem for Liberal Christian Faith." In *Liberal Protestantism: Realities and Possibilities*, pp. 145–66. Edited by R. S. Michaelsen and W. C. Roof. New York: Pilgrim Press, 1986.

Humphries, Jane. "Class Struggle and the Persistence of the Working-Class Family." *Cambridge Journal of Economics* 1 (1977):241–58.

Humphries, Jane. "The Working Class Family, Women's Liberation and Class Struggle: The Case of Nineteenth Century British History." *Review of Radical Political Economics* 9/3 (1977):25–41.

Isasi-Díaz, Ada-María. "Solidarity: Love of Neighbor in the 1980s." In *Lift Every Voice: Constructing Christian Theology from the Underside*, pp. 31–40. Edited by S. Thistlethwaite and M. Potter Engel. San Francisco: Harper and Row, Publishers, 1990.

Jaggar, Alison. "Feminist Ethics." In *Feminist Ethics*, pp. 78–104. Edited by C. Card. Lawrence: University Press of Kansas, 1991.

Jaggar, Alison. *Feminist Politics and Human Nature*. Totowa, NJ: Rowman and Allanheld, Publishers, 1983.

Jameson, Fredric. "Third-World Literature in the Era of Multinational Capitalism." *Social Text* 5/3 (Fall 1986):65–88.

Jameson, Fredric. *The Political Unconscious: Narrative as a Socially Symbolic Act*. Ithaca, NY: Cornell University Press, 1981.

Jameson, Fredric. "Postmodernism or the Cultural Logic of Late Capitalism." *New Left Review* 146 (July–August 1984):53–92.

Jay, Martin. *The Dialectical Imagination: A History of the Frankfurt School and the Insitute for Social Research, 1923–1950*. Boston: Little, Brown, and Co., 1973.

Jay, Martin. *Marxism and Totality*. Berkeley: University of California Press, 1984.

Johnson, Benton. "Winning Lost Sheep: A Recovery Course for Liberal Protestantism." In *Liberal Protestantism: Realities and Possibilities*, pp. 220–34. Edited by R. S. Michaelsen and W. C. Roof. New York: Pilgrim Press, 1986.

Keane, John. *Democracy and Civil Society: On the Predicaments of European Socialism, the Prospects for Democracy and the Problems of Controlling Social and Political Power*. New York: Verso Books, 1988.

Keane, John. *Public Life and Late Capitalism: Toward a Theory of Socialist Democracy*. New York: Cambridge University Press, 1984.

Kelly, George Armstrong. "Faith, Freedom and Disenchantment: Politics and the American Religious Consciousness," in *Religion and America: Spiritual Life in a Secular Age*, pp. 207-28.Edited by Mary Douglas and Steven Tipton. Boston: Beacon Press, 1983.

Kelly, George Armstrong. "Review of *The Naked Public Square*, by Richard John Neuhaus." *Society* 23 (November–December 1985):74–6.

Kennedy, Susan Estabrook. *If All We Did Was to Weep at Home: A History of White Working-Class Women in America*. Bloomington: Indiana University Press, 1979.

King, Jr., Martin Luther. "The Ethical Demand for Integration." In *A Testament of Hope: the Essential Writings of Martin Luther King, Jr.*, pp. 117–25. Edited by J. Washington. San Francisco: Harper and Row, Publishers, 1986.

King, Jr., Martin Luther. "I Have a Dream" (28 August 1963). In *A Testament of Hope: the Essential Writings of Martin Luther King, Jr.*, pp. 217–20. Edited by J. Washington. San Francisco: Harper and Row, Publishers, 1986.

King, Jr., Martin Luther. "Letter from Birmingham City Jail." In *A Testament of Hope: the Essential Writings of Martin Luther King, Jr.*, pp. 289–302. Edited by J. Washington. San Francisco: Harper and Row, Publishers, 1986.

King, Jr., Martin Luther. *Where Do We Go From Here: Chaos or Community?* New York: Harper and Row, Publishers, 1967.

Kirkland, Frank M. "Social Policy, Ethical Life, and the Urban Underclass." In *The Underclass Question*, pp. 152–87. Edited by Bill E. Lawson. Philadelphia: Temple University Press, 1992.

Kymlicka, Will. *Contemporary Political Philosophy: An Introduction*. Oxford: Oxford University Press, 1990.

Kymlicka, Will. *Liberalism, Community, and Culture*. Oxford: Oxford University Press, 1989.

Laclau, Ernesto and Mouffe, Chantal. *Hegemony and Socialist Strategy*. London: Verso, 1985.

Lasch, Christopher. *The Agony of the American Left*. New York: Alfred A. Knopf, 1969.

Lasch, Christopher. "The Communitarian Critique of Liberalism." *Soundings* 69/1–2 (Spring–Summer 1986):60–76.

Lasch, Christopher. "Conservatism Against Itself." *First Things* 2 (April 1990):17–23.

Lasch, Christopher. *The Culture of Narcissism*. New York: Warner Books, 1979.

Lasch, Christopher. *Haven in a Heartless World: The Family Besieged*. New York: Basic Books, Inc., 1979.

Lasch, Christopher. *The Minimal Self*. New York: W. W. Norton and Co., Inc., 1984.

Lasch, Christopher. "Popular Culture and the Illusion of Choice." *democracy* 2/2 (April 1982):88–92.

Lasch, Christopher. *The True and Only Heaven: Progress and Its Critics*. New York: W. W. Norton and Co., 1991.

Lasch, Christopher. *The World of Nations*. New York: Vintage Books, Random House, 1974.

Lawrence, Bruce. *Defenders of God: The Fundamentalist Revolt Against the Modern Age.* San Francisco: Harper and Row, Publishers, 1989.

Loury, Glenn C. "The Moral Quandary of the Black Community." *The Public Interest* 79 (Spring 1985): 9–22.

Loury, Glenn C. *One by One from the Inside Out: Essays and Reviews on Race and Responsibility in America.* New York: the Free Press, 1995.

MacIntyre, Alasdair. *After Virtue: A Study in Moral Theory.* Notre Dame, IN: University of Notre Dame Press, 1981.

Macpherson, C.B. *The Life and Times of Liberal Democracy.* New York: Oxford Unversity Press, 1977.

Marable, Manning. *Black American Politics: From the Washington Marches to Jesse Jackson.* London: Verso, 1985

Marable, Marable. *Blackwater: Historical Studies in Race, Class Consciousness, and Revolution.* Dayton: Black Praxis Press, 1981.

Marable, Manning. *How Capitalism Underdeveloped Black America.* Boston: South End Press, 1983.

Marable, Manning. "The Rhetoric of Racial Harmony." *Sojourners* (August–September 1990): 14–18.

Marty, Martin. "Religion in America since Mid-century." In *Religion and America: Spiritual Life in a Secular Age*, pp. 273–87. Edited by M. Douglas and S. Tipton. Boston: Beacon Press, 1983.

Marx, Karl, and Engels, Friederick. "Manifesto of the Communist Party." In *The Marx-Engels Reader.* 2d ed., pp. 469–500. Edited by R. C. Tucker. New York and London: W. W. Norton & Company, 1978.

McCann, Dennis P. *Christian Realism and Liberation Theology.* Maryknoll, NY: Orbis Books, 1981.

Meeks, Wayne. *The First Urban Christians: The Social World of the Apostle Paul.* New Haven, CT: Yale University Press, 1983.

Meilaender, Gilbert. "A View from Somewhere: The Political Thought of Michael Walzer." *Religious Studies Review* 16/3 (July 1990):197–201.

Merod, Jim. *The Political Responsibility of the Critic.* Ithaca, NY: Cornell University Press, 1987.

Michaelsen, R., and Roof, W. "Introduction." In *Liberal Protestantism: Realities and Possibilities*, pp. 3–15. Edited by R. Michaelsen and W. Roof. New York: Pilgrim Press, 1986.

Mohanty, Chandra Talpede. "Feminist Encounters: Locating the Politics of Experience." *Copyright* 1 (1987):30–44.

Mohanty, Chandra Talpede. "On Race and Voice: Challenges for Liberal Education in the 1990s." *Cultural Critique* (Winter 1989–90): 179–208.

Mouffe, Chantal. "Feminism, Citizenship, and Radical Democratic Politics." In *Feminists Theorize the Political*, pp. 369–82. Edited by J. Butler and J. Scott. New York: Routledge, 1992.

Mouffe, Chantal, ed. *Gramsci and Marxist Theory*. Boston: Routledge and Kegan Paul, 1979.

Mouffe, Chantal. "Hegemony and New Political Subjects: Toward a New Concept of Democracy." In *Marxism and the Interpretation of Culture*, pp. 89–101. Edited by C. Nelson and L. Grossberg. Urbana: University of Illinois Press, 1988.

Neuhaus, Richard J. *America Against Itself: Moral Vision and the Public Order*. Notre Dame, IN: University of Notre Dame Press, 1992.

Neuhaus, Richard J. *The Naked Public Square: Religion and Democracy in America*. Grand Rapids, MI: William B. Eerdmans Publishing Company, 1984.

Neuhaus, Richard J. "Religion and Public Life: The Continuing Conversation." *The Christian Century* 107/21 (July 11–18 1990): 669–73.

Nicholson, Linda. "Introduction." In *Feminism/Postmodernism*, pp. 1–16. Edited by L. Nicholson. New York: Routledge, 1990.

Nicholson, Linda, and Fraser, Nancy. "Social Theory Without Philosophy." In *Feminism/Postmodernism*, pp. 19–38. Edited by L. Nicholson. New York: Routledge, 1990.

Niebuhr, H. Richard. *Christ and Culture*. New York: Harper and Row, Publishers, 1951.

Niebuhr, H. Richard. *The Meaning of Revelation*. New York: The Macmillan Co., 1960.

Niebuhr, H. Richard. *The Responsible Self: An Essay in Christian Moral Philosophy*. New York: Harper and Row, Publishers, 1963.

Niebuhr, H. Richard. *The Social Sources of Denominationalism*. New York: Henry Holt and Co., 1929.

Niebuhr, Reinhold. *An Interpretation of Christian Ethics*. New York: The Seabury Press, 1979.

Niebuhr, Reinhold. *Moral Man and Immoral Society*. New York: Charles Scribner's Sons, 1932.

Niebuhr, Reinhold. *The Nature and Destiny of Man: A Christian Interpretation; Volume Two: Human Destiny*. New York: Charles Scribner's Sons, 1943.

Niebuhr, Reinhold. *The Self and the Dramas of History*. New York: Charles Scribner's Sons, 1955.

Offe, Claus. *Contradictions of the Welfare State*. Cambridge, MA: The MIT Press, 1984.

Ogden, Schubert. *Faith and Freedom: Toward a Theology of Liberation*. Nashville: Abingdon Press, 1979.

Okin, Susan Moller. "Humanist Liberation." In *Liberalism and the Moral Life*, pp. 39–53. Edited by N. Rosenblum. Cambridge, MA: Harvard University Press, 1989.

Okin, Susan Moller. *Justice, Gender, and the Family*. New York: Basic Books, Inc., 1989.

Ong, Aihwa. *Spirits of Resistance and Capitalist Discipline: Factory Women in Malaysia.* Albany: SUNY Press, 1987.

Owens, Craig. "Feminists and Postmodernism." In *The Anti-Aesthetic: Essays on Postmodern Culture*, pp. 57–82. Edited by H. Foster. Port Townsend, WA: Bay Press, 1983.

Pateman, Carole. *The Disorder of Women.* Stanford, CA: Stanford University Press, 1989.

Pateman, Carole. "Equality, Difference, Subordination: The Politics of Motherhood and Women's Citizenship." In *Beyond Equality and Difference*, pp. 17–31. Edited by Gisela Bock and Susan James. New York: Routledge, 1992.

Pateman, Carole. *The Sexual Contract.* Stanford, CA: Stanford University Press, 1988.

Plaskow, Judith. *Sex, Sin and Grace: Women's Experience and the Theologies of Reinhold Niebuhr and Paul Tillich.* Lanham, MD: University Press of America, 1980.

Pratt, Minnie Bruce. "Identity: Skin Blood Heart." In *Yours in Struggle*, pp. 9–64. Edited by E. Bulkin et al. Brooklyn: Long Haul Press, 1984.

Rasmussen, Larry. *Moral Fragments and Moral Community: A Proposal for Church in Society.* Minneapolis: Fortress Press, 1993.

Rawls, John. *Political Liberalism.* New York: Columbia University Press, 1993.

Rawls, John. *A Theory of Justice.* Cambridge: Harvard University Press, 1971.

Rich, Adrienne. *An Atlas of the Difficult World: Poems 1988–91.* New York: W. W. Norton & Co., 1991.

Richard, Pablo. "The Church, the Authoritarian State, and Social Classes in Latin America." *Lucha/Struggle* 9/1 and 9/2 (1985):35–9 and 29–39.

Roof, Wade Clark. "America's Voluntary Establishment: Mainline Religion in Transition." In *Religion and America: Spirituality in a Secular Age*, pp. 130–49. Edited by M. Douglas and S. Tipton. Boston: Beacon Press, 1983.

Rosenblum, Nancy. *Another Liberalism: Romanticism and the Reconstruction of Liberal Thought.* Cambridge, MA: Harvard University Press, 1987.

Rosenblum, Nancy. "Introduction." In *Liberalism and the Moral Life*, pp. 1–17. Edited by N. Rosenblum. Cambridge, MA: Harvard University Press, 1989.

Russo, Ann. "We Cannot Live without Our Lives." In *Third World Women and the Politics of Feminism*, pp. 297–313. Edited By C. Mohanty, et al. Bloomington: Indiana University Press, 1991.

Ryan, Michael. *Marxism and Deconstruction.* Baltimore: Johns Hopkins Press, 1982.

Sandel, Michael. *Liberalism and the Limits of Justice.* Cambridge: Cambridge University Press, 1982.

Sangari, Kumkum. "The Politics of the Possible." *Cultural Critique* 7 (Fall 1987):157–86

Segundo, Juan Luis. *The Liberation of Theology.* Maryknoll, NY: Orbis Books, 1981.

Shils, Edward. *Tradition.* Chicago: University of Chicago Press, 1981.

Simmons, Paul D. "The Narrative Ethics of Stanley Hauerwas: A Question of Method." Unpublished manuscript.

Skolnick, Arlene. *Embattled Paradise: The American Family in an Age of Uncertainty.* New York: Basic Books, Harper Collins Publishers, 1991.

Smith, Rogers. "'One United People': Second-Class Female Citizenship and the American Quest for Community." *Yale Journal of Law and Humanities* 1/2 (May 1989):229–93.

Smith, Ruth. "Feminism and the Moral Subject" In *Women's Consciousness, Women's Conscience: A Reader in Feminist Ethics,* pp. 235–50. Edited by B. H. Andolsen, C. E. Gudorf, and M. D. Pellauer. San Francisco: Harper and Row, Publishers, 1985.

Smith, Ruth. "Moral Transcendence and Moral Space in the Historical Experience of Women." *Journal of Feminist Studies in Religion* 4/2 (Fall 1988):21–37.

Smith, Ruth. "Morality and Perceptions of Society: The Limits of Self-Interest." *Journal for the Scientific Study of Religion* 26/3 (September 1987): 279–93.

Smith, Ruth. "Reinhold Niebuhr and History: The Elusive Liberal Critique." Unpublished manuscript.

Smith, Ruth. "Relationality and the Ordering of Differences in Feminist Ethics." *Journal of Feminist Studies in Religion* 9 1/2 (Spring/Fall 1993): 199–214.

Smith, Ruth, and Valenze, Deborah. "Mutuality and Marginality: Liberal Moral Theory and Working Class Women in Nineteenth Century England." *Signs* 13/2 (Winter 1988):277–98.

Spelman, Elizabeth V. *Inessential Woman: Problems of Exclusion in Feminist Thought.* Boston: Beacon Press, 1988.

Stacey, Judith. *Brave New Families: Stories of Domestic Upheaval in Late Twentieth-Century America.* New York: Harper Collins/Basic Books, 1991.

Stack, Carol B. *All Our Kin: Strategies for Survival in a Black Community.* New York: Harper & Row, Publishers/Harper Torchbooks, 1974.

Steinfels, Peter. *The Neo-Conservatives.* New York: Simon and Schuster, 1979.

Stone, Ronald. *Professor Reinhold Niebuhr: A Mentor to the Twentieth Century.* Louisville: Westminster/John Knox Press, 1992.

Stout, Jeffrey. *Ethics After Babel: The Languages of Morals and Their Discontents.* Boston: Beacon Press, 1988.

Sweet, Leonard. "The Modernization of Protestant Religion in America." In *Altered Landscapes: Christianity in America 1935–1985,* pp. 19–41. Edited by D. W. Lotz, with D. W. Shriver, Jr., and J. F. Wilson. Grand Rapids, MI: William B. Eerdmans Publishing Company, 1989.

Taylor, Charles. "Inwardness and the Culture of Modernity." In *Zwischen-betrachtungen im Prozess der Aufklärung*, pp. 601–23. Edited by A. Hönneth et al. Frankfurt: Suhrkamp Verlag, 1989.

Taylor, Charles. *Multiculturalism and "The Politics of Recognition"*. Edited by A. Gutman. Princeton, NJ: Princeton University Press, 1992.

Taylor, Charles. *Philosophy and the Human Sciences: Philosophical Papers*, vol. 2. Cambridge: Cambridge University Press, 1985.

Taylor, Charles. *Sources of the Self: The Making of the Modern Identity*. Cambridge, MA: Harvard University Press, 1989.

Thistlethwaite, Susan B. *Sex, Race, and God: Christian Feminism in Black and White*. New York: Crossroad, 1989.

Thompson, E.P. *The Making of the English Working Class*. New York: Random House/Vintage Books, 1963.

Tipton, Steven. "The Moral Logic of Alternative Religion." In *Religion and America: Spirituality in a Secular Age*, pp. 79–107. Edited by M. Douglas and S. Tipton. Boston: Beacon Press, 1983.

Toennies, Ferdinand. *Community and Society*. Translated by C. P. Loomis. New York: Harper and Row, Inc., 1963.

Townes, Emilie M. *In a Blaze of Glory: Womanist Spirituality as Social Witness*. Nashville: Abingdon Press, 1995.

Tracy, David. *Plurality and Ambiguity*. San Francisco: Harper and Row, Publishers, 1987.

Trimiew, Darryl. *Voices of the Silenced: The Responsible Self in a Marginalized Community*. Cleveland: Pilgrim Press, 1993.

Troeltsch, Ernst. "The Dogmatics of the '*Religionsgeschichtliche Schule*'." *The American Journal of Theology* 17/1 (January 1913):1–21.

Troeltsch, Ernst. *Protestantism and Progress: The Significance of Protestantism for the Rise of Modern World*. Philadelphia: Fortress Press, 1986.

Troeltsch, Ernst. *The Social Teaching of the Christian Churches*, 2 Vols. Translated by O. Wyon. Chicago: University of Chicago Press, Phoenix Edition, 1981.

Vaughan, Judith. *Sociality, Ethics, and Social Change*. Lanham, MD: University Press of America, 1983.

Walzer, Michael. "The Communitarian Critique of Liberalism." *Political Theory* 18/1 (February 1990):6–23.

Walzer, Michael. *The Company of Critics: Social Criticism and Political Commitment in the Twentieth Century*. New York: Basic Books, Inc., 1988.

Walzer, Michael. "A Critique of Philosophical Conversation." In *Hermeneutics and Critical Theory in Ethics and Politics*, pp. 182–96. Edited by M. Kelly. Cambridge, MA: The MIT Press, 1990.

Walzer, Michael. *Exodus and Revolution*. New York: Basic Books, 1985.

Walzer, Michael. "The Idea of Holy War in Ancient Israel." *Journal of Religious Ethics* 20/2 (Fall 1992): 215–28.

Walzer, Michael. *Interpretation and Social Criticism*. Cambridge, MA: Harvard University Press, 1987.

Walzer, Michael. *Obligations: Essays in Disobedience, War, and Citizenship*. Cambridge: Harvard University Press, 1970.

Walzer, Michael. *Spheres of Justice: A Defense of Pluralism and Equality*. New York: Basic Books, Inc., 1983.

Walzer, Michael. *What It Means to be an American*. New York: Marsilio, 1992.

Walzer, Michael. *What Kind of a State is a Jewish State?* The Shalom Hartman Institute, Center for Jewish Political Thought. New Jersey: Friends of SHI, 1989.

Warrior, Robert. "Canaanites and Conquerors." *Christianity and Crisis* 49/12 (September 11, 1989):261–4.

Washington, James M., ed. *A Testament of Hope: The Essential Writings of Martin Luther King, Jr.* San Francisco: Harper and Row, Publishers, 1986.

Welch, Sharon. *Communities of Resistance and Solidarity: A Feminist Theology of Liberation*. Maryknoll, NY: Orbis Books, 1985.

Welch, Sharon. "'Dreams of the Good': From the Analytics of Oppression to the Politics of Transformation." In *New Visions for the Americas: Religious Engagement and Social Transformation*, pp. 172–93. Edited by David Batstone. Minneapolis: Augsburg Fortress Press, 1993.

Welch, Sharon. *A Feminist Ethic of Risk*. Minneapolis: Fortress Press, 1990.

Welch, Sharon. "Sporting Power: American Feminism, French Feminism, and an Ethic of Conflict." In *Transfigurations: Theology and French Feminists*, pp. 171–98. Edited by M. Kim, et. al. Minneapolis: Fortress Press, 1993.

West, Cornel. "Demystifying the New Black Conservatism." *Praxis International* 7/2 (July 1987):143–51.

West, Cornel. "Philosophy and the Urban Underclass." In *The Underclass Question*, pp. 191–201. Edited by Bill E. Lawson. Philadelphia: Temple University Press, 1992.

West, Cornel. *Prophesy Deliverance! An Afro-American Revolutionary Christianity*. Philadelphia: Westminster Press, 1982.

West, Cornel. *Prophetic Fragments*. Grand Rapids, MI: William B. Eerdmans Publishing Co., 1988.

West, Cornel. *Race Matters*. Boston: Beacon Press, 1993.

White, Stephen. "Justice and the Postmodern Problematic." *Praxis International* 7/3–4 (Winter 1987/8):306–19.

Williams, Delores. *Sisters in the Wilderness: The Challenge of Womanist Godtalk*. Maryknoll: Orbis Books, 1993.

Williams, Raymond. *Marxism and Literature*. Oxford: Oxford University Press, 1978.

Williams, Raymond. *The Sociology of Culture*. New York: Schocken Books, 1982.

Wilson, William Julius. "The Political Economy and Urban Racial Tensions." *The American Economist* 39/1 (Spring 1995): 3–12.

Wilson, William Julius. "Studying Inner-City Dislocation: The Challenge of Public Agenda Research." *American Sociological Review* 56 (February 1991): 1–14.

Wolfe, Alan. *Whose Keeper? Social Science and Moral Obligations.* Berkeley: University of California Press, 1989.

X, Malcolm. *By Any Means Necessary.* New York: Pathfinder, 1970.

X, Malcolm. *The End of World Supremacy: Four Speeches.* Edited and with introduction by B. Karim. New York: Arcade Publishers/Little, Brown and Company, 1971.

Yoder, John Howard. "'Christ and Culture': A Critique of H. Richard Niebuhr." Unpublished manuscript.

Young, Iris Marion. "Beyond the Unhappy Marriage: A Critique of Dual Systems Theory." In *Women and Revolution*, pp. 43–70. Edited by L. Sargent. Boston: South End Press, 1981.

Young, Iris Marion. "The Ideal of Community and the Politics of Difference." In *Feminism/Postmodernism*, pp. 300–23. Edited by L. Nicholson. New York: Routledge, 1990.

Young, Iris Marion. *Justice and the Politics of Difference.* Princeton, NJ: Princeton University Press, 1990.

Young, Iris Marion. "Mothers, Citizenship, and Independence: A Critique of Pure Family Values." *Ethics* 105 (April 1995): 535–56.

Young, Iris Marion. *Throwing Like a Girl and Other Essays in Feminist Philosophy and Social Theory.* Bloomington: Indiana University Press, 1990.

Young, K., et al., eds. *Of Marriage and the Market.* London: CSE Books, 1981.

INDEX